OHIO

American Historical Press
Sun Valley, California

OHIO

THE BUCKEYE STATE

AN ILLUSTRATED HISTORY

EUGENE C. MURDOCK & JEFFREY DARBEE

Library of Congress Catalogue Card Number: 2007934393

EAN: 978-1-892724-55-7

Bibliography: p. 288
Includes Index

CONTENTS

INTRODUCTION

A veteran scout, refreshed from a month's stay at the Wyandot village, set out on foot for Shawnee Town, 150 miles away. Later he confided to his journal,

> . . . *all the way is a fine, rich, level land, well timbered with large walnut, ash, sugar trees, cherry trees, etc.; it is well watered with a great number of little streams and rivulets, full of beautiful natural meadows covered with wild rye, bluegrass and clover, and abounds with turkey, deer, elk and all sorts of game, particularly buffaloes, thirty or forty of which are frequently seen feeding in one meadow; in short, it wants nothing but cultivation to make it a most delightful country.*

In these words Christopher Gist, agent for the Ohio Land Company, described the Ohio country in 1751. He wrote more accurately than he knew.

Ohio was fortunate in many respects. It possessed an ideal geographical location. Tens of thousands of migrants crossed the mountains to the future "Gateway State," traveling by foot, horse, or boat. By its proximity to the older settled regions, by its abundant waterways, and by its mostly smooth tabletop terrain, Ohio, indeed, was the gateway to the transmontane West. No natural barriers obstructed the first interstate highway—the National Road—or the network of canals, or railroad links with all sections of the country. As historian George Knepper has written, "with very few exceptions all the major East-West lines of travel, transport, and communication passed through the state."

Not only was Ohio blessed with excellent geography, it also fulfilled Christopher Gist's promise of an agrarian utopia. The land of the Interior Plains, smoothly sculptured and enriched by the ancient glacier bulldozer, would—once the forests were cleared—make Ohio a bountiful agricultural region. The receptive soil, wide temperature range, ample rainfall, and extensive growing season guaranteed a prosperous farming future.

But what was to give Ohio its claim to economic greatness was something which Christopher Gist could not have foreseen. The state was endowed with vast reserves of mineral wealth, which in time would transform Ohio into a major manufacturing center. Coal in the southeast, iron ore in the south and east, clay in the central east, and gas and oil in the northwest, formed the foundation of Ohio's industrial strength. True, Hanging Rock iron ore—found in the environs of Ironton in the south—would be superceded by the rich ore brought into Cleveland from the upper Great Lakes. But this new development only elevated the state to the first rank in steel production. So it came to pass that Ohio, by its location and natural wealth, rose to economic preeminence.

Yet the first arrivals in the Ohio country, not long after Gist's memorable pilgrimage, faced a formidable task: they had to carve homesteads for themselves—and provide the means for survival—in a friendless wilderness. Indians, perhaps hostile, perhaps not, were ever present. These hardy pioneers, however, did not shirk from the challenge. Log cabins were built, crops sprouted from the ground, villages emerged, and a rough-hewn civilization developed on the frontier.

In 1803 Ohio became a state, the "Seventeenth Star," as it was called; the first to be formed from the Northwest Territory. Its growth was rapid and by mid-century Ohio could boast a population of over 1,950,000, compared to 42,000 in 1800. Roads and canals crisscrossed the state and railroads had recently appeared. With Cincinnati leading the way, Ohio had moved to third place among all states in manufactured goods. But the Industrial Revolution was still several decades away and agriculture continued to play the dominant role in the economy.

While historians debate whether the Civil War was a stimulus or a deterrent to industrial growth, two developments unrelated to the war sparked Ohio's economic boom of the postwar years. In the mid-1850s the first shipload of iron ore—132 tons—arrived in Cleveland. Things were never quite the same again. The trade developed rapidly and by 1875 over half a million tons came to town each year. The marriage of iron ore to coal, now abundantly available in eastern Ohio and western Pennsylvania, was soon consummated and the world's greatest steel center—the Cleveland-Youngstown-Pittsburgh nexus—was born.

At almost the same time crude oil was discovered in western Pennsylvania, and under the astute, though ruthless organizing skill of John D. Rockefeller, Cleveland became the world's greatest oil refining center. The rise of the oil and steel industries in Cleveland shifted the balance of economic power in Ohio almost overnight. No longer was the Ohio River and Cincinnati the focus of industrial life. Not that the central and southern parts of the state slipped backward; rather, the northeastern section raced madly forward.

In addition to steel and oil, other booming industries dotted the business map of Ohio in the late nineteenth century. Akron became the hub of the rubber industry; Toledo was a major glass center; Dayton had the National Cash Register Company; machine tools and automobiles were being manufactured in several cities. By 1900 Ohio was no longer an agricultural state. The majority of the population now lived in cities. The value of manufactured goods far outdistanced that of farm produce.

The structure of Ohio's economy, which had taken shape by 1900, remained relatively stable through the first quarter of the twentieth century. But it was dealt a savage blow by the Great Depression. While no state remained immune to the ravages of the economic cancer, Ohio seemed to suffer more than others. Its unemployment and welfare rates were rivaled by only a few states. Although

Ohio's industrial establishment was hurt by the Depression, World War II brought unprecedented prosperity to the state's factories, mills, and shops.

In the euphoria which followed the war it was hoped that American industrial growth would continue unabated, although major adjustments would have to be made to pick up the slack with the cancellation of war contracts. There was even concern that another major depression might occur; fortunately, that never happened. New plants were built and the economy prospered.

However, subtle changes were taking place which were eroding the bedrock upon which American industry was based. Markets were shifting as the population began to move into the South and West; new processes and materials were supplanting traditional ones; labor costs were beginning to escalate as unions became stronger. Still in the 1950s and 1960s Ohio's economy appeared relatively healthy.

The history of Ohio business is a tale of achievement. Following the conquest of the wilderness, the resourceful pioneers and their heirs proceeded to construct a mighty "inland empire," one of which Christopher Gist would have been proud. In the pages ahead the reader may follow the unfolding of this fascinating story.

Glass mosaic murals depicting Cincinnati workers were installed in the rotunda of Union Terminal in 1933. Created by Winold Reiss, these murals were made from actual photographs. They are now on display at the Greater Cincinnati International Airport. Pictured are two of the fourteen murals, depicting work at Cincinnati Milling Machine. Courtesy, Cincinnati Milacron

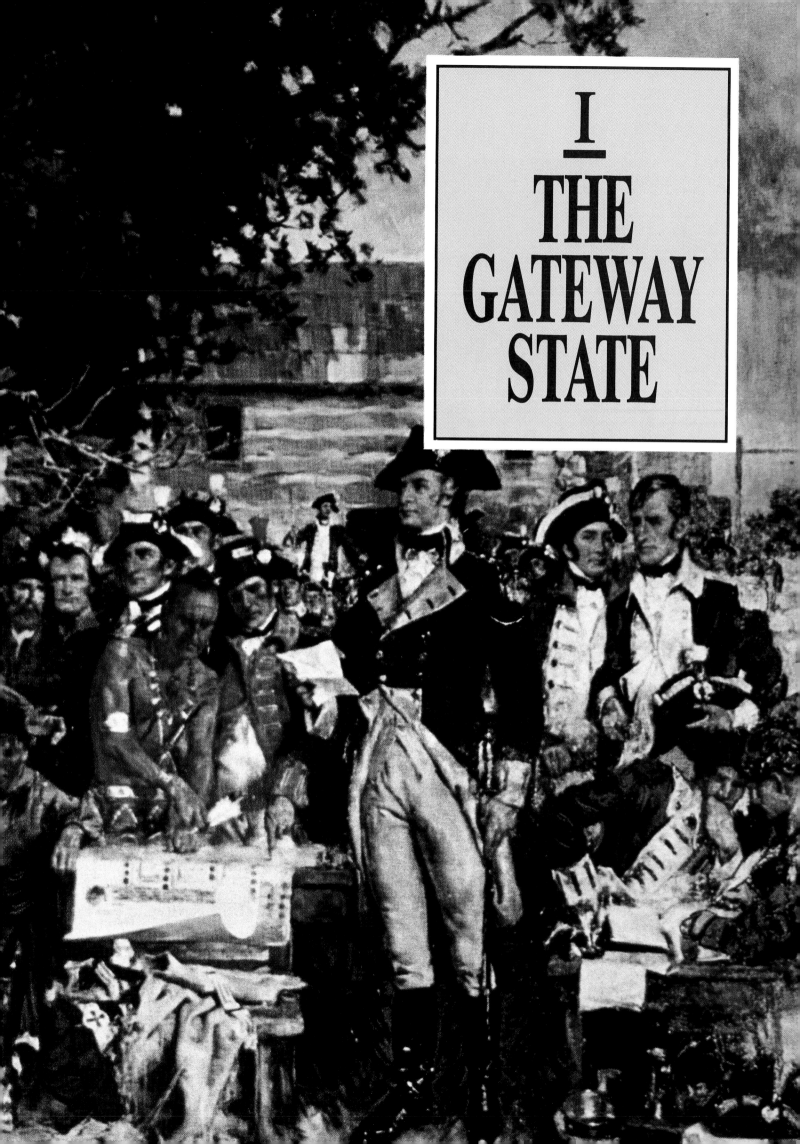

I
THE GATEWAY STATE

Howard Chandler Christie's famous painting, Treaty of Greene Ville, *shows Anthony Wayne, in 1795, standing at the right in uniform and the Indian chief, Little Turtle, offering him a symbol of peace. Surrounding the two men are famous historical figures such as William Henry Harrison, William Clark, Meriwether Lewis, Shawnee Chief Black Hoof, Blue Jacket, and Buckongahelas of the Delaware tribe. Courtesy, Ohio Historical Society*

Facing page: This map of the Ohio country shows boundaries and divisions, key forts, rivers, and villages in the new territory. Admitted to the Union on March 1, 1803, as the seventeenth state, Ohio was the first state to be formed from the Northwest Territory. Courtesy, Western Reserve Historical Society

That which would become Ohio was a land coveted by Indians, Englishmen, Frenchmen, and Americans. The passion for Ohio was not grounded in the area's wealth of mineral deposits, its fertile soil, or its virgin forests, but because of its convenient location. Ohio was a vast crossroads between East and West, a wilderness highway beyond the mountains. Whoever controlled Ohio controlled America. Well, almost.

Six Indian tribes roamed Ohio when the white man first arrived in the area. Most prestigious were the mighty Miami, a powerful tribe which dominated southwestern Ohio and much beyond. In the northwest were the Ottawa; in the northeast, the Wyandot and Mingo (mostly Seneca); in the south, the Shawnees; and in the Tuscarawas and Muskingum valleys were the reasonably friendly Delaware. But these tribes, strong as they were, had no future in Ohio once the white man arrived.

The British and French came into Ohio from different directions, but with the same determination to possess this valuable "heartland." The French arrived from the north through the Great Lakes, whereas the British migrated across the mountains and down inland streams. From 1689 to 1763 the British battled the French for control of what would be the United States. The British emerged triumphant at the conclusion of the French and Indian War in 1763, when the French were evicted from all of North America. Lands east of the Mississippi fell under the control of the British, while the Spanish dominated the lands west of that mighty river.

The British government was determined that the transmontane

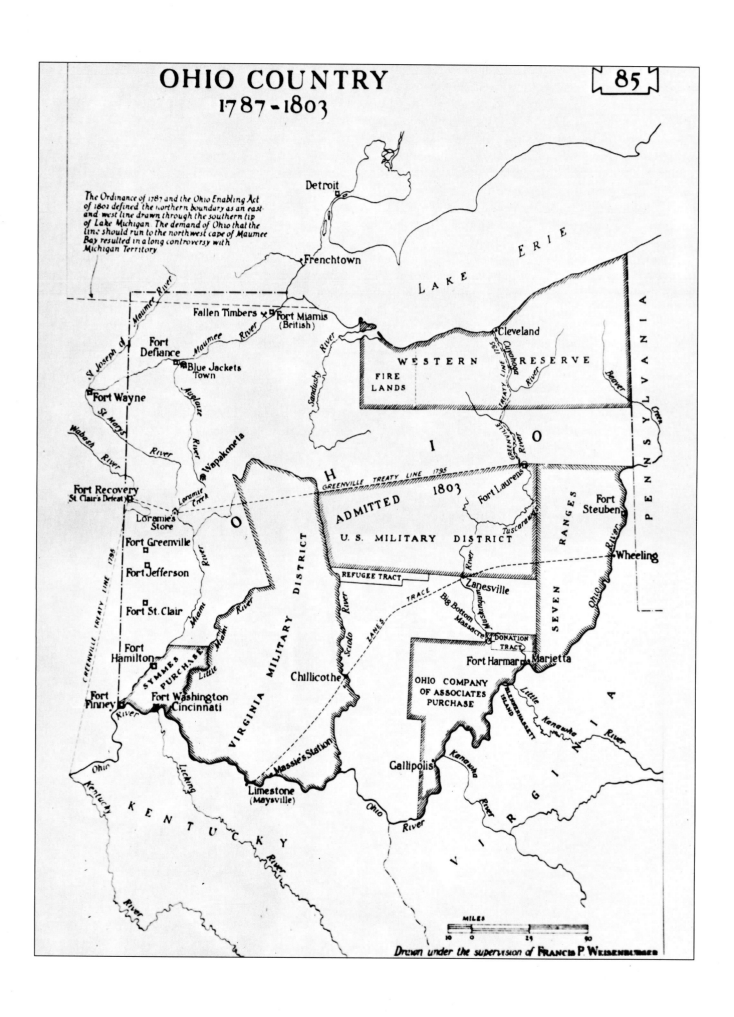

OHIO COUNTRY
1787-1803

The Ordinance of 1787 and the Ohio Enabling Act of 1802 defined the northern boundary as an east and west line drawn through the southern tip of Lake Michigan. The demand of Ohio that the line should run to the northwest cape of Maumee Bay resulted in a long controversy with Michigan Territory

LAKE ERIE

Detroit

Frenchtown

Fallen Timbers ✕ Fort Miamis (British)

Fort Defiance

Blue Jackets Town

Fort Wayne

Wapakoneta

Fort Recovery
St. Clair's Defeat

Loramie's Store

Fort Greenville

Fort Jefferson

Fort St. Clair

Fort Hamilton

SYMMES PURCHASE

Fort Finney

Fort Washington
Cincinnati

Limestone (Maysville)

Massie's Station

Chillicothe

Gallipolis

KENTUCKY

O H I O

Cleveland

WESTERN RESERVE

FIRE LANDS

Sandusky River

Cuyahoga River

GREENVILLE TREATY LINE 1795

ADMITTED 1803

U.S. MILITARY DISTRICT

Fort Laurens

Tuscarawas

SEVEN RANGES

Fort Steuben

PENNSYLVANIA

Beaver Creek

Wheeling

REFUGEE TRACT

VIRGINIA MILITARY DISTRICT

Scioto River

ZANE'S TRACE

Zanesville

Big Bottom Massacre

DONATION TRACT

Fort Harmar Marietta

OHIO COMPANY OF ASSOCIATES PURCHASE

Blennerhassett Island

Little Kanawha River

Kanawha River

V I R G I N I A

Ohio River

Miami River

Little Miami River

Licking River

Ohio River

GREENVILLE TREATY LINE 1795

Maumee River

St. Joseph R.

St. Marys River

Wabash River

Auglaize River

Loramie Creek

MILES
10   0   20   30

Drawn under the supervision of FRANCIS P. WEISENBURGER

region would be developed in a gradual, orderly manner. The Proclamation Line of 1763 prohibited British colonists from settling west of the Appalachian mountains and ordered squatters already there to vacate. When this proved unenforceable, Parliament enacted the Quebec Act in 1774 which annexed all of the Ohio country to the province of Quebec. The act further barred westward migration, denied claims of seaboard colonies to western lands, and reassured the Indians that their hunting grounds would remain inviolate—all of which aroused the colonists' anger.

The Quebec Act helped provoke the American Revolution. While no major battles were fought in Ohio, there was plenty of small-scale action

---

This painting by James A. Beard depicts weary travelers on their way to Ohio. At a fork in the road, the father leans on a post with signs pointing to North Carolina in one direction and Ohio in another. Courtesy, Cincinnati Historical Society

between Indians (supplied by their British allies) and the Americans. The year 1777 marked the beginning of a series of Indian raids across Ohio directed at white settlements in Pennsylvania, Kentucky, and northwestern Virginia, and subsequent retaliatory raids by white frontiersmen. Hostilities lasted well beyond the battle at Yorktown in October 1781. One of the worst massacres in American history took place in March 1782 at Gnadenhutten where a band of frontier cutthroats murdered almost 100 peaceful Christian Indians—men, women, and children.

Such raids and killings had little bearing on the outcome of the Revolution. The peace treaty with Great Britain was ratified in 1783. By its terms the British surrendered all of the land between the mountains and the Mississippi River to the Americans. Though Indians caused trouble periodically—encouraged by the British in Detroit and Canada—they only temporarily delayed the development of Ohio.

Of those who initially coveted the land, only the Americans now remained. The pioneers came from

This bedroom scene is from the Golden Lamb in Lebanon and is Ohio's oldest hotel. Photo by Rick Dieringer

Above: Corn is one of the crops grown in the rural regions of Greene County, east of Dayton. Photo by Connie Girard

Right: In Urbana, where this farm is located, vegetables and grains are the primary crops. Photo by Mark E. Gibson

Left: In the fall the southwestern Ohio Valley takes on many colorful hues. In the distance is the Eagle Creek covered bridge, outside Decatur in Brown County. Photo by Jana C. Morford

Below: Some inquisitive cows attempt to get closer to the camera in this Greene County farm scene. Photo by Connie Girard

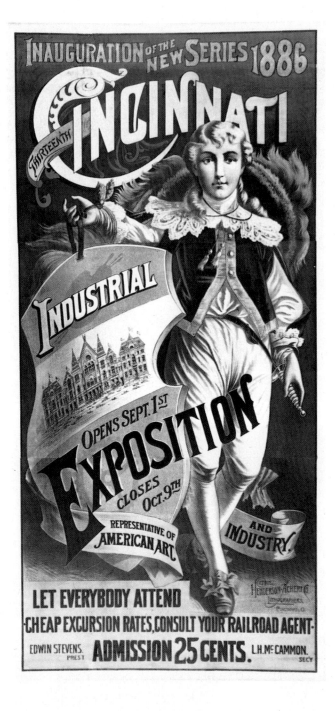

The Cleveland Industrial Exposition opened under the direction of the Cleveland Chamber of Commerce on June 7, 1909. This expo had a record attendance of 215,000, while thousands more were turned away from the twelve-day event. The purpose of the Industrial Exposition was "to teach Cleveland to know itself, and to teach the world to become better acquainted with Cleveland." Courtesy, Ohio Historical Society

The goal of the Industrial Exposition, held annually in the 1870s and 1880s, was to show the achievements of Cincinnati and the West. The 1879 exposition featured 1,000 exhibits and was attended by President Rutherford B. Hayes. The last Industrial Exposition was the elaborate 100-day Centennial Exposition of the Ohio Valley and Central States, held in 1888. Courtesy, Cincinnati Historical Society

many places. New Englanders settled in the lower Muskingum valley; New Jerseyites in the Miami valley; Virginians in the Military District between the Scioto and Little Miami rivers; and Moses Cleaveland and his fellows from Connecticut in the Western Reserve. Even from France came the unfortunate "500," who tried to establish homesteads in the unfriendly forests at Gallipolis. Ohio was the country's most impressive "melting pot." For this reason, perhaps, it has never been easy to label anything or any person as "typically Ohioan."

Not all the pioneers came to Ohio to settle. Some were merely passing through because Ohio's rivers and trails supplied the most direct route to lands further west. Whether one traveled from New England, New York, Pennsylvania, or Virginia, the most logical way west was through Ohio. Early in the nineteenth century the first important road to the west—the Cumberland or National Road —traversed the heart of Ohio. Once beyond the mountains, travelers passed through a gateway to the west, prompting some historians to call Ohio the "Gateway State."

What kind of land did the first pioneers gaze upon in Ohio? The terrain was relatively level, due to two glaciers which slid across most of the state during the last Ice Age. These huge masses of ice, inching their way down from Canada, leveled the land like monstrous bulldozers. Hilltops were sliced off and valleys were filled with rich, fertile soil. The only unglaciated part of the state is in the southeast, where the land is hilly, rugged, and less fertile.

When the settlers arrived, much of the state was heavily forested with stands of oak and maple, hickory and walnut, elm and—oh, yes—the buckeye. The grand Ohio forests, which extended throughout the glaciated as well as unglaciated regions, proved to be a hindrance to early arrivals. While the woods provided material for log huts and crude implements, for fences, furniture, and fuel, they also barred the cultivation of crops. Hence the trees came down so the crops could go in.

The first settlers were naturally unaware of the area's vast mineral resources. The unglaciated southeast had the richest store of subsurface wealth. Iron ore was found near Portsmouth and Ironton, and in the Mahoning valley; coal and clay deposits were extensive in the east central regions. Coal, still a major resource, was found in almost every county along the Ohio River from Columbiana to Lawrence, as well as in adjacent inland sections. Clay and clay products also were centered in the eastern sections, with Zanesville and East Liverpool as important centers. The southeast may not have been very good for farming, but it was excellent for industry.

The earliest people in the Ohio country, with no legal title to the land, were not bona fide settlers. They were "squatters." Historian Walter Havighurst has described them well:

> *Squatters were intruders on the public lands, ahead of legal survey and legal purchase. They had no maps or charts, no land warrants or certificates, and no specific destination. They simply made their way into wild country, looking for a southern hill-*

Although this man is under the homestead law, he can be likened to a squatter. Both groups of people came to the area, established themselves with homes, and began to farm. However, unlike the squatter who just moved into unoccupied territory and set up a claim, the homesteader held a grant of land from the U.S. government. Courtesy, Ohio Historical Society

Below: Manasseh Cutler, chaplain with the Massachusetts troops in the Revolutionary War, joined the Ohio Company in 1786 and helped to found Marietta in 1788. He served as a congressman from Ohio from 1801 to 1805. Courtesy, Ohio Historical Society

Bottom: This map of the Northwest Territory, made by Samuel Lewis in 1796, shows land grant divisions, early settlements, and the Greenville Treaty line. Courtesy, Cincinnati Historical Society

side with a trickling spring or a green opening where deer paths crossed. They came lightly laden—a rifle, ax, plow, and a bag of seed corn, a dog and a horse, and perhaps a few pigs and chickens.

Two different attitudes prevailed toward squatters. Some argued that those who settled first owned the land by right of occupation. Others believed such a policy led to disorder and chaos and said it was better to have an established plan: purchase the land from the Indians, survey it, and sell it at convenient land offices. In this fashion, titles would be unambiguous and revenue could accrue. In time, forced evictions, land sales by squatters to legitimate owners, and land purchases by the squatters themselves eventually cleared the land of these dubious claimants.

Squatters weren't the only ones to cause confusion over who owned land in Ohio. A number of eastern seaboard states, such as Virginia, New York, Connecticut, and Massachusetts, claimed ownership of western lands by their original charters. But

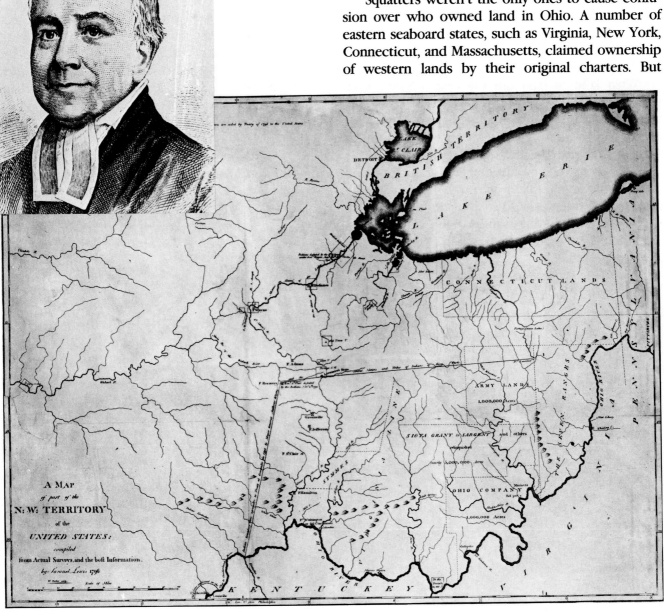

under pressure from the "have not" states, all western land claims were surrendered to the central government starting in 1784. Two exceptions to this influenced Ohio's future. A large section of land between the Scioto and Little Miami rivers, the so-called Virginia Military District, was reserved by Virginia as bounty land for its veterans of the Revolution. And in the northeast, a strip of land extending 120 miles west from the Pennsylvania boundary along the 41st parallel, the famous "Western Reserve," was reserved for Connecticut. By 1786 all land north and west of the Ohio River, reaching to the Mississippi River in the west and the Great Lakes in the north, the fabled "Northwest Territory," was property of the United States government.

In 1785 the Confederation Congress adopted an ordinance dealing with the newly acquired land. It provided for a system of rectilinear surveys to divide the territory into even, equal squares. These were called townships after the New England plan, measuring thirty-six square miles each. Townships were subdivided into thirty-six one-square-mile sections. Land was to be sold at auction for a minimum price of one dollar per acre, with a minimum purchase of 640 acres—not an inviting proposition when cash was in short supply. Section 16 of each township was reserved for public education and other sections were set aside for special purposes.

The 1785 ordinance eliminated the problem of disputed land claims which had plagued the older states, since now every inch of territory could be described specifically on property deeds. The first surveys in the Ohio country, the "Seven Ranges" along the Ohio River in the eastern part of the territory, were carried out in 1786 and 1787. However, so little land was sold to individuals because of the restrictive terms of the ordinance, a new approach was devised. Rather than trying to sell to cash-starved individuals, Congress decided to sell to companies interested in acquiring large units of land for either settlement or speculation.

In 1786 such a land company was formed in Massachusetts. The Ohio Company of Associates, organized in Boston, was composed principally of Revolutionary War officer veterans. But before negotiating for the land purchase, members of the Ohio Company wanted a civil government operating in the territory.

In July 1787 Manasseh Cutler, representing the Ohio Company, met with members of Congress. Within a week the Northwest Ordinance, which created the Northwest Territory and provided for an

orderly evolutionary process from territory to statehood, had been drafted. Three stages of growth were defined: In stage one (where the population of free adult males was less than 5,000) there would be no self-government, the territory being administered by a governor, three judges, and a secretary, all appointed by Congress. In stage two (from 5,000 to 60,000 population) the governor stayed on with veto powers, but a territorial legislature, partly elected and partly appointed, provided a certain degree of self-government. In addition, the territory was permitted a non-voting delegate to represent it in Congress. In stage three (over 60,000 population) the territory was entitled to statehood with all the powers of self-government that were available to the older states. The form of the Northwest Ordinance and the timing of its adoption, July 13, 1787, was a direct result of the interest and energy of the Ohio Company.

In the fall of 1787 the Ohio Company purchased over one and a half million acres of land at the confluence of the Ohio and Muskingum rivers. The price was half a million dollars when the contract was signed and another half million when surveys of the grant were completed.

The Ohio Company settlers left Massachusetts in two groups, one in the fall of 1787 and the other in February 1788. They wintered at Sumrill's Ferry on the Youghiogheny River south of Pittsburgh, where they constructed flatboats for the trip down the Ohio in the spring. All was ready by the end of March 1788 and the momentous expedition commenced on April 1. Forty-eight hardy pioneers, no women or children, led by Rufus Putnam, made the trip. When the company arrived at the mouth of the Muskingum on April 7, overhanging branches obscured the river's entrance. Helpful soldiers at Fort Harmar on the west side of the Muskingum tossed ropes to the voyagers and pulled them ashore. Some friendly Delawares were also on hand to welcome the immigrants.

Putnam established his headquarters on the east side of the river opposite Fort Harmar. He erected a long shed-like structure covered with tenting, which became known as "The Picketed Point." Temporary shelters built from timber which had been brought along for the purpose were put up. The nearby land was quickly cleared and crops were planted. Broad thoroughfares were laid out for the town, which modern visitors to Marietta still marvel at. Early in July the next batch of settlers, including the official governing members of the territory and the families of the first "48," landed on the banks

Above: This building, the oldest one in Ohio, served as the land office of the Ohio Company at Marietta. Settlers from the Ohio Company, founded in 1786, arrived at the mouth of the Muskingum River on April 7, 1788, and founded the town of Marietta. Courtesy, Ohio Historical Society

Right: Early settlers traveled downriver on flatboats which carried all their belongings. Upon reaching their destination, the boats were sometimes broken up and the wood used to construct cabins. Courtesy, Ohio Historical Society

of the Muskingum. General Arthur St. Clair, of Revolutionary War distinction and a confidante of Washington, headed the party and served as the first governor of the territory. On July 15, 1788, amid elaborate and colorful ceremonies, he formally proclaimed the government open for business.

Within the next year many more settlers arrived in the Marietta area and a number of new communities sprang up. Belpre, farther down the Ohio, was one of these, while Waterford, Plainfield, and Big Bottom were founded along the Muskingum. Managers of the Ohio Company made it inviting for people to settle in their tract. Lots of 100 acres were granted to settlers free if within five years they would construct homes, plant orchards, cultivate their fields, and develop grazing land for cattle. Heavy traffic traveled the Ohio past Marietta in the latter 1780s and many of the immigrants accepted the "homestead" challenge.

The second grant in the Northwest Territory went to a New Jerseyite of note, John Cleves Symmes, who was attracted to land along the Ohio farther to the west, between the Great and Little Miami rivers. In October 1788 he negotiated for a one-million-acre tract in the Miami valley. Considerable confusion developed in the next few years because Symmes sold land to settlers which was not legally his. By the fall of 1789, however, Fort Washington was constructed at Losantiville and St. Clair transferred his territorial headquarters from Marietta to the new location. He renamed Losantiville "Cincinnati," in honor of the veterans' organi-

Above: Arthur St. Clair, 1736-1818, fought in the American Revolution and later served in the Continental Congress which appointed him as the first governor of the Northwest Territory. He assumed office in 1788. St. Clair, however, was not popular among the frontiersmen, and his opposition to Ohio's statehood led to his removal from office in 1802 by Thomas Jefferson. Courtesy, S. Durward Hoag Collection, Cincinnati Historical Society

Top: The first pioneers in Cincinnati landed at Yeatman's Cove in December 1788. The party of eleven families and twenty-four men arrived via flatboats and called the settlement Losantiville. One month earlier previous settlers had established the town of Columbia, a few miles upriver at the mouth of the Little Miami River. Courtesy, Cincinnati Historical Society

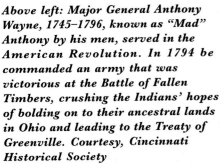

Above left: Major General Anthony Wayne, 1745–1796, known as "Mad" Anthony by his men, served in the American Revolution. In 1794 be commanded an army that was victorious at the Battle of Fallen Timbers, crushing the Indians' hopes of bolding on to their ancestral lands in Ohio and leading to the Treaty of Greenville. Courtesy, Cincinnati Historical Society

Above right: John Cleves Symmes, 1742–1814, became associated with the Northwest Territory when be was appointed a judge for the territory in 1788. Congress granted him a charter to develop land lying between the Great and Little Miami rivers, referred to as the Miami Purchase. Because of his neglect in securing legal claim to all of the land be sold, be was the victim of several lawsuits and died penniless. Painting by Charles Willson Peale. Courtesy, Cincinnati Historical Society

zation to which he belonged.

Further settlement in Ohio was delayed by the outbreak of the Indian Wars. All the tribes resented the steady encroachment of white settlers into their lands, but divisions among them prevented the formation of a united front against the newcomers. The Delawares and Wyandots met with St. Clair to preserve peace; the Miamis and Shawnees, however, refused to compromise. In 1790 sporadic fighting broke out, beginning four years of conflict between frontiersmen and Indians. Three campaigns were launched by the Americans against Indian strongholds in the western part of Ohio before the region was pacified. British agents in Detroit—they had remained there in violation of the 1783 peace treaty because of the lucrative fur trade with the Indians —gave moral and material support to their allies.

The first campaign, composed of 1,500 poorly trained troops, was commanded by Colonel Josiah Harmar. This force worked its way north as far as present-day Fort Wayne, but besides burning a few Indian villages and suffering several setbacks, had nothing to show for its efforts. It returned to Cincinnati with its forces decimated and its mission unaccomplished. In 1791 St. Clair himself led a force of 3,000, but the undisciplined troops were no match for their wily adversaries. After a devastating defeat at Fort Recovery early in November, the Americans were forced to withdraw.

THE PATRIOTS HOME

This picture illustrates important events in the life of William Henry Harrison, 1773-1841, hero of the Battle of Tippecanoe. Senator and congressman from Ohio, and later ninth president of the United States, Harrison used amusing ditties in his election campaign against Martin Van Buren such as, "Let Van from his coolers of silver drink wine/ And lounge on his cushioned settee./ Our man on his buckeye bench can recline./ Content with hard cider is he." Courtesy, Cincinnati Historical Society

With the news of St. Clair's humiliation, General Anthony Wayne, a hero of the Revolution, was charged to pacify the Ohio frontier once and for all. Borrowing an idea of St. Clair's, Wayne planned to erect a series of forts northward as he advanced toward the Indian strongholds in the Maumee valley. With a force of 2,500 Wayne arrived in Cincinnati in the spring of 1793 and began his advance in October. Eighty miles north of Cincinnati, Wayne established winter quarters at Fort Greenville. In the spring of 1794 he built Fort Defiance on the Maumee River. When peace talks with the Indians failed, the Americans pushed down the Maumee where they met the foe at Fallen Timbers. After a brief but momentous encounter on August 20, 1794, Wayne routed the approximately 2,000 Indians.

Humbled by this show of strength, the remaining Indians sought peace with Wayne. Most of the tribes were represented at Greenville a year later, in August 1795, when talks were held. The Treaty of Greenville, which resulted from these negotiations, provided for the surrender by the Indian tribes of all land claims east and south of a line drawn from modern Cleveland to the site of modern Bolivar on the Tuscarawas watershed, thence west to Loramie's post on the Great Miami, thence to Fort Recovery, and then southwest to the Ohio River. With Indian warfare over in Ohio, settlers began arriving quickly and steadily. The Western Reserve, the upper Ohio River, the Scioto valley, and the Miami valley all experienced a modest population explosion. Franklinton (Columbus), Chillicothe, Dayton, and Cleveland were among the new villages founded soon after the Indian fighting ceased.

But it was not only the cessation of warfare which stimulated settlement. A new law in 1796 slightly eased the financial strain for land-hungry pioneers. The measure provided that purchasers still had to buy 640-acre blocks at a minimum price of two dollars an acre, but the payments could now be made in installments over a twelve-month period.

Population growth was stimulated further when William Henry Harrison became Ohio's territorial delegate to Congress. Although he had no voting power, Harrison was influential in sponsoring liberal land legislation. The Harrison Land Law of 1800 reduced the minimum lot size for purchase to 320 acres. The price was still two dollars an acre, but buyers were now allowed four years to complete payment. Regional land offices were created at Steubenville, Marietta, Chillicothe, and Cincinnati.

Economic growth, stunted by the Indian Wars, also began to revive after the Treaty of Greenville. However, one important drawback to rapid development was the absence of good roads. Animal trails and Indian paths were the only routes available when white men first reached the area. While Indian paths crisscrossed the state in all directions, they were narrow and unsuitable for travel or transportation.

Most of the roads developed during the territorial period were crude refinements of these primitive trails. The only major road built in that time was subsidized by the federal government. In 1796 Ebenezer Zane was authorized to build a road from the Ohio border at Wheeling, Virginia, across the state in the direction of Chillicothe, and then southwest to Limestone (or Maysville), Kentucky. "Zane's Trace," as it was called, followed an old Indian trail most of the way. According to the plan, Zane was to establish ferries over the major rivers—the Muskingum, Hocking, and Scioto—which intersected the road and build hostelries at such crossing points. In exchange for all of this, Zane was granted sections of land at all of the river crossings. Zanesville grew out of one of these grants.

While Zane's Trace, completed in 1798, eventually became a major artery, at first it was not much more than a wide trail suited only for horse trains. The state of the road between Chillicothe and Cincinnati is revealed by the experience of a traveler in November 1801.

Set off very early, having 19 miles to ride before breakfast, and very soon I entered the White Oak Swamp,' which continued for 13 miles. The mire in the road was so deep that I found it impossible to pursue it without sticking fast, and had, therefore, to abandon it, and press through the dense and brushy forest on one side or the other. While in the midst of the swamp a violent storm of rain, with lightning and thunder, arose, which continued for two hours, the rain falling in torrents all the time. Of course, I was thoroughly wet, and even the feet of my boots were filled with water.

Reached Williamsburg about noon and breakfasted, and dried my clothes as well as I could, and proceeded on my journey.

This traveler, with incredible perseverance, reached his destination only two days later than planned. His experience was by no means unique.

Poor roads, distant markets, and the absence of a stable medium of exchange hindered Ohio's trade and commerce during its territorial stage. Yet the early settlers made up for what they didn't have with plenty of energy and ingenuity. And growth did occur, in spite of the handicaps which beset the pioneering Ohioans.

As trade began to emerge in the 1790s, Ohio merchants would make the arduous trip to Philadelphia or Baltimore for supplies. Following the arduous trip back to Ohio they would stock their shelves with the necessities so much desired by the frontiersmen. As agriculture and primitive industry became established in the territory and with ready cash in short supply, merchants began to accept local produce and products for exchange and export. Particularly after the Treaty of Greenville in 1795 and the Pinckney Treaty with Spain—which secured

Left: This sketch by Alfred R. Waud, included in the two-volume work entitled Picturesque America, 1872-74, *depicts Marietta's location where the Muskingum flows into the Ohio. Marietta, named in honor of Marie Antoinette, was settled by New Englanders who arrived on a flatboat called the* Mayflower. *Courtesy, Cincinnati Historical Society*

Below: This sketch is from an early history of Cincinnati by A.E. Jones. According to Jones, it was not uncommon to see women ride to town on horseback to trade farm products for store goods. Courtesy, Cincinnati Historical Society

America's right to navigate the lower Mississippi and deposit goods at New Orleans for transshipment abroad—the export trade on the Ohio-Mississippi route began to increase.

Cincinnati quickly emerged as the major commercial center in the West. Serving as the territorial capital for a few years and located on the Ohio near the mouths of two sizeable rivers, it attracted settlers more rapidly than any other early community. Farmers inland along the Great and Little Miami rivers began shipping their surplus to Cincinnati. On the opposite side of the Ohio, the Licking River provided a route into and out of central Kentucky. Merchants established wholesale and retail stores and commerce began to thrive. Beverley Bond, historian of the Old Northwest, describes the operations of Smith and Findlay and other commercial houses at this time:

> Customers . . . rapidly increased as settlement expanded, coming from Cincinnati, and from the near-by settlements, Columbia, North Bend, White's Station, from "up Miami," from "up Licking," and from Fort Hamilton. Much of this trade was wholesale, and the different Cincinnati houses were soon making shipments to retailers in Bardstown, Frankfort, and other settlements in the interior of Kentucky, and occasionally even to such distant points as Vincennes. Of home products, Smith and Findlay by 1795 sold whiskey and brandy in large quantities, along with imported gin, Lisbon and Madeira wines, coffee, lump sugar, Bohea tea, and chocolate. In their stock of hardware they included cups and saucers, looking-glasses, china plates, "pains" of glass, spoons and tableware. In the list of "dry goods" were shawls, pocket handkerchiefs, combs, Nankeen linen, coating, and corduroy.

Marietta was the next most important center of trade, servicing settlers on the Muskingum River and over on the Virginia side of the Ohio River, as well as supplying the ever-increasing number of travelers along the Ohio. Chillicothe, too, although founded slightly later, quickly grew as a center of trade for the mid-Scioto valley. Competing Chillicothe merchants advertised exotic beverages and comestibles, as well as the not-so-exotic "Overstreet's Chewing Tobacco, sold by the keg." Steubenville was another growing commercial district, as was Warren in the Western Reserve.

The shortage of specie and currency complicated the conduct of business. Without any medium of exchange, barter was the necessary alternative. Most area residents were farmers, so farm produce naturally made up the bulk of goods transferred to local merchants in exchange for other goods or credit. Dairy products, eggs, bacon, ham, and potatoes were high on the list of agricultural goods traded in, along with a few small manufactured items. Smith and Findlay disposed of some of these products locally, but shipped most to other markets down the river. Bond describes the nature of the barter trade as carried on by Smith and Findlay:

> Occasionally, horses were offered in payment, and Griffin Yeatman, a well-known tavern keeper in Cincinnati, partially settled his account with a yoke of oxen. Another account was credited with 19 pounds, 12 shillings, and 6 pence, for "22 sheep and a bell," others with a keel boat, a Kentucky boat, or a "periogg," and there was a credit item of 700 pounds in 1796 for houses and lots in Hamilton. Smith and Findlay gave credit, too, for ordinary labor, listing such items as the repair of the firm's boat, labor in the garden, or work in making caps and "callicoe" shirts. Most unusual of all was the account of a Cincinnati clergyman for six pounds five shillings which included items of whisky that totaled four and a half gallons in less than three months. This account the firm settled by "our subscription for preaching."

Other communities carried on in this way and as far as local trade was concerned barter seemed to meet the needs of the people. Merchants would advertise in the newspapers for the kinds of produce or livestock they would be happy to receive in exchange for their wares. A newspaper publisher even offered to cancel overdue subscription charges for a certain amount of "wheat, flour, corn, sugar, beef" and so forth. A Chillicothe dealer was willing to exchange everything he had for a herd of cattle. The list of exchangeable items covered just about everything produced in the territory.

Because of the scarcity of money throughout Ohio's territorial period, banknotes from eastern institutions (which were of uncertain value and could easily be counterfeited) began to circulate. The establishment of local banks which were fairly

Left: **The** Centinel Of The North-Western Territory *was the first newspaper published in Cincinnati; its purpose was to bring news to residents and acquaint them with happenings in the federal government. It also enabled Cincinnatians to "make themselves and their situations known abroad." Courtesy, Ohio Historical Society*

Below: Pictured is a banknote from the Miami Exporting Company, a company which was chartered by the State of Ohio in 1803 to build riverboats. Within four years the company, located in Cincinnati, left the shipping business and turned its interest to banking. Courtesy, Cincinnati Historical Society

well secured helped ease the money crisis. The first Ohio bank was the Miami Exporting Company. Formerly a Cincinnati mercantile house but recognized as a bank in 1803, it proved to be a successful venture and a boon to commerce. Other sound banks founded in the next few years were located in Marietta, Chillicothe, Steubenville, and Zanesville.

The immediate needs of the early settlers in Ohio as elsewhere were iron (necessary to forge tools and utensils), gristmills, sawmills, and salt. Gristmills were essential to grind wheat into flour and corn into meal. The Marietta settlers of 1788 got their corn and wheat in the ground the first year, but no mills were built until a year or so later. All grinding had to be done by hand. Several mills were built along the Muskingum River a short dis-

———

When settlers first arrived in the Ohio area, they found the land covered with trees. This made the clearing of land in preparation for planting difficult, but the ample hardwood available facilitated building. Courtesy, Ohio Historical Society

tance above Marietta in 1790 and 1791, but the outbreak of the Indian Wars made them difficult to use. An original "48-er," Jonathan Devol, built a floating gristmill in 1791 which was anchored between two boats in the Ohio River near Blennerhasset Island, a more secure location against Indian forays.

As settlement spread across southern Ohio and then along major rivers into the interior during the 1790s and early 1800s, the need for gristmills increased. Within two decades, hundreds of them had been built along creeks, streams, and rivers —wherever there was sufficient waterpower. In one case, a settlement's only access to water lay through a township on "congressional land." A petition was sent to Congress urging permission to build a mill on the reserved section, a petition which, happily, was granted. Usually a sawmill was built before or at the same time as a gristmill, in order to have lumber to construct the gristmill. The first sawmill in Ohio was erected on Wolf Creek, which flowed into the Muskingum River north of Marietta, at the present site of Waterford. This was also the location of the first gristmill built in 1790. Machinery for both mills had to be imported from the East. The millstones were so heavy that the flatboat carrying

them could not be anchored along the shore at Marietta. The stones were dropped into the water and hauled to land by a team of oxen.

Mills appeared somewhat later in the Western Reserve because of later settlement there. None existed prior to 1800, but by 1840 each county had about 14 mills. Prior to their appearance, the settlers, as in Marietta and other southern sections, had to grind their grain by hand. This laborious operation required two hours of manual grinding to secure a sufficient daily portion of flour for one person. An early Cleveland settler, John Doan, recalled the procedure:

> *In those days we ground corn in little hand-mills. There were two stones about two and one-half feet in diameter, one above the other, the upper being turned with a pole. The corn was poured through a hole in the upper stone.*

Salt was a necessity for the pioneers for food preservation and seasoning. Though there were numerous salt springs or "licks" in the eastern and southern parts of the territory, their exact location was not always known and it was necessary to import salt from across the mountains at steep prices—from six to ten dollars a bushel. It was important, therefore, to find and drill the local wells as soon as possible. A map from 1795 marked a few of the salt springs and creeks, but the pioneers knew nothing about the map or the springs.

The celebrated Moravian missionary David Zeisberger wrote in 1779 and 1780 about salt springs in the valley of the Muskingum. They were found along the banks of creeks or occasionally on a sandbar in the middle of a stream with pure water rushing past on both sides. The Indians of the Muskingum, however, did not use much salt. The arduous labor of boiling saline water apparently was not worth the effort. Rather than make it themselves, the Indians bartered for salt with white squatters who brought it with them.

Indians occasionally helped whites in locating salt licks. One man, a prisoner of the Indians who had been released after the Battle of Fallen Timbers, passed through Olive Green, west of present-day Caldwell, and informed the inhabitants of salt springs some miles away, which he had learned about from his captors. A group of men went off for a week and returned with a gallon of salt. Though it was not much, it was better than no salt at all. Two years later, in 1797, Indians assisted

settlers at Waterford in finding salt springs at modern Chandlersville, forty miles up the Muskingum River.

Ephraim Cutler, son of Manasseh Cutler, frequently took part in salt searches. On one such trip the party camped in a log cabin. Two traveling Frenchmen happened by and were taken in for the night. The evening entertainment for the company included singing "The Marseillaise" and other well-known songs of the day. One of the guests, a well-dressed, well-mannered person, devoted most of his time quizzing Cutler about conditions in the Ohio Company's grant and also at the settlement of the "French 500" at Gallipolis. Only as the Frenchmen were ready to leave the next day did Cutler learn that he had been conversing with the Duke of Orleans. He could not know, of course, that the Duke would later become King Louis Philippe of France.

As a result of his experiences, Cutler described the problems locating and manufacturing salt.

> *The article of salt was extremely difficult to procure. Nearly all the salt consumed west of the Alleghenies was brought over the mountains on pack-horses. The price was seldom less than five, and was sometimes even eight dollars a bushel. People were sent to Marietta to purchase it by the quart or gallon. It was not only excessively dear, but scarce and hard to be obtained; and our means of realizing money were very limited. When the springs were discovered a public meeting was called, and a "Salt-Spring Company" was formed from the settlements of Olive Green, Wolf Creek Mills, Cat's Creek, and Waterford, for the purpose of making salt. They were divided into four classes, bearing the names of these places, and at stated times they relieved each other in the work. We took possession of the spring, cleaned it out, set the large iron kettles, which we had for making sugar, into arches, and began boiling the water for salt. It was a slow, tedious process. During a week of hard work four men could make about six bushels. We succeeded, however, in making a full supply for the several settlements represented in the company, and had some to spare. Afterwards when our conveniences were improved we could, by our best efforts, make five bushels a day; and it as a great relief to the whole country.*

While salt was obtainable in the Muskingum valley the biggest source for Ohio salt was in Jackson County, later the home of the Scioto Salt Works. These springs were of ancient origin, even predating the glacial era. Fossil remains inform us that animals made regular pilgrimages to the area. Jackson County was Shawnee territory before white settlement, and the Shawnees allowed tribes from near and far to visit their springs. Located on a well-traveled Indian trail which ran from the Kanawha River in Virginia to the Maumee, the Shawnees had plenty of visitors. One historian of Jackson County has written that

> *these gatherings resembled the Russian markets of the nineteenth century. Many of these visiting Indians bought their salt, giving in exchange flint implements, tobacco, beads, pipestone and other articles of aboriginal commerce. It is told that tribes at war with each other would observe a truce during these visits. The squaws performed all work, chopping the saplings for fuel, drawing the water and watching the fires day and night, while the men spent their time hunting, fishing, playing ball, gaming and telling yarns. In later years, they tortured white captives in the presence of the assembled tribes. Even after the whites had taken possession of the licks the Indians used to revisit them every summer until about 1815.*

Manufacturing salt was a long, laborious process which took a lot of salt water to recover even a small amount of salt. In Jackson County it took fifteen gallons of water to recover a pound of salt and 600 gallons to recover a bushel. The most common method of securing salt was to pour the water into huge kettles placed over or next to a stone furnace. In the early years kettles were almost as scarce as the salt itself. In good weather the water was poured into long wooden troughs and placed in the sun. But evaporation was an even slower process than boiling.

The first so-called "industry" in Jefferson County was salt manufacturing. Salt springs were discovered late in the 1790s near Irondale on Yellow Creek and soon furnaces went up all over the area. One furnace built in 1802 was able to produce three bushels a day. A visitor who came to the furnace from afar found that there was such a long line of people waiting their turn for the salt that he was

Left: The old saltworks belonging to Stephen A. Guthrie, located in Muskingum County, are pictured here. The large vats were used for boiling water to obtain salt—a long and involved process. Fifteen gallons of water might yield only one pound of salt. Courtesy, Ohio Historical Society

Below: The terrain surrounding this farm at Armstrong Mills in eastern Ohio demonstrates the division of land into areas for crops, cattle grazing, and orchards. Courtesy, Ohio Historical Society

forced to return home "saltless."

In spite of Ohio's salt springs the output never was sufficient to satisfy the needs of early settlers. At the time statehood was proclaimed in 1803 the federal government granted to the state all the licks on "congressional lands." The state government unsuccessfully tried to operate the springs and then leased them to private interests. This method did not work well either and much of the state's salt supply continued to be imported from outside, chiefly New York. It was shipped from Buffalo to Cleveland and transported by teams of packhorses and oxen overland to the central and southern sections of the state. Kentucky and Virginia also sent salt to Ohio. But domestic production continued to grow and by 1830 there was no longer a shortage.

But in spite of a few primitive industries, Ohio, like everywhere else, was overwhelmingly farm country. Since the Indians had scarcely cultivated the land, Ohio agriculture really commenced with the arrival of the pioneers. The oft-told tale of the pioneer's life—carving a clearing out of the wilderness, the drudgery, the isolation, the illness, the unfriendly animals—needs no retelling. It was a hard life. But in time, the farm was a going concern, new buildings had been added, the crops and the cattle provided sustenance and profit, and the isolation was broken down.

Ohio farmers in the early years engaged in self-sufficient, general farming. The land was usually divided into three sections, one devoted to grain crops, particularly corn and wheat, another to pastureland for grazing cattle, and a smaller portion for an orchard. While this provided ample produce for family needs, a sufficient surplus also permitted the sale elsewhere of grain, meat, livestock, and dairy products.

Several regions became distinguished by specialized forms of farming. The "cattle kingdom" was centered in the Scioto River valley. In the nineteenth century, annual cattle drives took thousands of surplus livestock to eastern markets, difficult as such drives were. The Connecticut Western Reserve stood out in the dairy cattle industry, although dairying was carried on throughout the state. Wheat, while grown in most counties, was especially suited to the "Backbone" Region south of the Western Reserve, where the soil was good.

In the southwest, the Miami River valley was known as "swine country." A surplus of corn production provided ample feed for hogs and production soared. Cincinnati acquired its famous "Porkopolis" sobriquet because of its proximity to "swine

This sketch portrays settlers crossing the Ohio River from the Kentucky shore on flatboats. Courtesy, Cincinnati Historical Society

country." The first hogs which accompanied settlers into the Miami valley were "razorbacks," described as being "long-legged, slim-bodied, fleet-footed." Efforts at producing fatter, heavier hogs succeeded, and the new breed was called the "Miami Valley Hog." "The standardization of this breed," writes historian William T. Utter, "is Ohio's greatest contribution to American livestock" By the mid-1800s, farm output of grain, cattle, and dairy products had placed Ohio in the agricultural forefront of all states in the country.

Whiskey was also an important product in the country west of the Appalachians. Since shipping corn, rye, and barley, as well as fruit across the mountains to eastern markets was expensive, it was much more profitable to distill the product into whiskey and brandy which could be shipped at less cost. The newly formed United States Congress adopted a whiskey excise tax in 1791, in part to show the fiercely independent frontier farmers the power of the government. The farmers of western Pennsylvania ignored the whiskey tax and developed a prosperous commerce in the liquid merchandise. In the fall of 1794 a force of 15,000 militiamen from Virginia and Pennsylvania, accompanied by Secretary of the Treasury Alexander Hamilton, headed for Pittsburgh, the center of the "Whiskey Rebellion." Without bloodshed the frontiersmen were taught to behave and pay their taxes.

While agreeing that they must now pay the tax, farmers of the West still found it more profitable to distill the grain crops into liquor than to ship the crops themselves. Distilleries began to proliferate on the frontier, not only on the Pennsylvania-Virginia border, but in the Ohio country as well. A revenue officer was appointed for Ohio in 1795 to insure that distillers paid the whiskey tax. They did. One of the first Ohio distilleries was built in 1798 on the present site of Steubenville by a Mr. Snyder, a migrant from Uniontown, Pennsylvania, no doubt one of the "whiskey rebels." In addition to distilleries, breweries also made their appearance in the territorial period.

While the young economy was chugging along in low gear, the equally young territory was motoring toward statehood in high gear. Although Governor St. Clair opposed statehood, he may have hastened it along by his very perverseness. He had become increasingly autocratic as the years passed and had made important enemies in the process. The main reason for his opposition to statehood was his fear that Ohio would become another Republican state. A staunch Federalist, St. Clair was alarmed at Jefferson's election to the presidency in 1800 and was not about to strengthen the other party if he could avoid it.

By 1800 Ohio was sharply polarized along political lines. The Federalists with their strongholds in Cincinnati and Marietta stood against the Republicans centered in Chillicothe, the new territorial capital, in the Scioto valley. Despite Cincinnati's size and importance, the Republicans, led by such men as Thomas Worthington, held considerable power in the territory besides having close ties with Republicans in Congress. So bitter was St. Clair at the rising Republican tide that he proposed to divide the territory into three states with the Scioto River serving as the boundary line between the two easternmost states. In this way he hoped to dilute Republicanism on both sides of the river.

To overcome St. Clair's opposition, Republicans decided to ignore the governor and work through their friends in Washington. Worthington and Michael Baldwin were sent to the capital to plead their case for statehood. Resulting from this, Congress in April 1802 adopted an Enabling Act which permitted the people of Ohio to convoke a constitutional convention on their own initiative. In this

fashion the obstructionist tactics of St. Clair were circumvented. Ohio Republicans planned carefully and propagandized thoroughly for statehood prior to the October election, called for by the Enabling Act. As a result, they easily carried the vote and when the convention met on November 1 in Chillicothe, twenty-six of the thirty-five delegates were Republicans. St. Clair was permitted to address the assemblage and delivered such an intemperate speech denouncing the whole proceedings, that when word of it reached Jefferson, the President dismissed him from office. The convention voted for statehood and completed drafting the constitution in less than a month. Worthington was requested to take the document to Washington for final acceptance. Early in the new year of 1803 Congress approved statehood for Ohio and Jefferson proclaimed March 1, the date on which the General Assembly was organized, as the formal date of Ohio's admission into the Union.

Ohio's first state capitol was in Chillicothe in the state's first stone public building. Chillicothe was the capital from 1803 to 1810 and then again from 1812 until 1816, when the capital was permanently located in Columbus. Zanesville served as an interim capital from 1810 to 1812. Courtesy, Cincinnati Historical Society

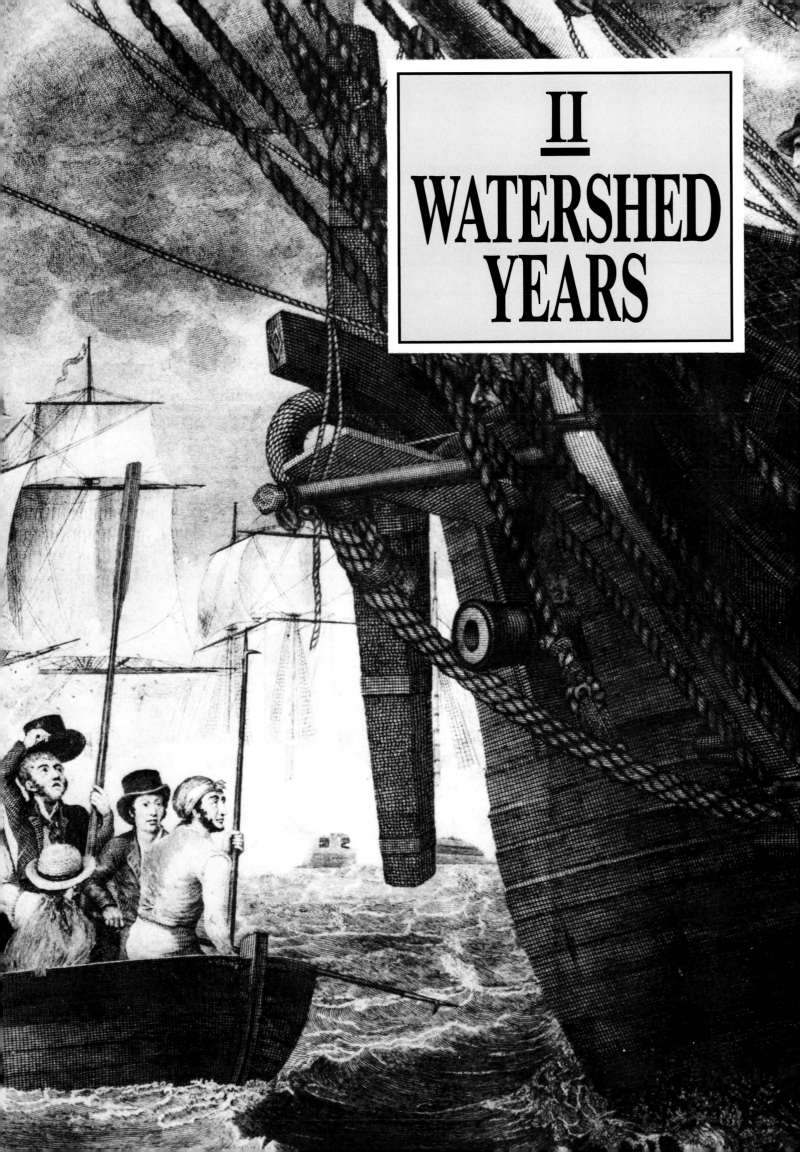

II
WATERSHED YEARS

"Dear General—We have met the enemy, and they are ours, two ships, two brigs, one schooner, and one sloop." So read the message Oliver H. Perry sent to General William H. Harrison upon the American victory over the British in the Battle of Lake Erie in September 1812. This victory gave the Americans control of Lake Erie, as shown in this engraving of Perry transferring his flag to the Niagara. *Engraving by A. Lawson, after a painting by F. Birch. Courtesy, Western Reserve Historical Society*

Facing page: The Cincinnati, Hamilton and Dayton Railroad, built in 1851, was instrumental in the growth of suburban towns north of the city. Trains passing through and stopping in these outlying neighborhoods enabled people to commute to the city for work. Courtesy, Cincinnati Historical Society

ny attempt to divide Ohio's early economic history into two distinct periods—one before and one after statehood—is bound to fail. After Ohio became a state, economic development continued steadily and unspectacularly. Roads and turnpikes improved, new industries were founded, and trade and commerce expanded, much as in the territorial stage. The first major watershed came after the War of 1812, when a more advanced stage of development commenced.

Local industries developed in the territorial years—household manufactures, cotton and woolen mills, gristmills, and salt works—continued to flourish after statehood, while a number of new kinds of manufacturing establishments—tanneries, factories for making grindstones and paper, and iron furnaces—made their appearance. The list of manufacturing plants was a lengthy one at the time war broke out. Although the 1810 census estimates the annual value of Ohio products at $2.9 million, this figure is much too low, since it omitted several important industries.

Shipbuilding was established early in Ohio and continued to grow well into the nineteenth century. The industry was stimulated in 1803 by the purchase of the Louisiana Territory from Napoleon. This opened up the Ohio-Mississippi river route all the way to the Gulf of Mexico. Most of the ships constructed at Marietta, Cincinnati, and a few other river ports were designed for river trade and transport, although a few did travel to foreign places.

Marietta was the first important shipbuilding center in Ohio, and Jonathan Devol, who built the floating gristmill in the Ohio River near

Cincinnati, Hamilton

AND

DAYTON

RAILROAD

BETWEEN

CINCINNATI

AND

DAYTON, TOLEDO,

DETROIT,

INDIANAPOLIS

RICHMOND, LOGANSPORT,

CHICAGO.

AND ALL WESTERN & NORTH WESTERN CITIES.

For Information Apply at the Principal Railroad Offices in the U.S. & Canada.

SAM'L. STEVENSON, *Gen'l Ticket Ag't.*　　　　*D. McLAREN Pres't*

In the mid-1800s, Cincinnati was one of the nation's largest boat builders, turning out approximately thirty boats a year. By 1880 nearly 1,000 steamboats had been built in the city. Pictured here is the construction of the steamboat Sunrise, *designed for carrying cotton. Courtesy, Cincinnati Historical Society*

———

Blennerhasset, was Marietta's first shipbuilder. A member of the Ohio Company and builder of the boats which brought the original contingent of settlers downstream in 1788, Devol continued his trade after he established his home in Marietta. In 1797 he built several mills and shipbuilding facilities on property he purchased on the Muskingum, a few miles north of Marietta.

Boats built by Devol and other early Ohio settlers were generally river barges and keelboats. A dispute has raged as to where the first oceangoing vessel was built on inland waters, but Marietta seems to have a good claim. The *St. Clair,* constructed there in 1800—not by Devol—traveled to Cuba with pork and flour under the command of

Commodore Abraham Whipple, a Revolutionary War naval hero. The War of 1812 put a damper on boat construction along the Ohio, but between 1800 and 1812 twenty-six vessels, including brigs, schooners, ships, and gunboats, were built in Marietta alone.

One Marietta shipbuilder became innocently involved in the Aaron Burr "conspiracy," which excited the western frontier in 1805-1806. When Burr visited Harman Blennerhasset, who lived in his beautiful island mansion below Parkersburg, in August 1806, Blennerhasset was completely won over by the suave former Vice President. Whatever Burr's intentions were, and historians have never completely agreed about the matter, boats were needed for his expedition down the Ohio and Mississippi rivers. Blennerhasset contracted with Colonel Joseph Barker, who had built the Blennerhasset mansion, to construct fifteen boats. Barker had a shipyard at his farm on the Muskingum. Ten of the boats were to be forty feet long, the others fifty feet long. One of the latter was to have "partitions, a fireplace, and glass windows" for the comfort of the Blennerhassets. The total cost was $1,390. By the late fall of 1806, however, rumors of Burr's "treasonous" plot were abroad and local militia at

Marietta were ordered to arrest suspicious persons. Only one of Barker's boats was completed when on the night of December 6, 1806, Blennerhasset was forced to flee his home to avoid arrest by Virginia militiamen from Parkersburg.

More serious trouble for the frontier came with the revival of Indian hostilities. Quiescent since the Treaty of Greenville, Indian tribes were restless because of further white encroachment on their lands in Indiana and Illinois. The celebrated Shawnee war chief Tecumseh tried to form an alliance among different tribes to block this advance, but was not successful. Raids on frontier settlements increased and the demand rose that the Indians be crushed. General William Henry Harrison made his

Above: Tecumseh, a Shawnee Indian war chief, organized a short-lived Indian confederacy against the encroachment of the white man on the Ohio territory and the lands beyond. He argued that all the land belonged to all tribes and therefore no single tribe could sell any part of it through a treaty. Tecumseh allied with the British during the War of 1812 and was killed at the Battle of the Thames in 1813. Courtesy, Ohio Historical Society

famous assault on the Indian base at Tippecanoe Creek on November 7, 1811, which delivered a sharp setback to the natives, but did not put the issue at rest.

The British in Canada were suspected of encouraging and supporting the Indian raids. Although the War of 1812 was supposedly caused by British depredations against American shipping on the high seas, the western cry of "Canada, Canada, Canada," was no doubt a more significant factor. A successful war against England and the acquisition of Canada would end once and for all the unholy alliance between the British and the Indians. While stirring

Left: Tenskwatawa, also known as the "Prophet," claimed to be a mystic and preached a return to ancient ways. He aided his brother Tecumseh in rallying tribes for an uprising against the white civilization. The Prophet's power was ended at the Battle of Tippecanoe when he made a premature and ill-advised attack on the forces of William Henry Harrison. Courtesy, Cincinnati Historical Society

naval battles were fought in the Atlantic early in the war, the most significant land fighting took place on the frontier.

The surrender of General William Hull and his force of 2,200 Americans, mostly from Ohio, at Detroit in August 1812 opened up the entire northwestern section of the state to invasion. Harrison, Hull's successor, held the line for the next year from his bases first at Upper Sandusky and later at Fort Meigs on the Maumee. On September 10 Oliver H. Perry won his great victory over the British Lake Erie flotilla at Put-in-Bay. This reopened the route to Canada and Harrison at once crossed the border. On October 5 he fought and won the Battle of the Thames and the war in the West was over. The Peace of Ghent, formally ending the war, was signed over a year later.

Some historians have asserted that whereas the American Revolution was a war for political independence, the War of 1812 was fought for economic independence. This is no doubt an oversimplification, but it does contain some truth. Overseas trade had been barred since Jefferson's "Embargo" policy was instituted in 1807, and this nec-

———

State banknotes were in great abundance in the early 1800s. This note from the Bank of Sandusky was issued in 1835 for five dollars, amid the rising number of counterfeit notes in the area. Courtesy, Ohio Historical Society

essarily stimulated domestic manufacturing. The factory system emerged, industry expanded, and local trade and commerce increased. After the war, when overseas trade resumed, Ohio was the best example of heightened economic activity in the West.

The momentum for economic growth drove the state forward almost too rapidly after the war. With the restoration of peace, settlers flocked into the state thirsting for land. The population of Ohio increased from 230,000 in 1810 to 580,000 in 1820. Land sales were big business. Federal land offices had never been as busy. One million acres were sold in the West in 1815 and over five million in 1819. Settlers could purchase 160 acres at a minimum of two dollars an acre, one-quarter down and the balance in four years.

Since the settlers had little money, they borrowed from the state banks and paid the government with state banknotes. This was fine as long as the state banks were strongly structured and their notes backed by gold or silver. In January 1815, however, specie payment was suspended by Ohio banks as a result of similar action a few months before by eastern banks. State banknotes could now be issued with no specie backing at all, and they were issued—in great abundance. A number of new banks were chartered in the state over the next few years, and while most of them tried to observe sound banking practices, others were not so careful. Some "banks" formed were not even chartered. In any case, all of them began issueing large amounts of unbacked paper money. With land sales skyrocketing, the federal land offices and treasury were soon filled with unbacked banknotes.

The Second United States Bank was chartered

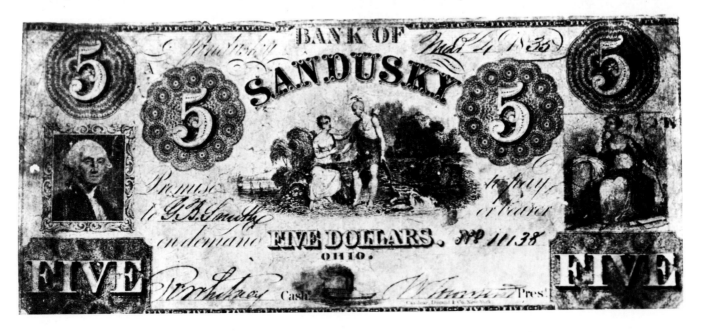

Above: The German Bank of Wooster in Wayne County issued this banknote early in the 1800s, when banknotes were quite popular. Courtesy, Ohio Historical Society

---

Left: This banknote is from the Bank of Manhattan, which was incorporated in the mid-1830s in the newly established village of Toledo. At that time, the Locofoco, an anti-bank faction of the Ohio Democratic Party, objected to the profusion of banknotes of denominations lower than five dollars. Their concern resulted in a state tax of 20 percent on banks, an increase of 15 percent, unless the banks ceased issuing bills less than five dollars. Courtesy, Toledo-Lucas County Public Library

in 1817 and two branches were created in Ohio at Cincinnati and Chillicothe. In July 1818 orders went out from the mother bank in Philadelphia to the western branches that only specie or its equivalent in United States notes would be accepted in the future. This precipitated a crisis. The branch banks, such as those in Cincinnati and Chillicothe, demanded specie from the state banks in exchange for their notes.

This sudden demand for specie payments was met with widespread protest. Requests for more time to shift to the new policy were rejected. Banks failed, mortgages were foreclosed, prices tumbled, and land speculators went to jail. Six years would pass before real prosperity would return, spurred then by canal construction. The "prosperity" of the post-War of 1812 years had been an artificial one, stimulated by a boom in public land sales based on cheaper paper money. "Probably half of the men living in Ohio," wrote historian William T. Utter, "were indebted to the Government for land purchases, and the fortunes of the other half were closely bound to theirs." But out of evil comes good. In 1820 a new land law reduced the minimum lot size to eighty acres at a dollar and a quarter an acre. Although no credit was allowed, for $100 a man could own his farm.

The rapid increase in population in the first years of the new century—from about 50,000 in 1800 to 230,000 in 1810—made it essential that more and better roads be built. When statehood was granted, the federal government allotted Ohio 3 percent of its annual income from all public land sales within the state to use for highway develop-

Above: The Cumberland or National Road became the main route of westward expansion in the first half of the nineteenth century. However, as this photo of Linnville, Ohio, reveals, the road could be a muddy mire in bad weather. Courtesy, Ohio Historical Society

Left: This tollgate, on the Lexington Pike outside Cincinnati, has seen many weary travelers as well as regular customers like this milkman. Courtesy, Cincinnati Historical Society

ment. The first fruits of this largesse in 1804 amounted to $17,000, with which the state legislature authorized the construction of several roads in and around Cincinnati. The legislature also required that all roads built with these monies meet certain width, strength, and grade standards. One specific clause required the removal of all stumps over one foot in height from the roadway.

The 3 percent fund provided the means for building a highway network over most of the state. By 1806 much of the south and central sections were linked and when war with England broke out in 1812 considerable construction had been completed in the Western Reserve. A traveler might now make his way from the Ohio River to Lake Erie over several different routes. Admittedly, this was not an easy nor comfortable trip, but it could be made. The legislature had expended by this time over $127,000 from the 3 percent fund and several hundreds of miles of roads had been built.

The state highway act of 1804 did not provide for the maintenance of the roads, leaving this responsibility in the hands of the county commissioners. The commissioners did very little to keep the roads in repair, judging from the complaints made about them. Because of this general dissatisfaction, two private turnpike companies were formed in 1809. One was authorized to construct a road in Trumbull County, the other a road from Zanesville to Columbus. These roads had to meet certain standards and be properly maintained. If this were done, tollgates could be built at eight-mile intervals and tolls charged for all users. But the real period of private turnpike construction came after the War of 1812.

The years following the war and before the depression of 1819 saw a sudden burst of turnpike construction, with twelve companies chartered in 1816 and 1817 alone. The new roads, which generally were improvements of the old, appeared in the more settled areas of the southeast and southwest, such as the links between Cambridge and Zanesville, Lancaster and Chillicothe, and Cincinnati and Hamilton.

Turnpike charters specified that the roads should be thirty-three feet wide, of which eighteen feet comprised the actual roadway. They were to be made of compacted stone, gravel, wood, or anything else which would provide a strong base, and graded gently from the crown to the sides for drainage. At every ten miles tollgates could be erected and rates charged for different forms of traffic. The charters also specified that the state could, at some future time, purchase these roads. Crude as these

Top: Thomas Worthington, governor of Ohio from 1814 to 1818, set the stage for future legislative approval of the construction of canals in the state. Courtesy, Ohio Historical Society

Above: Ethan Allen Brown, Ohio governor from 1818 to 1822, was known as the "Father of the Ohio Canals" and promoted internal improvements in the state. Upon his insistence, the legislature passed a law in February 1822 which provided for an engineer and a seven-member commission to determine the practicality and expense of various canal routes within the state. Courtesy, Ohio Historical Society

Above right: This map of Ohio counties shows the National Road, Zane's Trace, and the paths the canals followed. Major stopping points along each route are also depicted. Courtesy, Ohio Historical Society

early turnpikes were, they did provide an improved means of travel and transport for Ohio's burgeoning economy.

The completion of the National Road from Cumberland, Maryland, through the southwestern corner of Pennsylvania to Wheeling on the Ohio River in 1818 provided an important boost to trade. The demand that the road be continued across Ohio was made almost at once, but such expectations were stilled by the financial depression which broke out and lingered for almost six years. It was not until 1825 that federal appropriations permitted resumption of the construction of the road in Ohio. Tortuously working its way across the state, the National Road reached Zanesville in 1830, Columbus in 1833, Springfield in 1838, and the Indiana border in 1840.

While roads were improving, the construction of the Erie Canal in New York opened the eyes of Ohioans to the far more promising possibilities of a canal system. Governor Thomas Worthington (1814-1818), impressed by the importance of the Erie Canal to Ohio trade, called the legislature's attention to the matter. His successor Ethan Allen Brown (1818-1822) similarly understood the economic importance of the Erie Canal to Ohio and pressed hard for engineering surveys of possible canal routes. But local opposition—rising from Ohioans' fear that their communities might be bypassed by the canal—and economic problems stemming from the financial crisis of 1819 argued against appropriations for surveys.

In January 1822 the legislature overcame the obstacles and authorized surveys of several possible canal routes connecting Lake Erie with the Ohio River. A seven-member commission was created to supervise the surveys. The commissioners, men with broad experience in business and politics, understood the importance of a canal system to the state's economy. After extensive field studies, assisted by an engineer who had worked on the Erie Canal, the commission submitted its report to the legislature in January 1825.

The commission proposed two canals. The main one would begin at Portsmouth and follow the Scioto River to within twelve miles of Columbus, where it would veer eastward to the Muskingum River, and thence travel northward to Lake Erie at Cleveland. The estimated cost was roughly $2.8 million to $4 million. The second, or Miami Canal, would extend sixty-six miles from Cincinnati to Dayton and cost approximately $673,000. The report proposed that a new commission manage the canals and that a revision in property taxes be enacted to help fund construction of the two waterways. The

commission argued strongly that not only would the canal system stimulate the economy, but would rapidly develop the northern part of the state.

Although opponents of the canals made themselves heard, the bill passed both houses easily on February 4, 1825. Plans were made to break ground on July 4, and the ceremonies at Newark, a halfway point, were witnessed by a huge crowd. The guest of honor was DeWitt Clinton himself, creative genius of the Erie Canal, who had expressed great interest in and support for an Ohio canal. Clinton turned the first spadeful of dirt and passed the shovel to Ohio Governor Jeremiah Morrow, who had worked long and hard for the canals and had been a member of the survey commission. Although the ground breaking had taken place at Newark, actual construction began much farther north because of the need to move Ohio products to New York. A couple of weeks after the event at Newark, Clinton

———

The Ohio and Erie Canal was one of the many canals that facilitated the movement of large quantities of freight. Shown here is the George H. Watkins *unloading its freight and taking on additional cargo. Courtesy, Ohio Historical Society and the Columbus Dispatch*

was back in the state again, this time at Middletown, to turn the first shovelful of dirt for the Miami Canal.

No serious difficulties arose in marketing the canal bonds—New York bankers bought most of them—nor in securing laborers. Hundreds of farmers and their families who lived along the canal routes were hired, while hundreds of Irishmen who had worked on the Erie Canal came over to join the ranks (Akron was born amid the shantytowns of these Irish canal diggers). By the close of 1825, nearly 2,000 diggers were at work on the northernmost section of the Ohio-Erie Canal, from Akron to Cleveland.

While recruiting laborers was not difficult, it was not easy to retain them. Workers, whether wallowing in several inches of mud or hacking their way through thick woods and underbrush, toiled long hours. While the pay was good—eight to ten dollars a month plus food and shelter—it was not good enough to keep them on the job for any length of time. Farmers, in particular, were likely to run off periodically to attend to their land. And not infrequently contractors ran off without paying their workers. Disease was a constant concern. Historians Raymond Boryczka and Lorin Lee Cary write:

> *Recurrent epidemics of typhoid, malaria, and cholera—popularly termed "canal fever"—not only compounded workers' woes but also depleted their numbers. So many were stricken or frightened off during an 1827 outbreak, for example, that the state legislature authorized the use of convict labor on the Columbus Feeder Canal; and in 1829 disease temporarily halted construction throughout the state. Unsanitary conditions in the jerry-built shanties commonly provided by employers*

Left: In the early days of river transportation, horses and mules were used to pull canal boats. The fare and proposed speed of travel on canal boats were a "cent and a half a mile and a mile and a half an hour." The best time made on the Ohio and Erie Canal was 307 miles in eighty hours between Cleveland and Portsmouth. Courtesy, Cincinnati Historical Society

Above: The Miami and Erie Canal went through Cincinnati in an area predominantly occupied by Germans. They called the canal the "Rhine," and when returning from downtown they would say they were going "over the Rhine." In 1920 the canal was drained to provide a channel for a subway, which was never completed. Today Central Parkway covers the canal and the surrounding area is referred to as "over the Rhine." Courtesy, Cincinnati Historical Society

aggravated the situation. Under such trying hardships, cheap whiskey often became the canal workers' prevalent remedy and consolation. Whiskey dens sprang up around construction sites and, at least in the early years, contractors customarily provided three daily "Jiggerfuls" in order to mollify and retain their crews. Drunken brawls were the "unhappy consequences," frequently between rival Irish clan . . .

Two years to the day after construction began, on July 4, 1827, the canal was completed from Akron to Cleveland. The event was celebrated with even greater ceremony than the initial ground breaking. A convoy of flag-bedecked barges traveled the thirty-six-mile distance with excited residents cheering along the way. At Cleveland a big crowd welcomed the boats and a banquet concluded festivities. Big crowds awaited the canal's completion at

Canal boats had a solid and efficient, if not elegant, appearance. Passenger packets were patronized by the wealthy, whereas poorer individuals rode on freight barges. Packets provided separate cabins for men and women and a kitchen, usually in the stern. In fair weather, passengers could escape from the crowded quarters below and gather on deck to view the surrounding countryside. Courtesy, Cincinnati Historical Society

every point along the 308-mile route, as well as on the several "feeder" lines. It took three more years to complete the canal to Newark and it was not until 1833 that Portsmouth, the southern extremity, was reached.

Now the entire state from Lake Erie to the Ohio River could be traversed in eighty hours! Barges were lined up at every lock as the merchandise flowed to the South and Northeast in unprecedented volume. Formerly landlocked communities experienced a sudden birth of affluence. Land values along the canal quintupled in ten years' time. Walter Havighurst described the new prosperity:

At Canal Fulton in Summit County, Canal Street was lined with stores that had rear loading platforms on the water. Barge captains bought provisions and mule feed there, frequently on credit . . . Here on summer days town boys would drop off the overhead bridge onto southbound canal boats, riding to the lock a mile distant. As the return trip, on loaded barges, took twice as long, the boys generally walked back on the towpath. They could stop to swim and catch a few turtles and still beat the northbound boat to town.

One boy, a future president, got his start in life, as legend has it, as a mule driver on the towpath of the Ohio-Erie Canal. James Abram Garfield was his name.

But the colorful Canal Age was almost doomed before it began. The first railroad in Ohio was chartered by the state legislature even before the Ohio-Erie Canal was completed, although the marvelous possibilities of rail transport were only dimly seen then. Though canals were obsolete by the 1850s, they had performed a valuable function by contributing substantially to the growth of the state, both economically and numerically. Cities grew up overnight, a cash economy supplanted primitive barter trade, and the value of goods escalated. Ohio moved into the primal age of industrialism many years earlier than might have otherwise been the case, largely because of its canal system.

In time few people would argue that canals were superior to railroads in speed and volume of goods transported. However, there were various economic objections to railroads during the "period of incubation"—1830-1850—which helped delay their development. Those who had heavily invested in canals saw no good in the iron horse. Turnpike com-

Columbus, which has been called the "Crossroads of America," experienced a big population surge in the nineteenth century. The passage of railroads through the city played a big part in that growth. The city's Union Station, pictured here, was built in the mid-1800s. Courtesy, Ohio Historical Society

panes, tavern proprietors, and farmers in bypassed regions all raised cries of protest. Moreover, serious technical problems prevented the quick triumph of the railroad. Cast-iron wheels and rails were brittle and shattered easily, and no one yet knew how to convert steam power into motive power for the engine. The first steam-powered American locomotive operated successfully in an 1830 experiment, but not until steel rails could be manufactured cheaply after the Civil War would the railroad revolution take place.

Clumsy and unpopular as they were, railroads arrived in the watershed years. In 1830 the first small line in eastern Ohio was chartered, but not built. A wave of charter bills passed the legislature in 1832, including one for the Mad River and Lake Erie line, designed to run from Springfield to Sandusky. Difficulties over financing delayed ground breaking for the Mad River road for several years. In 1837 the legislature authorized the railroad directors to borrow $200,000 on the credit of the state. This plus stock subscriptions from each county through which the road would pass permitted construction to proceed. Sixteen miles of track north of Springfield was opened in 1838. Progress on the Mad River was slow from this point on and Sandusky was not reached until 1848. Meanwhile the Little Miami Railroad was being built south of Springfield to Cincinnati. It was also finished in 1848, which thus provided a continuous rail line across the state from Cincinnati to Sandusky.

During the 1840s other lines were completed, mostly in the northern part of the state. In 1847 the Cleveland, Columbus, and Cincinnati line was

chartered, demonstrating the rising importance of Cleveland. The section from Cleveland to Columbus was finished, 149 miles long, in February 1851. The fifty-four-mile stretch from Columbus to Xenia, which linked up with the Little Miami line, was completed in December 1850 permitting through travel from Cleveland to Cincinnati. Various state laws dealing with Ohio railroads were adopted as the network grew and the new constitution of 1851 established more uniform and standardized control over the entire system.

By mid-century Ohio had experienced a major watershed in its history. All parts of the state had been settled, even the swampy regions of the Maumee valley. A transportation network had been built linking all parts of the state and tying Ohio to eastern markets. Industry had expanded. The factory system had been founded and large urban centers dotted the map.

A glance around the state in 1830, a mid-point in Ohio's watershed period, reveals the progress that had been made up to that time. The Western Reserve was still thinly populated with only 1,000 people living in Cleveland, the principal village. But the Ohio-Erie Canal, then under construction, was about to infuse life and vigor into the Lake City. Canton to the south in Stark County was already firmly in place, while its neighbors Akron and Massillon would shortly prosper from the canal. Steubenville was one of the largest towns in the state and boasted an important woolen factory and other industries. In fact, next to Cincinnati, it was one of the leading manufacturing centers in the West.

Among the older cities, Zanesville, another

Facing page, top: This sketch from Martin's 1857 History of Columbus *shows the busy city market-house at the southwest corner of Town and Fourth streets in Columbus. Markets such as the one shown here were often located in a central spot where city dwellers could come to buy farm produce. Cincinnati's own Findlay Market dates from the mid-1850s. Courtesy, Ohio Historical Society*

Facing page, bottom: The state capitol and other government buildings in Columbus are shown here. From left to right are the U.S. courthouse state offices, and the Old State House which served as the capitol building until 1852. Courtesy, Ohio Historical Society

Above: This is how Columbus, south of High Street, looked in 1854 to artist Henry Howe. Note the wide street, laid out in 1816 when Columbus was chosen to be the state's new capital. The street was not paved until after the Civil War. Courtesy, Ohio Historical Society

manufacturing center, was the second largest city in the state in 1830, with a population of over 3,000. Marietta with a population of 1,200 was a lovely town based on shipbuilding and commerce, although some visitors were struck by signs of inactivity and decline. Portsmouth had 1,000 inhabitants and enjoyed a modest prosperity as the outlet for both the Scioto River and the canal. Also the center of the important "Hanging Rock" iron fields, Portsmouth was entering a kind of "golden age." To the north along the Scioto were the old villages of Chillicothe and Circleville where local trade and commerce continued to thrive. Chillicothe alone boasted four cotton mills. Columbus, the state capital, possessed about 2,500 people and was a center for trade and government. Many complained, however, that far too many pigs were permitted to run loose, a criticism made of a number of other places. From what can be gathered Columbus' principal industry seemed to be the state prison.

But without question the first city in every respect was Cincinnati. With an 1830 population of over 25,000, it was the number-one commercial center west of the mountains. Located at the lower terminus of the Miami-Maumee Canal, its prosperity was linked to trade, shipbuilding, and manufacturing. The city intrigued the eye with its beautiful banks, hotels, and private homes. It was a center of culture as well, claiming a university, theater, and museum. One visitor from abroad observed enthusiastically, "Cincinnati is in every respect an extraordinary city; the only one, perhaps, on record, which has in the course of 25 years, sprung up from nothing to be a place of great consequence."

The watershed years marked the transition from what was basically a domestic, small-shop form of industrial organization, to an embryonic factory system. This transition did not occur overnight, nor did it occur simultaneously throughout all fields of business activity. What might be called "factories" appeared early in the nineteenth century. Some of Ohio's early flour mills, textile mills, and iron works possessed many of the features of the factory system. A three-story woolen factory in Steubenville was powered by steam and had 115 laborers on its payroll. An "iron plantation" in Zanesville had 158 workers. Even more impressive was the Cincinnati Steam Mill, a nine-story structure built in 1814, which used steam engines to process wheat, wool, cotton, and pork products for markets as far away as the West Indies. However, the road to a more mature industrial society had not yet been paved.

New inventions, new techniques, and new processes were essential to the growth of the "modern" factory system. Americans contributed two important principles to the sophistication of production processes. One was the idea of the "interchangeability of parts," the other, the idea of "continuous process manufacturing." Eli Whitney is usually given credit for first successfully demonstrating the practicability of interchangeable parts when he manufactured guns for the United States government early in the nineteenth century. Continuous process, whereby a plant is so designed that the product is manufactured by a series of successive smooth-flowing operations—the modern "assembly line"—came later, toward the middle of the century. The early flour mills and woolen mills were not suited to continuous process.

A number of older industries continued to prosper and grow at least until the middle of the century. Take the iron business. The iron forge was almost as vital to the early settlers as the gristmill. Pioneers looked to the forge for tools, utensils, household wares, machinery, horse shoes, and nails. None were built in Ohio prior to statehood. Whatever iron tools and implements the people possessed were imported or made by the blacksmith with his small furnace and anvil. The first large furnace was built in the valley of the Mahoning River, near Poland, by Daniel Eaton. His output measured two tons daily, which was fashioned into kitchenware. The iron forge, which produced a better quality of iron than the furnace, appeared in two places in 1809. That year James Heaton constructed a dam, sawmill, and forge also in the Mahoning valley, at the site of modern Niles. Working the crude pig-iron through a laborious process of heating and cooling several times, Heaton produced a fairly good quality of iron, using charcoal for fuel. Also in 1809 Moses Dillon built a blast furnace and forge near Zanesville. By 1840 some twenty forges had been built throughout the state, fifteen powered by water, and five by steam, which was first used in 1815.

The most famous iron-producing area in early Ohio was the Hanging Rock region of south-central Ohio and northern Kentucky. The picturesque name given to the area, "Hanging Rock," was derived from a suspended rock on a cliff near Ironton. The region, roughly a hundred miles long and twenty-eight miles wide, embraced the Ohio counties of Lawrence, Scioto, Gallia, Jackson, Vinton, and Hocking, plus Carter, Boyd, and Greenup counties in Kentucky. Sixty-nine charcoal furnaces were built from the 1820s through the 1850s.

The needs of the workers of the Hanging Rock furnaces provided a good market for farmers in the area. Some farmers accumulated modest fortunes in selling their goods locally. In addition, iron manufactured at Hanging Rock became a major product of river transportation to Cincinnati, Pittsburgh, and other river ports. Approximately 100,000 tons were shipped annually.

The charcoal furnaces of Hanging Rock continued to dominate iron production in Ohio until the Civil War. The Hecla Furnace in Lawrence County, built in 1833, was the most famous of these, but many others were equally important.

Iron ore was discovered in the extreme northeast in 1812. This "bog iron" was dug from swampy land with a pick and shovel. By smelting, the organic matter was burned off and the ore reduced to iron. Though of low grade, bog iron was a tough material, particularly good for castings. The Arcole Furnace near Madison manufactured bog iron and prospered for about twenty-five years after its founding in 1831, but failed when charcoal became hard to obtain and as the supply of bog ore gave out. The nearby port of Madison Dock (Ellensbury), which prospered during the peak of the bog iron industry, became a ghost town.

As the years passed, new techniques, such as the "hot blast process" for smelting, were introduced. At Hecla and other iron centers in the south, forges utilized waterpower until the 1840s when steam power came into general use. It was more efficient

Iron miners pause after a hard day of mining at the Ohio Furnace in Scioto County. According to the Ohio Bureau of Labor Statistics *in 1879, miners faced "danger to life and limb . . . added to the awful and hardness and gloom of the coal mine . . . and the inhalation of noxious and poisonous gases [which] blanches the face and impoverishes the human blood." Courtesy, Ohio Historical Society*

than waterpower and permitted industrial site location far removed from rivers and streams.

Another important innovation in iron manufacture was the use of coal rather than charcoal for furnace fuel. It was responsible for opening up the iron industry in the Mahoning valley. Coal was more efficient in eliminating impurities in iron ore and also preserved timberlands. Mahoning valley's great importance as a center of iron and steel production stems from the late 1840s by which time four coal blast furnaces were in operation.

Coal had been discovered in Portage County and in the southeastern part of the state in the 1820s and production steadily increased in the next two decades. One pioneer merchant, Valentine Dexter Horton, settled in Pomeroy in Meigs County in

The Eagle Iron Works, owned by Miles Greenwood, was established in 1832 and manufactured, among other things, malleable iron castings, house locks and latches, vault and safe locks, shutter fasteners, garden seats, and iron house fronts. During the Civil War, Eagle Iron Works produced more munitions than the National Armory in Springfield. The company received 60,000 old flintlock muskets and converted them to modern weapons at the rate of 800 a day. Courtesy, Cincinnati Historical Society

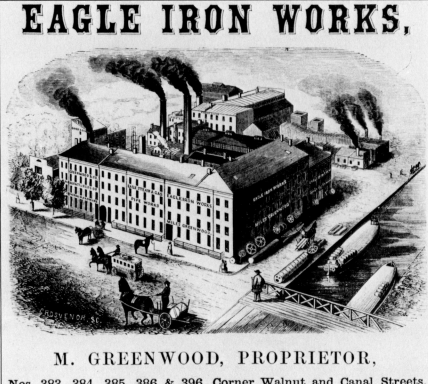

EAGLE IRON WORKS,

M. GREENWOOD, PROPRIETOR,

Nos. 383, 384, 385, 386 & 396, Corner Walnut and Canal Streets,

CINCINNATI, OHIO.

The Eagle Iron Works was established in 1832, by the present proprietor, in connection with Mr. Joseph Webb, for the purpose of a general Foundry business, although in a limited way, as the means of the proprietors would not admit of an extended business; and the articles of manufacture relied upon principally, were Stoves, Hollow Ware, Sad Irons, Dog Irons, Wagon Boxes, Plow Moulds, and some other ordinary articles in every day use; to which additions were made from time to time, of such things as were generally wanted, or made for special purposes.

The business was continued in this manner, and extended as the demands increased, for eight years, when Mr. Webb withdrew from the firm. The same year, 1840, it was determined to commence the manufacture of

BUTT HINGES.

This undertaking, for a time, met with but little favor from dealers, from whom it was but reasonable to expect a liberal patronage; but builders becoming aware of the superior quality of the Hinges made at this establishment, soon created a demand for them, which placed the manufacture and sales on a substantial basis, and has brought them into general use throughout the country.

1835 and began fairly large-scale operations. He shipped coal downstream to Cincinnati and other river ports. Mahoning valley coal, in addition to fueling the local furnaces around Youngstown, was shipped to both Cleveland and Pittsburgh along "feeder" lines of the Ohio-Erie and Pennsylvania-Ohio canals.

By 1850 Ohio ranked high among all states in certain forms of iron production. In that year it was number two in its output of pig iron and third in iron castings. The Hanging Rock furnaces contributed largely to this performance, shipping nearly 50 percent of its products to the foundries in Cincinnati. Several thousand workers were employed in the factories throughout the state turning out pig iron, castings, and other iron products.

Though Cleveland was growing, its minor indus-

trial importance at the time was evident in its mere handful of factories. The older cities were still the center of most industrial activity at mid-century. Steubenville, for example, located in the heart of the sheep-raising region of the state, continued to be one of the major woolen cloth manufacturing centers in the country with five factories in operation. Zanesville remained the hub of the ceramic industry—about 25 percent of the state's ninety-nine potteries in 1840 were located in Zanesville and its environs—although it would soon surrender its leadership to East Liverpool.

The first pottery in East Liverpool was founded in 1839 by James Bennett, a refugee from the Sheffield plants of England. The town's growth had been slow until the 1830s, when increasing commercial activity along the upper Ohio River instilled new life into it. Bennett, a skilled potter, utilized the rich clay deposits in the area and quickly made a name for himself. His brothers soon joined him, as did many other expert English potters. Soon "Bennett's Liverpool Ware" was selling up and down the river from Pittsburgh to St. Louis. By mid-century there were eleven potteries in the city, with 387 craftsmen producing $175,000 worth of goods annually. With the coming of the railroad, East Liverpool earthenware was being sold in Chicago, New Orleans, and other distant markets.

Rich clay deposits were discovered in Summit County (Akron) as early as 1828. By the 1840s there were so many potteries there that business

Above: William and John Hill Garrard manufactured crucible steel at the Cincinnati Steel Works Plant. This advertisement shows the steel plant, known for making top quality steel from 1832 to 1837, at its ideal location on the Miami Canal. Courtesy, Ohio Historical Society

Left: Businesses like the Miners' Supply Company sprang up in response to the local economy. This outlet in Coalton provided necessary equipment for the industry and its employees. Courtesy, Ohio Historical Society

began to suffer. In order to avoid mass bankruptcies, an agreement was reached among them. Thus a "pool," perhaps one of the earliest business combinations anywhere, was formed in 1841. Although this arrangement may not have lasted very long, it put the pottery business back on its feet. Edwin H. Merrill and his associates and Enoch Rowley and his brothers-in-law made reputations for themselves in the manufacture of different forms of stoneware. Rowley came from Staffordshire, England, as had the Bennetts in East Liverpool, and like the Bennetts, began the successful production of yellow and Rockingham ware.

Dayton, aided by the completion of the Miami Canal, also enjoyed an age of growth and prosperity during the watershed years. Cotton spinning, agricultural equipment and carpet factories, flour mills, dis-

tilleries, foundries, and paper mills were all flourishing there.

Dayton was also the home of many dairy farms. The emergence of the dairy industry occurred during the 1820s. Centered in the Western Reserve, dairying prospered because of the region's rich grassland and the internal migration of practiced New England dairy farmers. As of 1850 the total production of Ohio cheese amounted to twenty-one million pounds, with eighteen million of that emanating from the Reserve, or, as some called it, "Cheesedom." The canals and later the railroads carried cheese from northeastern Ohio to the East, South, Far West, and overseas.

But no matter how prosperous, all other Ohio cities paled before mid-century Cincinnati, which was the dominant commercial and industrial city of

The Cincinnati Butchers' Supply Company opened in 1886 producing machinery used in the packing industry. For over fifty years, this business was located on Central Avenue, close to the pork packers and slaughterhouses. The wagon pictured here was typical of the company's advertisements describing its equipment. Courtesy, Cincinnati Historical Society

Facing page: In a short period of time Cincinnati became a major manufacturing center. Increasingly dependent on river transportation, many companies, like the Straub Company, were situated close to the Ohio River. Courtesy, Cincinnati Historical Society

Our Meat Market on Wheels

Customers waited upon without leaving Wagon.

the West. About one-half of Ohio's seventeen million dollars of capital investment was centered there. The slaughtering and packing of pork was the major business in this city of many businesses. Although begun only in the early 1830s, the industry in two decades was packing approximately 27 percent of all meat products of the West. So many hogs went to slaughter annually in Cincinnati, that one swinish observer was moved to remark, "that if put into sausages of the ordinary diameter, it would make a girdle long enough to encompass the whole globe along the line of the equator." Cincinnati packers developed a mammoth conveyor system which later manufacturers would adapt for their own assembly lines. The numerous byproducts recovered in the slaughtering process such as lard, soap, candles, and glue, gave birth to new industrial organizations, such as Procter & Gamble.

While pork was the largest industry in Cincinnati, it was by no means the only one. Thousands of workers were employed in foundries, engine plants, boot and shoe and ready-made clothing shops, and furniture factories. Foundries were primarily concerned with stove production and could turn out 1,000 of them in a day. Cincinnati was the major western center for the manufacturing of clothing, using both the factory and "putting-out" systems, the latter occupying the time of 9,000 women working at home. Thousands of pieces of furniture, particularly bedsteads and chairs, were produced annually and marketed in the West and South. Of course, no description of Cincinnati industry in the

mid-nineteenth century could neglect breweries and distilleries, which were fueled by the large-scale German immigration of the 1840s. In 1850 Ohio was second in the country in gallons of beer and liquor produced and thirsty Cincinnati was the main reason.

The mid-1830s witnessed another age of wild land speculation in the West, prompted by another wave of "wildcat" banking and indiscriminate issue of state banknotes. This resulted from President Andrew Jackson's removal of federal monies from the Second United States Bank to favored "pet banks." There were nine of these in Ohio. Using these funds as security, state banks began issuing large amounts of notes, much in excess of the federal deposits. The land-office business was far greater than that which preceded the panic and depression of 1819. To stop the rampant speculation, President Jackson in the summer of 1836 issued his famous "Specie Circular," ordering that henceforth only specie would be accepted at government land offices. This had a sharp impact on the national economy, similar to that of the edict of the United States Bank in July 1818 calling for specie payments. Within a year the country had sunk into another lengthy depression.

While Ohio suffered through the next four or five years, the situation was not as critical there as in other parts of the West. Land sales were not great and its economy had attained a greater degree of maturity. The state was also still largely geared to agriculture which softened the blow for many. In

Pictured here are the employees of the Jackson Brewery in Cincinnati. Many of these workers were immigrants from Austria. Courtesy, Cincinnati Historical Society

fact, it has been suggested that some Ohioans were not even aware that there was a depression. The pinch was felt most keenly in canal construction. Some projects were temporarily suspended. Money was secured from different sources, but the state's credit was so damaged by 1841 that it was unable to market its bonds anywhere. But one big success was scored. In April 1840 the Pennsylvania and Ohio Canal was completed, providing a clear route from Pittsburgh to Cleveland.

The financial setbacks of 1819-1825 and 1837-1843 had hurt Ohio's economy and delayed growth. But by mid-century these difficulties were all but forgotten as the state rushed forward on many fronts. Better transportation had expanded markets in all directions. New inventions and processes had built the foundation for an industrial complex that would rank Ohio among the country's leaders. The greatest growth was still ahead, but what had been achieved so far was impressive. The total value of manufactured goods tripled between 1825 and 1850. Ohio was still an agricultural state in 1850, but industry was on the march. The watershed years witnessed the origins of this turnaround.

Cleveland's Public Square was the center of the city's community life and was the scene of many important gatherings over the years. In 1865 a pavilion was erected on the square to receive the body of President Lincoln, which was viewed by more than 100,000 mourners. In 1881 James Garfield's body was also brought to the square. Courtesy, Western Reserve Historical Society

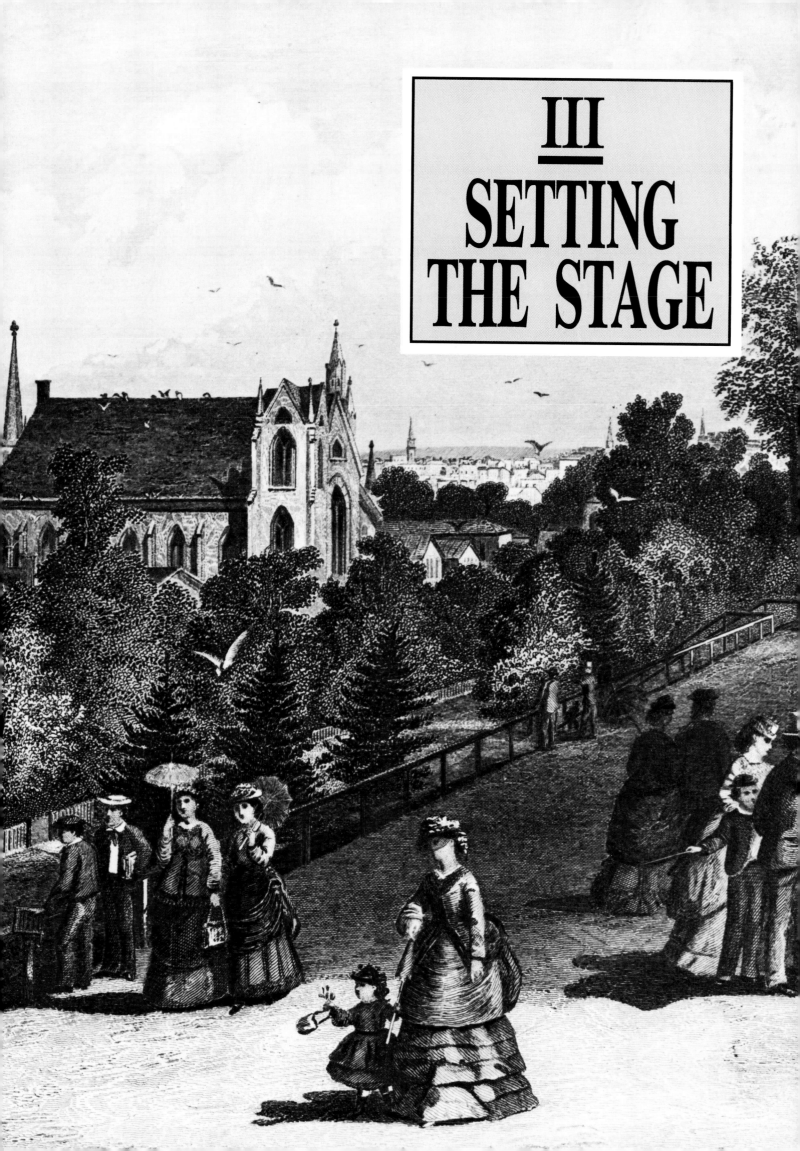

III
SETTING THE STAGE

Cleveland derived its importance from its location on the Great Lakes and at the head of the Ohio Canal. Its railway connections with cities to the east and west aided Cleveland's development. By the 1870s it was rapidly emerging as an industrial center. Courtesy, Ohio Historical Society

Facing page: On September 5, 1862, volunteers marched across a pontoon bridge over the Ohio River to help defend Cincinnati from the threat of a Confederate attack. Cincinnati and its neighbors in northern Kentucky were spared when the Confederates turned back and marched out of Kentucky. Courtesy, Cincinnati Historical Society

While the second twenty-five years of the nineteenth century saw Ohio transformed from a frontier to a settled state, the following quarter-century marked perhaps an even greater watershed in the state's history. Building on the rudimentary foundations of the earlier age, a mighty industrial empire was being constructed, one which would place Ohio among the national leaders.

Prior to this "Industrial Revolution," Ohio, as well as the rest of the country, had to contend with civil war. Though economic historians argue over the affect the war had on industry, the weight of opinion appears to hold that the war neither retarded nor accelerated industrial production. However, it may have stimulated certain industries and impeded others. Ohio wool growers, for example, prospered during the war because of the military need for uniforms and blankets. On the other hand, cotton textiles were severely hurt with the restriction on the cotton trade. A study of wartime industrial progress in the Miami Valley reveals an upsurge of "inventive-innovative" activity with respect to farm equipment, durable consumer goods, and publishing.

Those who argue that the Civil War stimulated industry have only to examine the economic growth of Akron to document their case. The region's second railroad—Atlantic and Great Western—came to town on April 17, 1863. While this road, absorbed by the Erie system in the 1890s, was in financial trouble for many years, it was fundamental to the industrial expansion of the city. Coal also played a part in Akron's growth. Ample supplies of cheap coal, found in abundance in Summit County, gave the local economy a substantial

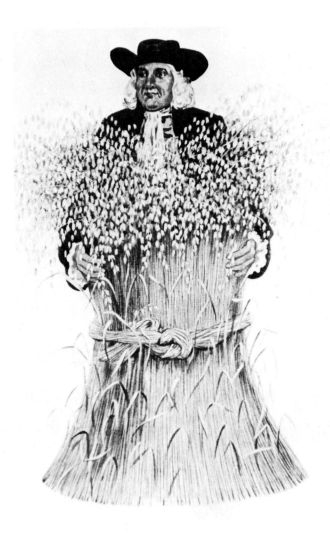

During the Civil War a German merchant named Ferdinand Schumacher started the German Mills in Akron. After many mergers, the firm became part of the Quaker Oats complex. Courtesy, Cincinnati Historical Society

advantage over other aspiring communities. Ten coal companies were in business there in 1868 and the output of their mines increased steadily in later years.

The heightened demand for foodstuffs during the Civil War stimulated another important industry in Akron—agricultural equipment. Patents for Cyrus McCormick's harvesting machines expired in the 1850s and many new companies were now manufacturing mowers and reapers. The Champion Company of Springfield was an important producer of farm equipment, but Akron boasted two manufacturers in the field. Ball, Aultman, and Company of Canton really started the industry in Akron by opening a branch plant there in 1863. Soon the Akron facil-

ity had outgrown its parent. John R. Buchtel and Lewis Miller played central roles in the solid growth of the Buckeye Mower and Reaper Works, by which name the Ball, Aultman offshoot was known. John F. Seiberling, whose son would later create the Goodyear Tire and Rubber Company, founded another mower and reaper plant—the Empire Mower and Reaper Works—in the late stages of the Civil War. While Seiberling's plant had its ups and downs, Buckeye Mower and Reaper grew steadily and by the end of the century was among the largest manufacturers of farm equipment in the world.

Ferdinand Schumacher, a German immigrant, was another Akron resident to prosper directly from the Civil War. He had "invented" oatmeal in the late 1850s, but sold it only locally. Through the intercession of his good friend and fellow German immigrant Erhard Steinbacher, Schumacher received a large order from the army quartermaster for oatmeal for the troops. It proved popular with the men in blue and within a year after the war began, Schumacher was having trouble keeping up with the demand for his oatmeal. The army also needed "pearl barley," and turned to Schumacher to supply it. He built the Empire Barley Mill to meet this need. He also wisely cultivated the civilian market in the postwar years and by 1870 was the unquestioned "cereal king" of the country. In the 1880s, however, other cereal companies were on the scene. To avoid competition a giant "trust," the American Cereal Company, forerunner of Quaker Oats, was formed in 1888 with Schumacher as its head.

Another major Akron industry which blossomed during the Civil War—although apparently independent of wartime economics—was the match business. The architect of this new enterprise bore the improbable name of Ohio Columbus Barber. In 1857, at the age of sixteen, Barber became a salesman for his father's small break-even match plant in Akron. He was a born huckster and by 1863 he and a friend, John K. Robinson, were running the company. Incorporated in 1867, the Barber Match Company began selling its matches under the name "Diamond," because the matchsticks were cut in diamond shapes. By 1871 the company's 150 employees, truly sweatshop laborers, were turning out two million boxes of matches annually. Within another decade the company controled one-fifth of the country's match output. Barber and Robinson, along with other leaders in the industry, in 1881 put together a gigantic trust, the Diamond Match Company, which, according to historian Karl

*Above: Before the onslaught of the rail-
road, coaches were often the means
of transportation between cities. The
trip to Lebanon, roughly thirty miles
from Cincinnati, took seven hours,
while the return journey took eight.
Courtesy, Cincinnati Historical Society*

———

*Top: Shown here are hoppers being
used to fill waiting trucks with shipments from train cars in the Pennsylvania Railroad yard at Court and Gil-
bert streets in Cincinnati. Before the
building of Cincinnati's Union Terminal, in the early 1930s, each railroad company had its own station.
Courtesy, Cincinnati Historical Society*

Grismer, held a "virtual stranglehold in the match
industry."

Despite his success, Barber exemplified the
most exploitive type of nineteenth-century businessman. He employed large numbers of women and
children, worked them long hours, and paid them
less than subsistence wages. For eleven hours of
daily labor men received $1.21, women seventy-
seven cents, and children sixty-six cents. At the
same time Buckeye Mower and Reaper was paying
its employees $2.27 a day. Moreover, work in a
match factory was exceedingly hazardous to the
laborer's health. Many workers contracted phosphorous necrosis, a painful, degenerative disease of the
jaw caused by the yellow phosphorous used in
match making. When the victims were forced to
quit their jobs, they got no aid, comfort, or recom-
pense from the company. Of course, Barber was no
more callous than other employers in this regard.
The age of "welfare capitalism" had not yet arrived.

After the Civil War, railroads figured prominently in the changes overtaking the national econ-

omy. Though railroads first appeared in the 1830s and 1840s, construction was limited. A number of technical problems inhibited rapid growth and canals were still thought to be a more dependable means of transport. However, the decade of the 1850s marked a sudden explosion in railroad building. Total railroad mileage throughout the country in 1850 was 9,000, but by 1860 the figure had jumped to 30,000. The Civil War brought new construction to a halt, but in the postwar years railroad building was resumed on an unprecedented scale. The demand for transcontinental lines and the avail-

———

This lithograph commemorated the completion of the Cincinnati Southern Railway and a celebration held at Music Hall in March 1880. Cincinnati, sometimes referred to as the "Gateway to the South," had important business ties to the Southern states before and after the Civil War. Courtesy, Cincinnati Historical Society

ability of the more durable steel rails prompted a large expansion of the railroad network.

Ohio not only reflected the national growth, it may have even been in the forefront of the railroad revolution. In 1850 it possessed only 300 miles of track, but by 1860 the figure had increased to nearly 3,000. At first it was thought that the railroads would be geared to the canal and river systems as an internal feeder network, but it soon became clear that east-west through lines would control the flow. Four such national systems had appeared by the 1880s: the New York Central, the Erie, the Pennsylvania, and the Baltimore and Ohio. One important internal line was the Columbus and Hocking Valley Railroad, built from the state capital to Athens in 1869-1870. This road opened up the coal resources of the Hocking valley in the southeast which would prove so vital to the steel industry developing in the north.

Cincinnati, bypassed by the major east-west rail lines, turned southward and sought to restore its prewar commercial ties with that region. Construction of the Cincinnati Southern Railroad was begun in

Left: This photograph of Cincinnati was taken in 1865 from the John A. Roebling Suspension Bridge during its construction. Although no fighting took place on her soil, Cincinnati was instrumental in the North's ultimate victory in the Civil War. Cincinnati factories produced a wide variety of goods for the war effort, including shoes, clothing, wagons, harnesses, boats, and guns. Courtesy, Cincinnati Historical Society

Below left: Busy with passenger and commercial riverboat transportation, Cincinnati failed to establish itself as a railroad city in time to keep up with other cities in the state and surrounding areas. Courtesy, Ohio Historical Society

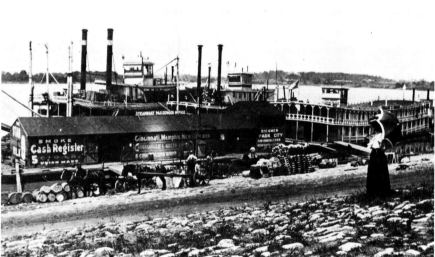

1873 and completed to Chattanooga, Tennessee, 336 miles away, in the next few years. Though the road prospered in both freight and passenger traffic, Cincinnati was partial to river commerce and failed to establish itself as an important railroad city.

Nevertheless, by the 1880s Ohio was crisscrossed by a network of local and interstate rail lines that bound the state more closely together than it had ever been before and integrated it tightly with national markets. The growing pains of the industry, however, troubled Ohio as it did other states. The celebrated abuses of rebates, the "long and short haul" discrimination, free passes to politicians, excessive rates, and the move to monopoly were resented by Ohioans much as they were by western farmers, the chief victims of such practices. Their complaints were by no means satisfied with the passage of the Interstate Commerce Act in 1887, but at least a first step toward ensuring railroad responsibility had been taken.

More visible to the general public than the involutions of rebates, rates, and combinations, were the plethora of railroad accidents, which seemed to occur with frightening frequency. Neither employees, passengers, nor innocent bystanders were spared. Even the introduction of air brakes, automatic couplers, and other safety devices did not slow down the rise in casualty figures. In 1873, 210 deaths and 398 serious injuries resulted from Ohio train accidents. In 1900 more than 500 died from train crashes and the injured list ran to over 7,000. Maimed arms and legs and broken backs were suffered by hundreds of railroad employees caught between or under cars involved in accidents. Probably the worst wreck took place in December 1876 near Ashtabula where a train crashed through a bridge into a gully sixty feet below. Close to 100 passengers were either killed in the fall or in the fire which followed. In addition to human casualties, thousands of cattle, horses, sheep, and pigs

68

Right: As a publicity stunt, the Hocking Valley Railroad staged a wreck on May 30, 1896. Hailed as the "first made to order railway collision," the incident drew spectators to Buckeye Park, twenty-five miles south of Columbus. Several photographs were taken before, during, and after the collision. Courtesy, Ohio Historical Society

were destroyed by speeding trains.

Closely linked with the rise of railroads and industry was the rise of the city. Ample work forces to man the emerging red brick factories were found in the cities. With businesses located there, cities became the centers for trade, finance, transportation, and government. The rise of urban centers in the last part of the nineteenth century was so spectacular that what little efforts were made to accommodate the mounting multitudes fell far short of what was necessary. Thus while cities mushroomed, the services they supplied for their citizens were grossly inadequate. This was a problem to be faced by the Progressives. But on the emerging industrialists, such matters weighed only lightly. Cities were their playgrounds and production, profits, and power their lodestars.

One can trace the process of the "urban revolution" by an examination of the Ohio scene. The change was most notable in the northeastern part of the state which had been something of a wasteland in the earlier years. True, the canals had given birth to commercial activity in the northeast, but the southern part of the state remained clearly in the ascendant. However, with the rise of the iron and steel industry in the 1870s and 1880s in the Cleveland-Youngstown orbit, a dramatic shift occurred. Cleveland jumped from a population of 17,000 in 1860 to 160,000 in 1880 and more than doubled that figure by 1900 when it reached 381,000, finally passing Cincinnati as the largest city in the state. Meanwhile Toledo, Youngstown, and Akron, which were barely on the map when the Civil War broke out, had moved forward to become the third, sixth, and seventh largest cities in 1900, with populations of 131,000, 44,000, and 42,000, respectively.

Cities of the southeast and southwest, centers of trade and primitive industry in the first half-century of statehood, fell behind the rising metropolitan areas in the north. Springfield became a center for the manufacture of farm equipment while Dayton was a major producer of office machines, but for the most part such historic towns as Marietta, East Liverpool, Steubenville, and Portsmouth grew slowly, if at all, and were overshadowed by the northern cities. Marietta never went above the 16,000 mark in the 200 years after its founding. East Liver-

Above: Located near clay deposits, East Liverpool was one of the country's most important pottery centers. By 1877 pottery making was a major industry, employing thirty-two workers. Pictured here is a construction crew in front of some bottle kilns, few of which remain. Courtesy, Ohio Historical Society

Left: Pictured here are employees of a clay shop in East Liverpool. The pottery industry often employed entire families, including many children under the age of fifteen. Women and children were given menial and routine tasks. Workers endured health hazards such as poor ventilation in buildings, temperature extremes, and overcrowding. Courtesy, Ohio Historical Society

pool, still a major pottery producer, grew from 1,600 in 1850 to 5,600 in 1880. Steubenville's figures for those years were 6,000 and 12,000, and Portsmouth's, 4,000 and 11,000. There was growth, but these figures hardly compared with those of Youngstown, Toledo, and Akron. Cincinnati, the most important center of trade and industry in Ohio and the West in 1860, surrendered its position of preeminence to Cleveland, its upstart rival on the shores of Lake Erie.

Ironically, at mid-century there had seemed little likelihood that Cincinnati's grandeur would ever be dimmed. One could hardly have anticipated that the "Queen City" would ever fall behind Cleveland. It should not be inferred from this that Cincinnati had declined as an industrial center in the third quarter of the century. In fact, the city had grown substantially since 1850. By 1880 Cincinnati's industrial plant had practically doubled from thirty years earlier. The size of the work force in factories, the value of manufactured goods, and the number of industrial plants were almost twice that in 1880 as in 1850. Through its 3,000 factories spread among 125 different industries, Cincinnati ranked sixth nationally in output and was the most diversified industrial center in the West.

The problem with these promising figures is that the city seemed to be standing still in a period of monumental change. Its major industries were principally the same ones that had marked its rise to supremacy earlier. Cincinnati was still among the national leaders in the manufacture of wagons and carriages, in meat packing and slaughtering, in the number of foundries and machine shops, and in shoes, clothing, and furniture. But these were hardly among the newer heavy industries which were reshaping the national economy. While Cincinnati may have led Cleveland in the number of industrial establishments even after 1900, the value of the goods produced in Cleveland far exceeded that of Cincinnati.

Even in areas where Cincinnati had long been a leader it began to fall behind. Symptomatic of the city's malaise was the pork packing business. Between 1840 and 1860 Cincinnati was the leading pork packing center in the country; it was justifiably called "Porkopolis." In 1840, 1,200 workers in forty-eight packing plants turned out pork and pork products valued at three million dollars. The industry expanded steadily over the next two decades until the annual value of pork and pork products had risen to six million dollars in 1860.

Then something went wrong. Ohio's railroad network which began to take shape in the 1850s did not favor Cincinnati. None of the major trunk lines passed through it. With the construction of the Mad River and Lake Erie line from Springfield to Sandusky, hog farmers in southwestern Ohio began shipping their swine north to the railroad links with eastern markets. It was also more economical to send hogs by rail and they arrived at their destination in better condition than when driven overland to market. Cincinnati merchants and packers failed to recognize the importance of the railroad until new transportation routes and markets had become fixed. The lack of significant growth in the city's economy after the Civil War can be attributed in no small part to its limited railroad structure. Moreover, the corn-growing belt began to shift westward. Corn and hence hogs could now be raised more cheaply in Indiana and Illinois, so hog production in southwestern Ohio declined. This is not to

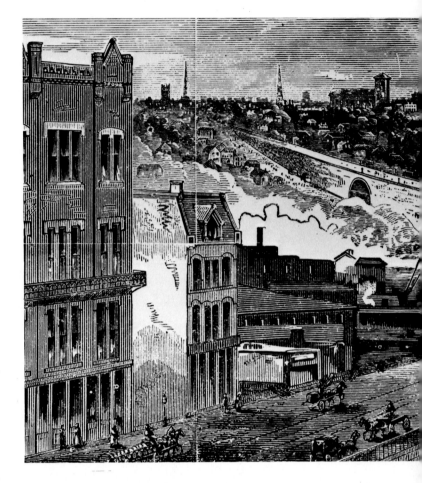

Above: By 1878 in Cleveland's industrial sector, what had once been pastureland was covered with oil refineries and manufacturing plants. An observer pointed out that "blackness, dirt, and decay were visible everywhere." Courtesy, Ohio Historical Society

Right: The first electric trolley car line, owned by the East Cleveland Railway Company, opened in 1884. Citizens of the day expressed concern over the safety of these electrically operated cars. This streetcar traveled along Euclid Avenue in Cleveland, which at one time was home to the city's wealthiest residents. Courtesy, Cleveland Public Library

Above: Some of the city's most wealthy and famous residents lived in the grand mansions on "Millionaires' Row" along Cleveland's Euclid Avenue. Some of the residents were Tom L. Johnson; William Chisholm, president of Cleveland Rolling Mill; Sylvester Everett, whose brownstone mansion was said to be the most expensive home erected in Cleveland; nineteenth-century author and Secretary of State John Hay; Amasa Stone; and John D. Rockefeller. Courtesy, Western Reserve Historical Society

say that hog production in Ohio died out. It continued to thrive throughout the state, but no longer did it occupy its once paramount place in the economy. Cincinnati had given way to Chicago as the nation's number-one packing center.

While Cincinnati was experiencing economic problems, Cleveland was being transformed into a major industrial city. Cleveland's rapid rush to a position of leadership in industrial America was due largely to the accident of location. Its prospects had not been bright in the early days. There was even a dispute with Newburg over which town should be the Cuyahoga County seat. But then came the canals, then the railroads, then the iron ore, and then John D. Rockefeller. Rockefeller was not the only great industrialist spawned by the Lake City, but he was the most imaginative one during the oil boom. Then there were the daring entrepreneurs of the steel industry, who sensed that Cleveland could become the happy meeting point for the rich iron ore of upper Minnesota and the plentiful fuel sources of eastern Ohio and western Pennsylvania. Oil and steel, the catalysts of change, elevated Cleve-

land to the industrial forefront.

What was Cleveland like before industry took over? Having only a population of 6,000 in 1840, it was simply a pleasant country village. The center of town was Public Square, which had been set aside by the founding fathers. Whitewashed rail fences marked off the four sections of the square, which were bisected by Superior Street running east-west and Ontario Street running north-south. The business section extended east for several blocks along Superior and then disappeared into the countryside. West of Public Square, the "Flats" along the

Above: This farm scene was common throughout the Ohio countryside in the 1930s. Courtesy, Ohio Historical Society

———

Top: Cleveland's Tom Loftin Johnson, steel manufacturer and street railway magnate, served as a congressman and then as mayor of Cleveland for eight years. In 1903 he ran an unsuccessful campaign as Democratic candidate for governor. A tribute to him on his statue in Cleveland's Public Square reads: "He found us leaderless and blind. He left a city with a civic mind." Courtesy, Ohio Historical Society

Cuyahoga River, which separated Cleveland from Ohio City on the west bank, were acquiring a busy air. Foundries, soap factories, breweries, and carriage works were a portent of things to come. Canal traffic emptied at the foot of West Superior. Still, Cleveland was only the "capital" of the Western Reserve, the center of a dairy and farming community which gave little thought to an industrial future. Though benefiting from the canal and lake trade, Cleveland had no railroads to speak of and was content being the commercial center of the region.

Yet in thirty years the city was unrecognizable to returning visitors. The tremendous population increase, accompanied by the appearance of a dozen railroads, innumerable steel plants, oil refineries, and sundry other industrial facilities, had totally transformed Cleveland. Smoke and soot clouded the air while shanties and hovels cluttered the ground. The business center had spread out along the main thoroughfares east, southeast, and

Left: By the end of the nineteenth century, Ohio no longer led the nation in agricultural production, but farming was still an important ingredient in the lives of Ohioans. Pictured here is a group of men, women, and children threshing grain in Guernsey County. Courtesy, Ohio Historical Society

Below: By the end of the nineteenth century, Ohio led the nation in the manufacture of farm machinery with products such as mowers, reapers, steel plows, cultivators, and binders. The Champion Company of Springfield, producer of this thresher, became the foremost manufacturer of farm equipment. Courtesy, Ohio Historical Society

By the end of the Civil War and throughout the rest of the nineteenth century, agriculture was Ohio's most important industry. This 1860 diploma from the Ohio Board of Agriculture shows the emphasis placed on agriculture. Courtesy, Ohio Historical Society

west. The view of the "Flats," in the opinion of one observer,

> *though far from beautiful, is a very interesting one. There are copper smelting, iron rolling, and iron manufacturing works, lumber yards, paper mills, breweries, flour mills, nail works, pork packing establishments, and the multitudinous industries of a great manufacturing city . . .*

In contrast to the dirt and congestion of downtown, Euclid Avenue had become "Millionaire's Row," the setting for the city's industrial elite. Amasa Stone, Samuel Andrews, John D. Rockefeller, and Tom L. Johnson, among others, occupied regal mansions on spacious grounds, carefully concealed from the curious proletariat by nicely groomed shrubbery and trees. By the end of the century Cleveland's position as a major industrial center was established.

With the rise of industrial cities such as Cleveland came the demise of agriculture. Though farming still dominated Ohio's economy in 1880, its advantage was lessening. Leading all states in 1850, Ohio dropped to a secondary position in the next twenty years, as the farm belt became firmly fixed in the Great Plains. Agricultural output did increase over the years, but in comparison with industrial production, it fell badly behind.

The post-Civil War years were generally difficult ones for agriculture. Probably the worst farm depression in the nation's history—to that time—struck in the 1880s and 1890s, when prices dropped steadily. The most badly afflicted areas were the Great Plains, particularly the states of Kansas and Nebraska. Exorbitant railroad rates, usurious interest charges, and unfavorable weather had placed the plains farmers in desperate straits. It was during those days, the story goes, that Minnesota farmers found that it was more economical to burn their wheat for fuel rather than ship it to market by rail. The agricultural nightmare gave birth to the Populist Movement, which exercised a significant political influence in the 1890s.

While Ohio suffered from the general decline in farm prices in the late nineteenth century, the problem never achieved the crisis proportions of the western states. For example, Ohio wheat production maintained a fairly stable level during the 1880s and 1890s, although the price per bushel went down continuously. In 1894, the worst year of the depression but a banner year for wheat production —fifty-one million bushels were harvested—farmers got only fifty-one cents per bushel. The other staple for Ohio agriculture, corn, remained at high levels of production throughout most of the period, although the early 1890s were poor years.

Railroads, the principal reason for the westward shift of the farm country, also broke down the regionalism of Ohio farming. No longer was corn produced only in the southwest, wheat in the "backbone," and dairy products in the Reserve. While those regions still led in their specialties, farmers had learned that it was far wiser to diversify their crops. Railroads had overcome the isolation of rural sections and opened up all parts of the state to broader markets. Diversification rather than specialization marked the new age.

Other signs of agricultural change in the post-Civil War era were the advent of new farm machinery, selective breeding of livestock, and the advancement of education. The last point was symbolized by the founding of Ohio State University in 1870 for the purpose, among other things, of promoting agricultural education. Although dirt farmers were slow to accept new academic theories about agriculture, the importance of education finally came across.

In one obvious way the dawning Industrial Revolution proved a boon to agriculture. The manufacture of agricultural equipment and machinery became big business and was instrumental in bringing about more economical and efficient farming practices in the latter half of the nineteenth century. But farming as a way of life had given way to urbanism. No longer was the "sturdy yeoman" of Jefferson's time the bulwark of American society. The great entrepreneurs—the Rockefellers, the Carnegies, and the Morgans—had supplanted the rugged, democratic, independent tiller of the soil as the shaper of the country's future.

With the Civil War over, no distractions barred Ohio's full industrial development. All of the factors essential to a massive leap forward were present. The stage was set. Ohio would figure prominently in the momentous period of economic growth which lay ahead.

IV
STEEL
AND OIL

These complex machines were used by the American Steel & Wire Company in the 1930s. This Cleveland firm later became a subsidiary of U.S. Steel. Courtesy, Ohio Historical Society

Facing page: In 1880 Otis Iron Steel Company was the first firm in America organized to produce acid open-hearth steel. Later, the company dropped "Iron" from its name. Pictured is one of the steps in steelmaking, as the finished heat of steel is tapped from the open hearth into a ladle. Courtesy, Cleveland Public Library

The most spectacular event in American history in the last part of the nineteenth century was the Industrial Revolution. An industrial pygmy prior to the Civil War when compared to a number of European countries, the United States advanced so rapidly within the next four decades that by the turn of the century its works dwarfed the accomplishments of all other nations. The Industrial Revolution gave employment to millions of workers, native and foreign born, immeasurably raised the country's standard of living, provided the people with undreamed of conveniences and luxuries, and generated a galaxy of hard-nosed businessmen who would dominate the nation's economic and political life for the next generation and beyond.

What made the United States such "fertile ground" for this revolution? Six factors explain the phenomenon. Several of them may have existed in Europe, but nowhere did all of them prevail, and in such abundance, as in America. "Fertile ground" was certainly one of them. The nation's richness in natural resources—coal, iron, timber, petroleum, and waterpower—was unparalleled. A supply of cheap labor was also a necessity. This was available from the hordes of immigrants pouring into the Atlantic ports. In addition, native inventiveness was needed to solve technical and engineering problems. Yankee ingenuity met this need.

But resources, labor, and creativity were not sufficient in themselves. Imaginative and, yes, ruthless men were required to mobilize the basic ingredients, organize them, push them forward. "Captains of Industry," "Robber Barons," "Great Entrepreneurs," call them what you will, rose to fame and power as they manipulated the

Datus and Irad Kelley made their island, located north of Sandusky in Lake Erie, a thriving community. Kelley's Island became known for its vineyards, peach orchards, red cedar, and a stone quarry, as seen in this picture. Mark Twain also helped immortalize the island when he wrote, "You can't fool me with Kelley Island wine; I can tell it from vinegar everytime—by the label on the bottle." Courtesy, Western Reserve Historical Society

new machinery into high gear. Buyers of the many goods and services were also necessary. Railroads had knit the country from coast to coast, nationalizing markets and tremendously expanding production figures in the process. Finally, the American government was very supportive of industrial growth. Through protective tariffs, railroad land grants, and other favors, industry benefited handsomely at the hands of government.

These six factors forged the Industrial Revolution, and Ohio was blessed with all of them. It had the resources, the labor, the inventors, the entrepreneurs, the markets, and the federal favors. The state was rich in coal, iron, oil, natural gas, and timber. (Actually, much of the iron and oil came from elsewhere, but they were drawn to Ohio.) Among the great inventors were Charles Brush, Thomas Edison, and Charles Kettering. John D. Rockefeller, Marcus A. Hanna, and Harvey Firestone exemplified the entrepreneurs.

Ohio's population figures nearly doubled between 1880 and 1920. A good bulk of the growth was due to immigration from southern and eastern Europe. Whereas prior to 1890 immigrants to the United States were drawn largely from northwestern Europe—Germany, Great Britain, and Scandinavia—from 1890 to 1920 most came from Italy, Greece, Hungary, Bohemia, Poland, and Russia. This was the "new immigration." Because these people arrived without funds, could not speak English, and formed ethnic communities in the large cities, they caused a backlash of nativist opposition leading to the restrictive immigration legislation of the 1920s. Yet these factors made the "new immigrants" an ideal labor source for the burgeoning industries.

They could be paid subsistence wages and dismissed if they caused trouble. Most of the immigrants gravitated to the industrial centers. Jobs were available there despite the exploitation, and the newcomers found security among their fellow countrymen who had preceded them.

Cleveland is the best example of the immigrant impact on Ohio. In 1900 it passed Cincinnati to become the largest city in the state. By 1910 its population exceeded the half-million mark and by 1920 reached 796,841, making it one of the largest cities in the country. Because of the city's heavy industry and its easy access to Atlantic ports, large numbers of new immigrants began arriving in the city in the 1880s and 1890s. In 1890, 97,000 of the city's 261,000 people were foreign-born, while another 98,600 were native-born of foreign or mixed parentage. This constituted 75 percent of the total population. This percentage remained constant for the next three decades, although the city's population more than trebled in that time. In the 1905 municipal election, men of forty-four nationalities voted and 36 percent of the electors voting were born in Europe. The only ethnic groups one historian could not find in Cleveland at that time were Australian Bushmen, Hottentots, and Eskimos.

By no means did all new immigrants settle in Cleveland. Youngstown's percentage figures were almost as high for that forty-year period, from 1880-1920. The peak was in 1890, when 70 percent of the city's population of 33,220 was foreign-born and native-born of foreign or mixed parentage. By 1920 the proportion had dropped to 60 percent while its population had increased to 100,000. Toledo and Akron also had large immigrant

Above: Ohio inventor Powell Crosley, Jr., stands in his first WLW studio in 1922. Called "the Ford of the radio business," Crosley not only manufactured radios but experimented with the development of airplanes, invented a four-cylinder auto engine capable of getting thirty-five to fifty miles per gallon, and designed a refrigerator called the "Shelvador" which featured shelves for storage in the door. Courtesy, Cincinnati Historical Society

Above left: Charles F. Brush, 1849-1929, brought electric lights to American streets. In 1879 he demonstrated the use of arc lights for street illumination in Cleveland, his hometown. Courtesy, Ohio Historical Society

Left: Despite his poor eyesight, Charles F. Kettering became an inventor and important figure in the automobile industry. He invented the electric starter for automobiles, introduced ethyl gasoline and quick-drying lacquer finish for auto bodies, and made improvements in the diesel engine. Courtesy, Ohio Historical Society

Above: Thomas Alva Edison, born in Milan, Ohio, in 1847, is foremost among Ohio-born inventors. Although he lived and worked outside the state most of his life, Ohio still claims him as one of her own. Courtesy, Ohio Historical Society

populations. Cincinnati, however, showed a reverse trend. While its population rose only from 255,000 to 401,000 from 1880 to 1920, its immigrant element dropped sharply from 71 percent to 41 percent. Cincinnati remained an important city, but its relative economic influence declined over those years, a point seemingly supported by the immigration statistics. The centers of heavy industry in the northern half of the state were home for the majority of Ohio's new immigrants.

But the growth of large cities was not entirely due to foreign immigration. The latter third of the nineteenth century was marked by a steady influx of young men and women from the countryside. To them, the lure of the city proved irresistible. Its conveniences, its educational and cultural opportunities, its excitement, and, above all, its job prospects, attracted young people in ever-growing numbers. Ohio clearly reflected this national trend. While remaining one of the nation's important agricultural states well into the twentieth century, its rural areas showed little, if any, population increase. Boryczka and Cary observe: "Rural Ohioans outnumbered other Buckeyes for the last time in 1900; indeed, the rural population barely grew at all between 1880 and 1890 and thereafter declined steadily."

By 1920, drawing from both native and foreign sources, Ohio could boast seven cities with more than 100,000 population and a few others approaching that figure.

Ohio, perhaps better than any other state except Pennsylvania, epitomized the flowering of the Industrial Revolution. While the romance of iron, steel, and oil occupied centerstage in the unfolding drama, other industries flourished as well. The manufacture of agricultural machinery and equipment,

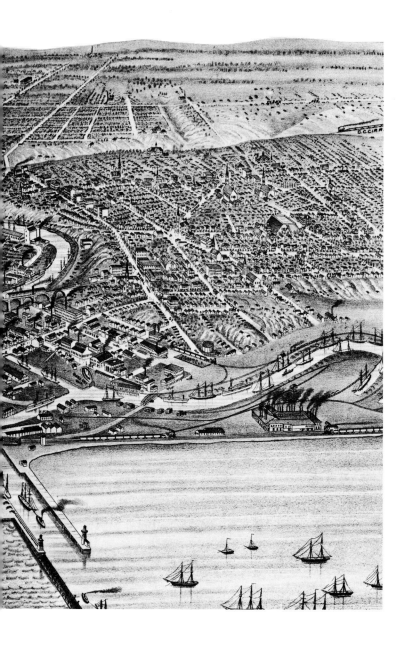

Above: This bird's-eye view of Cleveland in 1877 reveals a bustling riverfront city. Courtesy, Western Reserve Historical Society

---

Left: Henry A. Schauffler was a pioneer in missionary work among "Bohemians," or Czechs, living in Cleveland. These immigrants settled on Hamm Avenue in the 1880s. Schauffler's schools were mainly to train religious workers, and in 1883 he founded Bethlehem Church to be used exclusively for Slavic mission work. Courtesy, Western Reserve Historical Society

glass and timber products, and office machinery, and the rise of the machine tool, rubber, and automobile industries, only suggest the scope of industrial activity in Ohio. By 1891, when industrialism was gathering momentum, capital investment in Ohio industry amounted to $185 million, while the total value of the products from the more than 12,000 factories was $259 million. These figures multiplied in the decades ahead.

The steel industry was the common denominator for the Industrial Revolution. It was central to all that followed. First, it supplied the strong durable rails so urgently needed for the expanding post-Civil War railroad network. The transcontinental lines linked the East and Midwest with the Far West, and nationalized markets. Prior to the Civil War it was difficult to market one's goods beyond the local setting, unless a river or canal was nearby. Even then, river and canal commerce was slow. Railroads made it possible to sell goods anywhere in the country, quickly and easily. Moreover, steel made possible the manufacture of all kinds of machines, implements, vehicles, buildings, and appliances for commercial and home use. The pace of business and the standard of living improved sharply because of the steel industry.

Steel manufacturing prior to the Civil War was a difficult and costly process, and simply impractical as far as large-scale industrial use was concerned. The knowledge of how to produce steel—by removing impurities from iron—was available, but the technique for doing it was not. The big breakthrough occurred in the mid-1850s when two men, one an Englishman, Henry Bessemer, the other an American, William Kelly, independently invented a relatively easy method of extracting silicon and carbon from iron. Bessemer in 1855 devised a converter into which the molten iron was poured. A violent blast of cold air at the base of Bessemer's converter caused a tremendous fire and minor explosion, which forced out the carbon and silicon. When the converter was tipped, liquid steel ran into the molds. Although Kelly had developed the same method, Bessemer received most of the credit for devising the new process.

But the Bessemer converter was slow to catch on. The first experiments with it failed because, as it turned out, the wrong kind of iron ore was used. Only ore with less than .05 percent phosphorous was suitable for the converter, otherwise the phosphorous spoiled the steel. Lawsuits over patent

Above: This picture shows children playing near Hiram House, Ohio's first social settlement for immigrants. George A. Bellamy, who began the settlement, hoped to encourage good citizenship and improve community welfare. Bellamy was the first to begin Americanization classes in Cleveland. Courtesy, Western Reserve Historical Society

———

Right: Cincinnati had five inclines which provided cheap and convenient transportation from the downtown basin to the hilltops. The Mt. Adams incline, pictured here, was built in 1876 and continued to operate until 1948. At the top of the hill and to the left of the station stood the Highland House, a popular restaurant and beer garden. Courtesy, Cincinnati Historical Society

Above: It took a lot of hard work to build the railroads across the state of Ohio. The Cleveland *Daily True Democrat wrote about the work that was done on the line between Cleveland and Columbus. "Not far from this city may be seen, and could have been during all the past winter, a solitary man, with pickaxe and spade, digging into the bowels of the earth. Every now and then he would raise his eyes to the task before him and groan in agony." Courtesy, Western Reserve Historical Society*

Above right: The first local railroad ad in a Cleveland newspaper appeared in the Plain Dealer *on June 29, 1850. It advertised the Cleveland, Columbus, Cincinnati Railroad which traveled as far south as Wellington at twenty m.p.h. In 1865 six railroad lines operated daily in and out of Cleveland and by the 1880s, when this photo of the Cleveland and Pittsburgh Railroad was taken, Cleveland was serviced by eleven railroads. Courtesy, Western Reserve Historical Society*

rights further delayed full-scale trials of the process. By the late 1860s these problems had been resolved and the first Bessemer plant in the United States was constructed by the Pennsylvania Steel Company, a subsidiary of the Pennsylvania Railroad. Far more significant was the founding by Andrew Carnegie, America's foremost "ironmaster," of the Edgar Thomson Company outside Pittsburgh in 1873. This marked the first major use of the Bessemer-Kelly method, which would become widely adopted by the end of the century. Carnegie dominated the steel industry for a generation. His company and its subsidiaries were worth more than $400 million at the time he sold out to the newly formed United States Steel Corporation in 1901.

Meanwhile, another steel-making method, the "open hearth" process, had found favor with many manufacturers. The open hearth furnaces took much longer to make a batch of steel than the Bessemer-Kelly method—eight to ten hours compared to fifteen to twenty minutes—but their capacity was much greater. In addition, the extended length of time permitted workmen to regularly test the mix and make any adjustments needed to attain a better quality of steel. This constant checking could not be done under the Bessemer-Kelly process. Whereas the latter remained the most common means of manufacturing steel throughout the nineteenth century, it gradually gave way to the open hearth method in the twentieth.

Ohio moved into the Bessemer age a few years before Carnegie, but not on as large a scale. In 1868 the Cleveland Rolling Mill Company at Newburg installed two six-ton converters. Its main product initially was steel rails, but it expanded the inventory to include wire, screws, and agricultural equipment. Later, an open hearth furnace was installed and the company was absorbed by the American Steel and Wire Company. Bessemer converters were also placed in the Otis Steel Company of Cleveland, the Bellaire Nail Works, and the Mingo Junction works of the Laughlin and Junction Steel Company in the 1880s. Republic Iron and Steel at Youngstown adopted the system in 1901. But by then, the open hearth process had gained adherents. Burgess Steel and Iron in 1871 was the first to install the new system, followed by Otis in 1875. Canton and Portsmouth firms adopted the method in 1880 and by 1905 at least a dozen open hearth furnaces were operating in Ohio.

Coincidental with the development of improved ways of manufacturing steel came the discovery of vast new iron ore deposits in northern Michigan and Minnesota. Whereas Ohioans had played no role in developing the Bessemer-Kelly and open hearth processes, they had a great deal to do with the finding of the untapped lodes in the north country. These Ohioans were mostly Clevelanders involved in Great Lakes shipping, eager to improve their commercial prospects. Lake Superior iron ore made Cleveland, Youngstown, and Pittsburgh the greatest steel domain in the world.

The first news of important mineral reserves around Lake Superior reached Cleveland in the 1840s. The famous local geologist Charles Whittlesey published several papers based on his findings which greatly intensified interest on the subject, particularly in Cleveland. Fifty-two tons of copper ore arrived in Cleveland from the Upper Peninsula in the summer of 1848. Cleveland developers unearthed several million dollars worth of ore containing silver and copper by the mid-1850s. How-

Pictured here is the Van Dorn Iron Works in Cleveland, which manufactured products varying from garden furniture to jail cells. Van Dorn also made ornamental ironwork, streetcar vestibules, bicycle parts, and metal office furniture. Courtesy, Western Reserve Historical Society

ever, the discovery of vast lodes or iron ore directed attention away from silver and copper.

The first major iron range was developed at Marquette, Michigan. Clevelanders were soon on the scene. The Cleveland Iron Company, formed in 1849 and reorganized as the Cleveland Iron Mining Company in 1853, played the most important role in the early days. Samuel L. Mather and W.J. Gordon, prominent Cleveland businessmen, were the principal organizers of the company. They built forges on the shores of Lake Superior, cast the iron into ingots and blooms, and shipped them back to Cleveland. Very soon, however, it was found more economical to send the ore directly to Cleveland and let blast furnaces there make the pig iron and derivative products. This decision was abetted by the construction of a canal at Sault Sainte Marie in 1855, making it possible for larger ships to travel from Lake Superior to Lake Erie.

As more mines were opened, more mining and

shipping companies appeared. An important new mine was opened at Menominee, Michigan, in 1870, but by far the richest and most productive lodes were those at Gogebic (opened in 1884) and in Minnesota at Vermilion (1884) and Mesabi (1892). As the ore poured forth in ever-increasing volume, bigger ships were needed to carry the cargoes. The locks at the "Soo" and adjacent rivers were deepened and widened to accommodate the heavier flow. The Cleveland Iron Mining Company, as it expanded its holdings, added steadily to its fleet of ships—from wood to iron to steel—and later, as the Cleveland-Cliffs Company, became the foremost organization in Great Lakes shipping. Mark Hanna, after marrying into the Daniel Rhodes family, which was rich from a prosperous Cleveland coal and iron business, soon took over the company, expanded its operations, and became another Great Lakes shipping magnate. Samuel Mather and Colonel James Pickands formed the Pickands Mather Company in 1883 to exploit the new mines to be opened at

Below right: After 1880 iron works along Lake Erie shifted from the production of steam boilers and machinery for wooden vessels to the construction of iron- and steel-hulled ships. This ship under construction belongs to the Cleveland Shipbuilding Company, which in 1897 began to build the largest dry docks on the Great Lakes at Lorain, Ohio. Courtesy, Western Reserve Historical Society

Below: Cleveland's position as a port on the Great Lakes, its service by trunk line railroads, and its nearness to coal, limestone, and oil deposits had much to do with the city's emergence as Ohio's premier manufacturing city. Today, Greater Cleveland extends 100 miles along the shore of Lake Erie and more than forty miles inland. Pictured here is a ship being loaded on the Cuyahoga River before heading out on the Great Lakes. Courtesy, Western Reserve Historical Society

Gogebic. Pickands Mather also developed its own fleet of lake ships, a subsidiary known as the Interlake Steamship Company. Most of these ships were built by the American Shipbuilding Company of Cleveland, one of the largest firms in the country.

Greater Cleveland's rise to industrial supremacy was due to its location. The city's growing importance as a commercial center and lake port had resulted from the coming of the canal, followed swiftly by the railroad in the 1850s and 1860s. Now it was a major entrepot for Lake Superior iron ore. Pittsburgh, 130 miles to the southeast, had become the nation's number-one steel manufacturing center as a result of Andrew Carnegie, who secured his ore from regional and eastern sources and his coke fuel from the Connellsville area. Youngstown, too, midway between Cleveland and Pittsburgh, had a long history of iron production although its local sources had been depleted. It is no mystery, then, that a natural iron and steel nexus was formed along the Cleveland-Youngstown-Pittsburgh line. Jones and Laughlin, Republic Steel, and Youngstown Sheet and Tube were only the best known of the major steel companies established on the Ohio-Pennsylvania frontier.

An important advance in steel production was the introduction of, first, coal, and then coke for fuel. Charcoal had been the principal fuel in the glory days of Hanging Rock, but its relative inefficiency and total dependence on timber stands, which were vanishing, necessitated a substitute. Coal was burned in eastern iron mills in the 1830s and its use spread west of the mountains with the discovery of coal reserves in western Pennsylvania and eastern Ohio. It was found that coke, derived from coal, provided a better fuel for smelting iron. After the Civil War, coke came into favor throughout most of the iron and steel industry. Early in the twentieth century Ohio had established itself as the second state in the country, next to Pennsylvania, in both iron and steel production. One authority on the subject, Bert S. Stephenson, writing of the Ohio scene in 1905, observed that Cincinnati was

> . . . *a maker of machine tools and heavy machinery. Columbus became famous for its malleable castings, its car couplers, chains, mining and hoisting machinery. Dayton and Columbus developed large car building plants, turning in later years to the manufacture of the all-steel car. Youngstown and the Mahoning Valley built up immense works for the production of*

Above: A worker at Youngstown Sheet and Tube directs the pouring of molten iron into an open hearth furnace. Youngstown has been called the "prototypical industrial city" because it was dependent upon steel production for its existence. Courtesy, Ohio Historical Society

Top: The Jones and Laughlin Steel Corporation merged with Otis Steel in 1942, thus uniting America's two oldest steel companies. Pictured is the entry end of an eighty-four-inch tandem temper mill at the Cleveland Works of Jones and Laughlin. This highly mechanized machine was used to facilitate production. Courtesy, Cleveland Public Library

Above: Among Cleveland's fifteen ranked manufacturing plants in the 1880s was the Bowler Foundry, pictured here. Courtesy, Western Reserve Historical Society

Right: This photo, taken underground in a Hocking Valley Coal Mine, is possibly the first "flashlight" photograph of a mine. Mining in this coal-rich area was dangerous work. Miners toiled in gloomy environments, rarely seeing the sun because of their work schedules. In 1873 more than 250 Ohio miners were killed, and 750 suffered injuries in mining accidents. Courtesy, Ohio Historical Society

sheets, plates, and steel rails and a string of prosperous establishments for the working of steel into finished and semi-finished forms eventually stretched along the Ohio River. Almost every city of size now has its important iron, steel or manufacturing works, and Ohio products in these lines have won for themselves more than a nation-wide reputation.

The impact of iron and steel on Cleveland is reflected in city directories for the boom years of the late nineteenth century. On the eve of the Civil War only a handful of companies were connected with the industry, which employed well under a thousand workmen. It was quite different in the 1890s, as Harlan Hatcher reports:

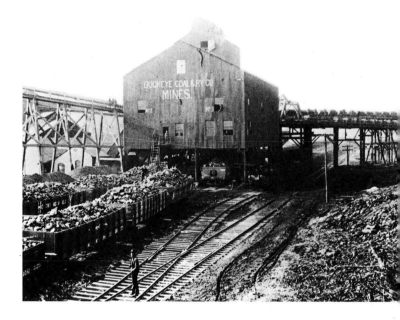

Above: Railroads facilitated the movement of goods across the state. Buckeye Coal depended on trains to ship coal to its customers. Coal was moved along on the conveyor to the building where it was loaded into waiting train cars. Courtesy, Ohio Historical Society

———

Left: Mining companies built communities for workers because coal mines were often located in remote areas. Unfortunately, these houses, only meant to provide temporary shelter, were usually built rapidly and poorly and soon deteriorated into shanties. Courtesy, Ohio Historical Society

The list covered pages. There were 462 establishments, a heavy percentage of which were working with iron and steel. The Cleveland Rolling Mills employed 5,000; American Wire Company, 463; Ohio Steel Works, 623; Globe Iron Works and Shipyard, 543; Cleveland Malleable Iron Company, 550; Union Rolling Mill, 335; the Central Blast Furnace and the Riverside Blast Furnace, 323—to mention samples of the transformation wrought in these few years. By 1910 . . . there were 14 large iron and steel works and rolling mills, and 231 foundries and machine shops in the city doing $76,000,000 worth of business annually. Cleveland had become the first ranking industrial city in Ohio.

. . .

The oil industry began at the same time as the steel industry and almost at the same place. Western Pennsylvania was the birthplace of both and nearby Ohio cashed in on the fruits of both. For years prior to the Civil War, rivers and creeks in the region of Titusville, eighty miles north of Pittsburgh, had been exuding a greasy, scummy substance, which local farmers skimmed from the surface of the water and used as both a medicine and lubricant. At length an enterprising man named George H. Bissell decided to learn if this "petroleum" possessed commercial value. He sent a sample of the stuff to the celebrated Yale chemist Benjamin Silliman. In 1855—the very same year of Bessemer's patent —Silliman published a paper in which he said that

Above: The Cleveland Rolling Mill, a family business started by Henry Chisholm, was incorporated in 1863. Manned by Welsh, Irish, and Scottish workers, the company paid inside men and rollers between $3.50 and $7 a day and laborers $1.65 a day. William Chisholm took over as president after his father's death on May 9, 1881. Courtesy, Western Reserve Historical Society

Right: This picture shows trains being assembled at the Lima Locomotive Works. The company, originally called the Lima Machine Works, turned out its first three locomotives in 1879 and in 1893 exhibited its 450th locomotive at the World's Columbian Exposition. Courtesy, Ohio Historical Society

ing for oil around Oil City, Titusville, and their environs. Fortunes were made, lost, and remade almost overnight. Crossroad villages mushroomed into crowded, boisterous, money-mad centers of wealth, with gambling, drinking, and other kinds of dens. As quickly as they had risen, many such places died out as the oil dried up. Lucky farmers on whose property gushers were struck became rich beyond their dreams if they went into the oil business. The conservative ones no doubt regretted having sold out to budding entrepreneurs.

In Trumbull County the crossroads village of Mecca struck oil in 1860 not long after engineer Drake had begun the business. The word quickly

petroleum would make an excellent illuminant, and that a number of valuable byproducts, such as naphtha, kerosene, paraffin, and lubricating oil, could be recovered from it. Encouraged by this report, Bissell raised the necessary funds and hired an engineer, Edwin L. Drake, to sink the first well at Titusville. It was August 1859 and the oil industry was born.

In contrast with steel, the oil industry had no mass market. Gasoline automobiles would not appear in significant numbers for another half-century. In spite of that, however, oil boomed. Following Drake's successful gusher, there was a "gold rush" descent on the oil country. Visions of instant wealth flashed through the minds of hundreds drill-

got out—"Thar's oil in Meccy!" Within several months 700 wells had been drilled and the town was booming. Three post offices were required to handle the mail. The boardinghouses, hotels, saloons, and gambling halls echoed with talk of quick wealth. The overflow of speculators and prospectors filled the hotels of nearby Warren. Alas, it was only for a moment. The oil simply was not there. The boom ended and most everyone left. A few houses were moved to Warren, while others were abandoned to the elements.

The domain of oil rapidly spread to southeastern Ohio and panhandle West Virginia. Within a dozen years the 4,000-square-mile tri-state area dominated the industry. By 1872 forty million barrels had been pumped from the wells there and oil had become a major product in the national economy—number four on the list of exports. Because of the oil fever in Marietta, during Civil War years local papers regularly ran stories of people going into the oil business and of new wells being drilled. Oil news was not as important as war news, but it was a matter of intense interest.

Crude oil must be refined before it is commercially usable, much as iron ore must be smelted. Refineries appeared in the oil fields almost as soon as the oil. Most of them, however, were ill-suited for the purpose. Under-financed and poorly situated for transporting the oil to major markets, the field refineries could not hold their own against larger competitors in big cities. Pittsburgh and Cleveland became the two principal refining centers for the oil industry and small refiners were driven out of business. Pittsburgh appeared to have an advantage because of its proximity to the field, but Cleveland gradually pulled ahead. Early in 1865 thirty refineries producing coal oil, gasoline, paraffin, kerosene, and tar were operating in Cleveland. The number doubled within a year. By the early 1870s the race for supremacy had been won by the Lake City. The reason for Cleveland's success lay in its superior transportation links to eastern markets. Whereas in Cleveland the New York Central and Erie railroads, plus the Erie Canal, provided competitive routes, Pittsburgh relied solely on the Pennsylvania Railroad.

The man who capitalized on Cleveland's competitive advantage was not necessarily unique in the annals of industrial history, but he became the most celebrated entrepreneur or "Robber Baron" in America. John D. Rockefeller was born in Upstate New York in 1839, the son of a sharp, somewhat irresponsible traveling patent medicine salesman. The family moved to Cleveland in the early 1850s when young Rockefeller was thirteen. He finished his common schooling and became a clerk in a local produce commission firm, an early wholesale house. Possessing a shrewd, calculating mind and an observant eye, he quickly mastered the basics of bookkeeping and the mechanics of business management. His passion for thrift, economy, and efficiency, inherited from his mother, was quickened in this early business experience.

Growing to maturity in Cleveland just when the oil refining business was being established there, Rockefeller had a ringside seat at the unfolding of the Industrial Revolution. He had no intention of

Industrialist and philanthropist John D. Rockefeller, 1839-1937, established the Standard Oil Company in 1870. By the time he retired in 1897, he was the world's richest man with a fortune estimated at $1 billion. After his retirement Rockefeller devoted much of his time to setting up endowment funds and is said to have given away $550 million in his lifetime. Courtesy, Ohio Historical Society

missing out on the opportunities available to an industrious young man with sense and vision. Having carefully husbanded his earnings, he formed a produce commission partnership with a man named Clark in 1863. The business was quite successful, grossing nearly half a million dollars in its first year, returning more than 100 percent on the original investment. Rockefeller's mind, however, was on oil. Using proceeds from his firm, he formed a new partnership in 1865 with Stanley Andrews for the purpose of refining oil. The organization did well in the

This 1928 photo of a clean and bright Standard Oil of Ohio (SOHIO) truck was made by Palm Brothers, a Cincinnati firm specializing in decalcomania. Courtesy, Cincinnati Historical Society

next five years, adding steadily to its resources, expanding operations, and taking on new partners, such as Henry Flagler. By 1870 the partnership was prepared for the next step.

In January of that year Rockefeller and his associates announced the formation of the Standard Oil Company of Ohio. Capitalized at one million dollars, the new firm was the largest refiner in the largest refining center in the world. It produced initially about 1,500 barrels of oil daily, one-seventh of the output of all Cleveland refineries. With his passion for economy and efficiency, Rockefeller recognized the need to build up large cash reserves in the event of a depression, or if an inviting opportunity for growth appeared. Hard times struck very soon, in 1873, and small refiners were poorly fixed to weather the difficulties facing them. On the other hand, Standard Oil was in a position to buy up the weaker refineries at bargain prices until it had a near monopoly on Cleveland's refining business. The company could now organize its operations on such a broad scale that costs for refining and distributing oil were reduced substantially below those of their competitors.

Further steps to drive out competition involved the use of rebates, drawbacks, and kickbacks in the shipping of oil. Standard Oil was not the first company to employ these devices, but it was the first to manipulate them to the great disadvantage of its rivals. The "rebate" was simply the return to the company of a portion of the shipping charge it paid to the railroad. Because Standard Oil's business was so vast, it was a matter of some consequence that the railroads not lose it. Any favors might help. Standard officials persuaded the railroads to grant their company rebates while denying them to other oil refiners. The company also convinced the railroads to grant it "drawbacks," or a percentage of the shipping charge paid by other refiners. "Kickbacks" to railroad officials sweetened to some degree the unpalatable necessity of making rebates and drawbacks to Standard Oil.

Through such practices, Standard Oil by 1880, ten short years after its founding, was in sole control of 90 percent of the refined oil business in the United States. One by one, its competitors, lacking the resources to withstand these cutthroat methods, had fallen before it. By 1875 Standard Oil's cash resources had climbed to thirteen million dollars, and by 1882 the figure had reached forty-five million. Over eleven million dollars had already been paid out in dividends. The ruthless techniques employed by the company in destroying its competition—rebates, drawbacks, and kickbacks were but a few of many—can hardly be defended by even its most sympathetic critics. However, other "Robber Barons" were doing the same things in the violent dog-eat-dog world of modern business. No rules existed by which to play this new game, so most of its practitioners resorted to any method they could think of to destroy their competition.

So vast had become the Standard Oil empire, extending far beyond the boundaries of Ohio, that a new plan of organization was needed. Thus in 1882 the Standard Oil Trust was established, although the public knew nothing about it for several years. By this device, stock in all Standard companies—numbering around twenty—was transferred to nine trustees, in exchange for twenty trust certificates for each share of stock. This permitted the trust to manage all Standard Oil properties as a single unit, providing the centralized control so dear to Rockefeller and his fellows. Greater economy and efficiency was attainable now than when the companies operated independently. The Standard Oil Trust, capitalized at seventy million dollars with annual earnings of about ten million dollars, became the prototype for the trust movement

Blacksmiths were important and necessary craftsmen before the advent of automobiles. This photograph, taken in the 1890s, depicts a blacksmith shop in Portsmouth. Courtesy, Ohio Historical Society

which ran rampant throughout American business over the next decade. The very term "trust" has become a part of our language, implying a massive monopoly.

Trusts were outlawed by the Sherman Anti-Trust Act of 1890 and the Standard Oil Trust was dissolved in 1892. For seven years the company's leaders—Rockefeller, Andrews, Flagler, H.H. Rogers, John D. Archbold, and others—ran the organization much as they had the trust, under a "gentleman's agreement," an informal arrangement whereby all decisions were made in concert. In 1899 they came up with another device which would shape the course of American business organization for much of the twentieth century: the holding company. By

this scheme Standard Oil of New Jersey bought controlling stock in all other Standard Oil companies and the entire empire was run through Standard Oil of New Jersey. Centralized management had again been achieved. In 1911, however, the United States Supreme Court ordered the dissolution of the Standard Oil holding company as it caused unreasonable restraint of trade under the Sherman Act. The empire was thereupon broken up into its constituent companies.

The breakup of the Standard Oil empire in 1911 gave birth to another large, independent oil company in Ohio. The discovery of oil in 1885 in the northwestern part of the state led to the formation of the Ohio Oil Company in 1887. The company's energies were devoted chiefly to the production of oil rather than the refining and marketing ends of the business. At the time Standard Oil was extending its activities into the area and was impressed by the efficient operations of Ohio Oil. It was so impressed, in fact, that in 1889 Standard Oil bought out Ohio Oil. With its headquarters now located in Findlay, Ohio Oil in the next few years was producing 50 percent of all the oil in Ohio and Indiana.

Granted considerable autonomy under Standard Oil ownership, Ohio Oil moved into the newly opened oil fields of Illinois and by 1908 had a pipeline running from the Mississippi River to the Pennsylvania border. The company was looking well beyond the Mississippi to the Rocky Mountains and Texas for new oil fields when the Supreme Court issued its dissolution order against Standard Oil. Thus on December 9, 1911, Ohio Oil once again became an independent organization. For another decade it confined itself to oil production, but in the 1920s it began to revamp its structure toward total integration—production, refining, and marketing. In 1962 the Ohio Oil Company became the Marathon Oil Company.

By the time of the dissolution, Standard Oil had played an important part in the nation's history and its Ohio origins were almost forgotten. The oil business had expanded far beyond the fields of Pennsylvania and the refineries of Cleveland with the discovery of great new reserves in Texas, California, off the Atlantic and Gulf coasts, in South America, and in the Middle East. New companies were organized which would in time rival and surpass Standard Oil as drillers and refiners of oil. Nevertheless, Standard Oil of Ohio remained a prominent Ohio corporation, and its claim to being the first company in one of the world's major industries assured it a special place in history.

V
RUBBER AND THE REST

This picture, looking north on High Street, shows busy downtown Columbus. By 1914 Columbus ranked among the top forty industrial cities in the country. Transportation has been a basis of the city's industry: Columbus was home to buggy and wagon factories, and has manufactured railroad, automotive, and airplane parts. Courtesy, Ohio Historical Society and the Columbus Dispatch

Facing page: This eye-catching ad for nonskid "quick detachable clincher" tires, designed by the Firestone Tire and Rubber Company, appeared in the October 22, 1910, issue of The Outlook.

While John D. Rockefeller and Standard Oil were going national, another Ohio industry was being founded, one which would forever retain its Ohio identity. In fact, this industry would always be identified with one particular Ohio city. There was no special reason why Akron should become the "tire capital" of the world. Cleveland, Youngstown, and Pittsburgh were suitably situated to form the heart of the iron and steel business, but why did the rubber industry come to Akron? Rubber manufacturing required crude rubber, coal, cloth, and ample supplies of water, but these were not indigenous to Akron; many places had them. Akron was chosen because of one man, who deliberately selected the city as the site of his rubber plant.

Benjamin F. Goodrich arrived in Akron in November 1870. He knew something about the area having attended Cleveland Medical College (now the Case Western Reserve School of Medicine) before the Civil War. After the war, he stopped practicing surgery, worked briefly in the Pennsylvania oil fields, and then, in 1867, opened a real estate business in New York City. Two years later he exchanged $10,000 worth of real estate for $14,000 in stock in the Hudson River Rubber Company at Hastings-on-Hudson and moved the plant to Melrose, north of Albany. While the company's products were of high quality, Goodrich found that eastern competition in the rubber business was keen. After learning that there were no rubber companies west of the mountains, Goodrich decided to look for prospects in Ohio. While visiting friends in Cleveland, he saw a circular put out by the Akron Board of Trade extolling the city's bright promise for

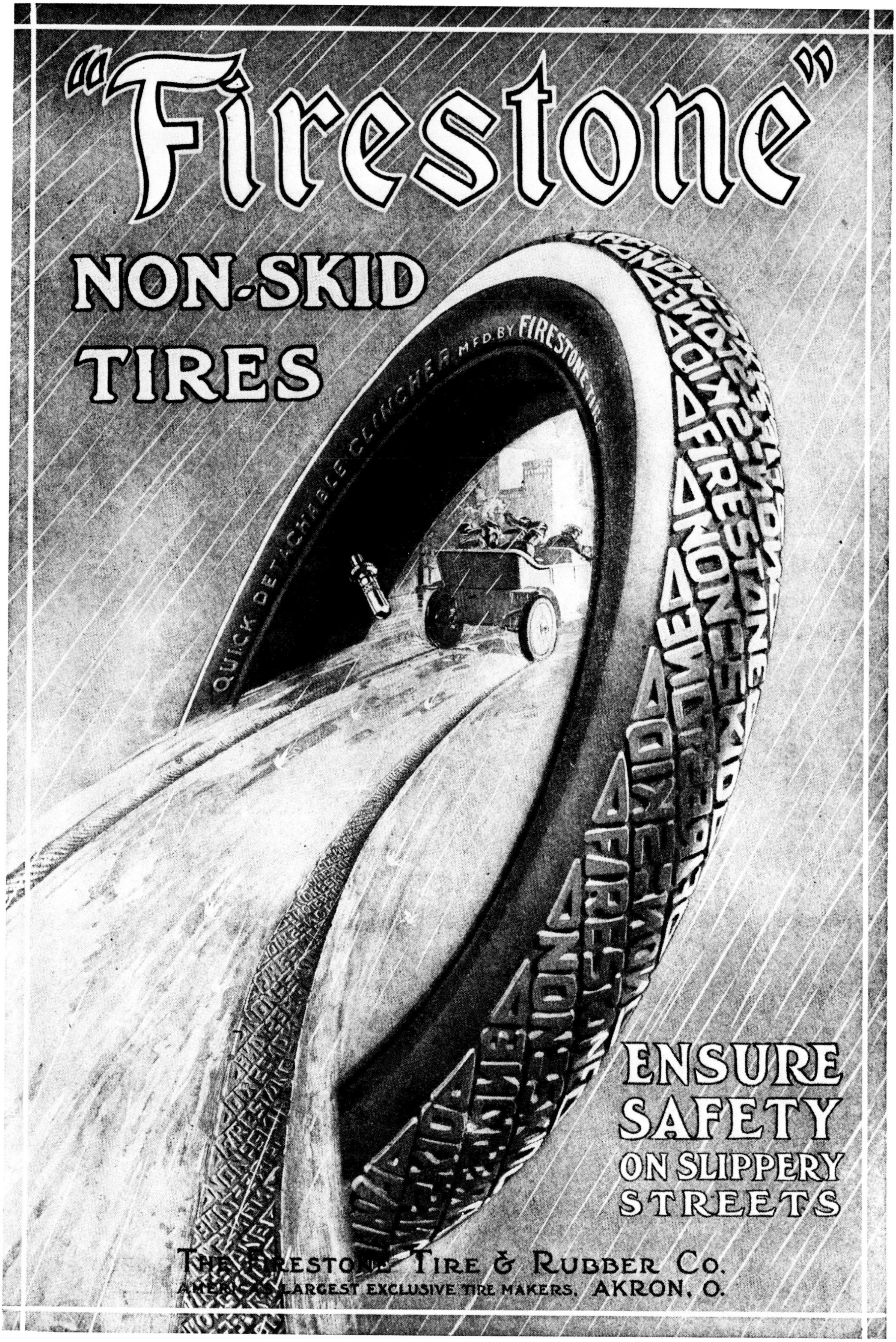

"Firestone"

NON-SKID TIRES

ENSURE SAFETY ON SLIPPERY STREETS

THE FIRESTONE TIRE & RUBBER Co.
AMERICA'S LARGEST EXCLUSIVE TIRE MAKERS, AKRON, O.

"I can make a hose which will stand up under any test," said B.F. Goodrich, a doctor who went on to open the first rubber factory in the Midwest. Within a few years the Goodrich Company was among the leading industries in Akron, the soon-to-emerge "Rubber Capital of the World." Courtesy, University of Akron Archives

future industry. He decided to check it out.

Goodrich liked what he saw in Akron. He spoke with a local businessman about relocating his rubber company there and was invited to address a large group of civic leaders at an evening meeting. He discussed his own history and explained why he wished to move his plant to Akron: there was plenty of coal and water, good transportation links, and a sizeable, available work force. And since no rubber companies existed west of the mountains, the market potential was good. Where would he get his supplies? The rubber would come from Brazil, the cotton from textile mills in the East. What would he make? Many products could be made from rubber, but what he was most interested in were fire hoses. He had seen a neighbor's house burn to

the ground because a fire hose had burst. His promise was simple: "I can make a hose which will stand up under any test. It will sell—and sell at good prices. I'm sure of it."

The rubber industry was a fairly new one. It dated only from 1839 when Charles Goodyear perfected the vulcanization process, making it possible to work the rubber more readily, enhancing its practical usage. But the industry developed slowly because rubber's usefulness was underestimated. Raincoats, shoes, overshoes, hot-water bottles, and caps were the principal items made. Rubber tires had been used but infrequently. Queen Victoria supposedly had solid rubber strips glued onto the wheels of one of her early carriages, and an Englishman had designed a primitive pneumatic tire in 1845, but it was of no real value.

The breakthrough in the rubber tire business occurred in 1888 when an Irish veterinarian named John B. Dunlop developed a clumsy pneumatic for his son's bike. Displeased with the heavy, solid rubber tires which slowed the bike's speed, he wrapped a tube of rubber around the tire rim, inserted a valve, and encased the whole tire in strong cloth. He inflated the tube and the experiment worked. The tire provided a smoother, faster ride. Pneumatic tires, first manufactured in the United States in 1891, ignited the bicycle mania of the 1890s. Everyone who was anyone had to have a bicycle on which he could enjoy the soft ride provided by the pneumatics. Manufacturers had trouble keeping up with the demand and popular songs were composed about the new fad.

Akron's business community, seeking to lure industry to town, was impressed with Goodrich. The president of the Board of Trade traveled to Melrose to make sure all Goodrich had said was true and found that it was. Goodrich needed $15,000 in financial backing. His new friends were able to collect only $13,600, but Goodrich decided to go ahead anyhow. The Melrose plant was dismantled and the machinery shipped to Akron. The new factory opened in March 1871 with a work force of twenty. A local newspaper announced that the company was ready to manufacture a host of items, including billiard cushions and fruit jar rings. As promised, though, Goodrich specialized in fire hoses.

Business was not good at first. The company was not well known and did not push its products aggressively. The depression of the mid-1870s led to a crisis in 1875 when bankruptcy threatened. George T. Perkins, one of Goodrich's original

backers, supplied sufficient capital to keep the company functioning until 1878 when an even more serious crisis faced the company. On this occasion another early backer, George W. Crouse, guaranteed the company's financial stability and the worst was over. From then on the company grew steadily. In 1880 it was incorporated as B.F. Goodrich Company, capitalized at $100,000. Although Goodrich died in 1888, the organization was so firmly established that the transfer of control to others went smoothly. By 1891 Goodrich had risen to fourth place among Akron companies. The following year, the company, with about 400 employees, reported sales of $1,413,000, and profits of over $250,000.

Despite this good financial report the next few years were not easy ones for Goodrich. The nation's worst depression until that time struck within a few months and the demand for most rubber products dropped off sharply. However, offsetting this decline was the growing call for pneumatic bicycle tires. By 1896 business had so improved that the company was making more money than it had before the depression. Goodrich during these years continued

As tire manufacturing progressed from manual methods to semiautomatic processes, employees at the Goodyear tire plant in Akron often faced pay cuts or lay-offs. Their discontent resulted in the great Akron rubber strike in 1913, which lasted a month and a half. Courtesy, Goodyear Tire and Rubber Company Archives

to market solid-rubber tires for the carriage trade, but this was not a major money-making branch of the business. The first agreement for a pneumatic automobile tire, a field which would revolutionize the tire business, was made with the Winton Company of Cleveland. The owner, Alexander Winton, blew one of the tires when he was out driving and patched the hole with molasses. Too much molasses went into the tube and it blew again, decorating Winton with a complete coat of the sticky stuff. Molasses and all, Goodrich had produced the first set of pneumatic automobile tires and a milestone had been reached. The big business, however, was still in bicycle tires.

Many other rubber manufacturing firms were now responding to the demand for pneumatic bicycle tires. One of these plants, the Diamond Rubber Company, was built literally next door to Goodrich. Diamond Rubber had purchased a building recently abandoned by the Diamond Match Company which had moved to Barberton. Capitalized at $50,000 when it opened in March 1894, Diamond Rubber was founded by former Goodrich employees (ex-Goodrich workers were prominent in many of the new rubber companies). Diamond had difficult times in the depression of the 1890s, and went through several reorganizations. But forceful leadership and innovations in rubber research put it on a solid financial footing. Goodrich's major competition came not from Diamond, however, but from two "new kids on the block"—Goodyear and Firestone.

The Seiberling family had long been active in Akron's business and civic affairs. John Seiberling had owned agricultural machinery, flour milling, and traction companies during the 1870s, 1880s, and 1890s. He had been one of the backers of Goodrich's rubber company in 1871 and even organized his own rubber company. But financial problems during the depression in the mid-1890s forced him to dispose of all his properties. However, one of John's sons, Frank, who had worked with his father, had gotten the rubber "itch." In 1898 while in Chicago selling his father's Empire Mower and Reaper Works, he learned of a vacated factory complex in East Akron which was up for sale. He raised $56,000 to acquire and renovate the abandoned building and to purchase equipment. With an additional $93,000 to begin operations, raised through a stock sale, Frank Seiberling was prepared to start up his own rubber company.

Frank named his new company for Charles Goodyear, whose vulcanization process had made possible the growth of the rubber industry. The Goodyear Tire and Rubber Company was incorporated on August 29, 1898. Operations began in early December. Specializing in pneumatic bicycle and carriage tires, Goodyear had sales of $508,000 in 1899 and doubled this figure in 1900.

But things are not always what they seem. From the very outset Goodyear was plagued with bitter legal controversies over patent rights. Goodyear applied for a license to use the "Grant patent," which involved a method of securing a carriage tire to the wheel rim. The company's request was turned down, even though others who had applied for the license had received it. As a result Goodyear made a modification in the Grant process and pro-

———

As time went on, Firestone diversified its production and began to manufacture other items besides tires. Pictured here are women at work in the Firestone Spark Plug Factory in Akron. Courtesy, Ohio Historical Society

Above: The B.F. Goodrich Company made products other than tires, as seen in this ad for Goodrich Trouser Guards. The ad guarantees that the trouser guards will not rust or "soil the pantaloons." Courtesy, University of Akron Archives

Above right: The Seiberlings provided financial backing for Melvin Vaniman's airship, pictured here at Atlantic City on July 2, 1912, before taking off on a trans-Atlantic flight. The airship met with tragedy when it later burst into flames, taking the lives of all five passengers, including Vaniman. Courtesy, University of Akron Archives

ceeded to manufacture the tire on the theory that its method was different. This was at once challenged in court. Goodyear was allowed to continue manufacturing the tire while the litigation proceeded, but all revenue from sales was held in escrow. In May 1902 a federal appeals court ruled for Goodyear and the escrow funds were released.

Harvey Firestone, born in 1868 on a farm in eastern Ohio, attended a business college in Cleveland and obtained a job with the Columbus Buggy Company. He learned about the tire business in 1892 when he was the company's representative in Detroit. Later he was a partner in a small rubber company in Chicago. He sold out for a nice profit and with the boom in bicycle tires reaching a peak he decided to enter the business. Since Akron was a rising tire town and near his home he set up shop there. The Firestone Tire and Rubber Company was chartered in August 1900. The tires were actually manufactured in Chicago, but the marketing was

million dollars. The work force had grown to 1,000. Since this extensive growth was well beyond the company's original capacity, buildings were added. But this enlarged complex was still inadequate. A new four-story plant opened its doors on June 8, 1911. Within another year or so some 2,900 workers were turning out 7,500 tires daily.

Meanwhile Goodrich and Goodyear were rapidly moving forward. Goodrich's sales had risen more than fifty times between 1900 and 1911, increasing from $491,000 to $27,406,700. Profits had quintupled over the same period. In 1912 Goodrich absorbed its friendly neighbor and rival, Diamond Rubber. While Goodrich made products other than tires, Goodyear had moved to the front as the country's leading tire manufacturer. In 1912, with a work force of 6,880, Goodyear's sales had reached $25,232,000 with profits of $3,000,000. Goodrich, Goodyear, and Firestone were the giants in the rubber and tire capital of the world, but there were a dozen or more lesser firms in the rubber business in the Greater Akron area.

Again the question is asked: Why did Akron of all places become the heart of the rubber industry? Karl H. Grismer, who has written an excellent history of Akron and Summit County, provides some clues. He points out that Akron's prosperous future could hardly have been predicted in 1890. Of ninety-four rubber plants across the country at that time, Akron possessed only B.F. Goodrich. However, economic conditions in the city in the mid-1890s made it fertile ground for any kind of new industry. Many companies had gone out of business and there were a host of empty factory buildings about town. "Every new concern," Grismer writes, "which started between 1894 and 1902 located in buildings once occupied by companies which had gone bankrupt or had left the city. In every case the buildings were acquired at prices far below the cost of construction."

The empty factories left a large number of unemployed workers who were ready to work at almost any wage. This large pool of cheap labor was readily seized upon by the rubber companies. Not that they were ruthless exploiters of labor—in fact, all of them later developed substantial programs providing for the workers' well-being. Yet when the rubber companies were fighting for survival they needed cheap labor. Grismer reports that Akron firms paid their workers about 20 percent less than their competitors in other places. This gave them an obvious advantage with respect to production

handled by Firestone. Although business was good, all the profits went to the Chicago manufacturer. Thus the company was reorganized in 1903 and Firestone went into the tire manufacturing business for itself.

Firestone entered the tire business at the dawning of the automobile age. Early auto tires were not of a very high quality. The life of a tire was about 1,000 miles at best and frequent punctures or blow-outs meant frequent changes. Most tires at the time were "clinchers," which were very difficult to remove after a puncture. What was needed was a tire which a motorist could remove, repair, and reinstall while on the road without exhausting himself. Goodyear and later Firestone both came up with a new type of rim and "straight-side" tire which was easier to handle. This advance led to Goodyear's supremacy in auto tire manufacturing, but it also gave a great boost to Firestone.

By 1910 Firestone's sales were in excess of five million dollars, returning a profit of over one

costs. In addition, the ample supply of coal and water and Akron's convenient location were important assets. The Cuyahoga River came down from the north and the Erie Railroad came in from the east. Of course, being adjacent to Detroit would be an unexpected bonus.

The managers of the rubber companies were all very smart and talented men, each trying to gain an advantage over his rivals. Grismer writes that

they fought constantly for leadership in sales, in profits, and even in such minor matters as amateur athletics. Every one of the rubber barons strove constantly to produce a better tire than his competitors—a tire he could crow about at the country club and in his national advertising. He stopped at no expense in employing top-flight chemists and physicists for his research laboratory, and in making countless experiments. All the leading companies had fleets of test cars barreling through the country, day and night, in all kinds of weather and over all kinds of roads, to determine in what respects their tires were weak or strong and how much mileage they would give. Whenever one company came out with a new tire, the others immediately got samples to tear apart in their laboratories and find out how they were made. To keep track of what their competitors were doing, they allegedly employed "spies" who got jobs in the rival plants and carefully reported all tidbits of information pertaining to new developments. Because of this intense rivalry, the quality of Akron-made tires improved steadily, and shortly became better than the tires made by firms in other cities. Motorists everywhere began demanding Akron tires —and in the race for supremacy in the rubber industry other cities dropped by the wayside.

With the growing demand, new techniques were perfected, production increased as costs were cut, plants expanded, and thousands upon thousands of workers were hired. The city population jumped from 27,600 in 1890, to 42,700 in 1900, to 69,000 in 1910, to 208,000 in 1920. All this seems to explain why Akron became the "tire city," the "rubber capital of the world."

But the rubber industry would never have blossomed as it did without the automobile. At first con-sidered an impractical plaything, then a luxury for the rich, and finally a necessity, the automobile transformed America in the twentieth century. The automobile industry not only zoomed to the top as the nation's number-one business, providing thousands of jobs to workers in auto and auto-related industries, it changed the lifestyle of America. The automobile brought the country to the city and the city to the country. No, life was never quite the same after the arrival of the automobile.

The gasoline auto appeared after considerable experimentation with other methods of locomotion. Autos powered by steam were manufactured by many companies in the 1890s, the most famous being the Stanley Steamer. Burning kerosene heated the tank of water and the resultant steam energized the motor. It took too long to raise a head of steam, however, and steam cars disappeared around World War I.

Developed at about the same time as the steam car was the electric automobile. Some 35,000 of these were manufactured in the United States between 1896 and 1915. The electric car was popular, especially with ladies because it was easy to handle and made little noise. The problem with the electric was that it could not attain speeds much above twenty miles per hour and the battery required frequent recharging. Gas autos were not bound by these limitations and electrics disappeared shortly after the steamers. But the Electric Vehicle Association did not lose hope, urging as late as 1913 that "before you buy any car, consider the electric."

Very few gas cars were on the road in 1900, but as inventions and refinements expedited manufacture and lowered the cost of cars, sales picked up rapidly. Ransom E. Olds designed a primitive assembly line in 1901 and within two years was manufacturing over 5,000 cars annually. Henry Ford developed a moving assembly line and brought out his first Model-T in 1908. By 1916 he was selling the car for under $400. The Model-T was discontinued in 1927 to make room for the Model-A, but in that twenty-year span over fifteen million of them were sold, over half the total number for all companies. Auto sales were off in World War I, but the boom resumed after the war, with almost two million being sold in 1920.

Although Detroit quickly asserted leadership in automobile manufacture, in the early years of the industry Ohio ranked next to Michigan in the output of cars, auto bodies, and auto parts. For a time it competed on an even basis with Michigan for first

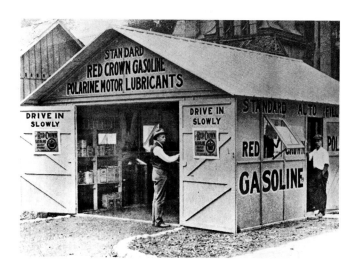

Left: With the advent of the automobile came the gasoline station. This early Columbus station offered drive-in service. Courtesy, Ohio Historical Society

———

Below: Pictured here is an advertisement for the Buckeye Buggy Company of Columbus, boasting the largest selection of carriages in the state. Companies that began manufacturing carriages typically progressed to making automobiles years later. Courtesy, Ohio Historical Society

BUCKEYE BUGGY CO.,
COLUMBUS, OHIO,
Large · Manufacturers · of · Fine · Vehicles.

A Great Point of Interest to Visitors is their 3½ Acres of NEW Factory Buildings, Just NORTH of Union Depot, on High Street. Largest Repository in Ohio, Showin 125 Vehicles to Select From.

BUCKEYE BUGGY COMPANY.

Baker Electric Vehicles

The Aristocrats of Motordom

The Electric Sensation of 1909

The Baker Electric Runabout has unusual speed and a mileage capacity of one hundred miles. It is swift, noiseless, and easy of control in congested streets.

The Ideal Car for Professional and Business Men

Our catalogue describing our latest models of Baker Electric Runabouts, Victorias, Coupés, Roadsters, Broughams, Landaulets, etc., mailed on request.

THE BAKER MOTOR VEHICLE COMPANY, 42 W. 80TH ST., CLEVELAND, OHIO.

place in car production, but fell behind when Ford brought out his Model-T.

Many Ohio auto companies grew out of electric car, carriage, and bicycle companies. The Winton Company of Cleveland went from the bicycle to the carriage, and then to the gas auto. The Columbus Buggy Company manufactured carriages, then electrics, and finally gas machines.

Two famous Cleveland firms never got beyond the electric stage. The Rauch and Lang Company started making carriages before the Civil War, turning to electrics at the end of the century. This company was not interested in the assembly-line philosophy, boasting that it required ninety days to make a single car. But the end product was worth it, the public was assured, for the car was absolutely safe and so simple to drive that a twelve-year-old could handle it. The Baker Motor Vehicle Company of Cleveland also specialized in electric cars. Claiming to be "the oldest and largest manufacturers of elec-

tric motor cars in the world," Baker called itself "the aristocrats of motordom." It was asserted in 1909 that one battery charge was good for 100 miles. By 1911 the figure had improved to 244.5 miles per charge. At the peak of its popularity, Baker Electrics sold for $3,000 while Henry Ford's Model-T cost only $500.

Cleveland's three largest automobile manufacturers, three of the largest in the state, were Peerless, White, and Winton. Peerless, whose slogan was "all that the name implies," manufactured six-cylinder cars, both open and closed models, in addition to a line of trucks. The cars were not cheap, averaging between $4,300 and $7,200. The company stressed silence and comfort as the hallmarks of its product.

The White Motor Company began turning out steam automobiles in 1899 and continued to make them for about ten years. They boasted of their superiority over gas cars and pointed with pride to their victory in an endurance run against gas autos

The 1908 *Peerless*

All That The Name Implies

is fitted for the ╱ roughest work
and proportioned to satisfy the keenest
sense of refinement and comfort.

A larger Tonneau, longer wheel-base, slightly
longer springs and a double ignition system
are simply the 1908 slight developments of the
principles of past Peerless construction.

They like it best who know it most intimately.

Write for our 1908 Catalogue "O" which fully
describes and illustrates the Peerless Models.

PEERLESS MOTOR CAR CO., 2445 Oakdale St., Cleveland, O.

Member A.L.A.M.

Above: Assembly of automobiles at Willys-Overland in Toledo originally took place in individual stalls, but by 1913 the plant had developed assembly lines. Here a worker guides an auto body onto a frame. Courtesy, Ohio Historical Society

Below right: With the advent of the automobile, accidents became inevitable. Several curious boys gathered to view the damage done to this vehicle in 1920. Courtesy, Western Reserve Historical Society

at Harrisburg, Pennsylvania, in May 1908. By 1910, however, they were extolling the virtues of their gas engine cars, although they still produced some steam cars. In two more years they were exclusively into gasoline cars. To assist women in learning how to drive their fashionable "town cars," the company prepared "a dainty booklet for dainty women." White was now manufacturing trucks and taxicabs as well as cars. It became famous in World War I for its trucks, which earned the Croix de Guerre from the French government. The statement put out by the company read:

The Croix de Guerre has been awarded the First and Second Groupments of the Great Headquarters Reserve No. 1 of the French Army, each operating 500 or more White Trucks. Citations for distinguished service accompanied the order, supplemented by a later citation to the entire Reserve No. 1,

operating 2,500 White Trucks. This is the first and only instance on record of motor transport formations in any army receiving this honor. The White trucks were all veterans, many in continuous service since 1914.

Winton got started as a bicycle company in 1890 and progressed onward to the gas automobile after the turn of the century. In 1896 and 1897 their "12 stylish models" of bicycles were selling for $100. As the bicycle mania ebbed and the automobile mania grew, the Winton Bicycle Company became the Winton Carriage Company and then the Winton Motor Car Company. Its principal product was the "Winton Six," an open touring car which sold in 1910 for $3,250. Winton got plenty of free publicity in 1903 when Tom L. Johnson, Cleveland's famous mayor, drove his Winton around the state during his campaign for governor. The company may not have been happy about this publicity, however. The "Red Devil" ran into trouble outside of Ravenna in early September. The weather was bad and the machine went off the road into a ditch. Johnson and his party eventually made it to town on the back of a hay wagon. A week later the car's battery went dead near Newcomerstown and a local farmer came to the rescue. In another week the mayor drove the machine into a stone culvert while trying to take a cigar out of his pocket. Finally, near the end of September, the "Red Devil" suffered a general breakdown at Georgetown on the Ohio River and

had to be abandoned. Driving an automobile in those pioneer days may have been an exhilarating experience, but it could also be an exasperating one.

Another famous Ohio car was the Willys-Overland of Toledo. Toledo had come a long way since its incorporation in 1835. Growth was great after the Civil War, in particular, with railroads and iron ore stimulating industrial activity. One of the companies established by the turn of the century was Pope Motor, which was purchased by John Willys in 1909. A native of New York State, Willys had grown up in the bicycle business, but quickly recognized the possibilities of the automobile. Under his leadership Willys-Overland became Toledo's number-one business concern and its product was well regarded throughout the auto business. Within

two years it was manufacturing twenty-two low-priced models. Its promotional literature boasted that its five factories were the best equipped in the world and that there were "20,000 delighted owners" of Overland cars.

Toledo boasted not only Willys-Overland, but other important industries, some related to the automobile business, some not. One of the most famous was the Champion Spark Plug Company, run by the Stranahan brothers, Robert and Frank. By the late 1920s Champion was turning out fifty million plugs a year, which supplied two-thirds of all autos and airplanes throughout the world. Another concern which rose to a dominant position in its field was the Electric Auto-Lite Company, which produced batteries and ignition and lighting systems for automobiles. Other companies manufactured auto parts and auto supplies. Proximity to Detroit helped Toledo's auto-related industries.

Perhaps Toledo's most famous industry in the twentieth century resulted from the discovery of a large natural gas field in northwestern Ohio in the 1880s. In 1888 Edward D. Libbey, a successful New England glass manufacturer but beset with labor problems, came to Ohio to explore the prospects of relocating his company. Attracted by the community and cheap fuel, he founded the Libbey Glass Company in Toledo. Within a decade his high quality "Libbey Cut Glass" was known at home and abroad. An inventor, Michael J. Owens of Newark, Ohio, joined the company in the 1890s. In the next

These were employees of the Federal Glass Company of Columbus, which was started by George and R.J. Beatty, descendants of a family prominently identified with the glass industry since 1848. They manufactured mainly household glass and initiated the process of making handblown glassware from continuous tanks, rather than from clay pots. Courtesy, Ohio Historical Society

few years he developed a machine which produced bottles, tumblers, and glass chimneys. While putting many skilled glassblowers out of work, Owens' machine greatly increased Libbey revenues. In addition to cut-glass pieces, bottles, containers, and window glass, Libbey also was manufacturing "shatterproof" windshields for the growing auto industry. Akron may have been the "tire capital of the world," but Toledo was the "glass capital of the world." After World War II Toledo's professional baseball team was even given the unlikely nickname of "Glass Sox."

Like Toledo, Cincinnati also had a highly diversified economy throughout the Industrial Revolution. The city never was caught up in iron and steel or rubber as was the northern part of the state. It simply continued on its way manufacturing carriages, furniture, machine tools, paper, clothing, soap, and other sundries, much as it had before the Civil War. It could claim having more industries than any other city in the state, although they were

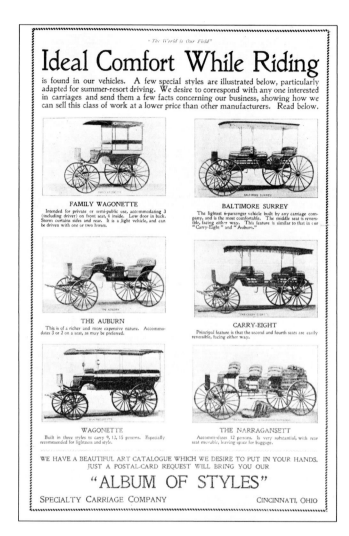

not among the so-called "heavy" industries. Cincinnati missed out on the automobile much as it had missed out on the railroad. Both Henry Ford and the Packard brothers of Warren, Ohio, had tried to raise funds for their experimental cars in Cincinnati because of its strength in the carriage industry, but they were turned down and shifted their attention to Michigan. When the carriage business declined, Cincinnati had no automobile industry to replace it, as it might have had.

But Cincinnati did not miss out on soap. Procter & Gamble, the world's premier soap maker, was founded in 1837 by two young immigrants from Great Britain. James Gamble arrived in Cincinnati a very sick sixteen-year-old lad in 1819. The family, late of County Fermanagh, Ireland, had come to the United States hoping to improve their prospects at Shawneetown, Illinois, which developers had proclaimed an "El Dorado." James' illness from fever compelled the family to stop at Cincinnati, and they liked the place so much they decided to stay. In 1821 James became apprenticed to a soap maker, a position he held for eight years. In 1829 he formed a soap and candle partnership with Hiram

Above: The Libbey Glass Company was founded by Edward Libbey, a New England glass manufacturer. Soon Libbey Cut Glass was famous around the world and, as this 1901 ad proudly proclaims, it took first prize at every exposition it entered. Courtesy, The Outlook, *1901*

Above left: The carriage and wagon industry began in Cincinnati in the early 1800s. Before the end of the century, Cincinnati led the world in the manufacture of wagons and carriages. This ad in the April 23, 1896, issue of The Outlook *illustrates six styles of carriages available from the Specialty Carriage Company in Cincinnati.*

Knowlton and in 1833 married Elizabeth Ann Norris. Meanwhile, William Procter, whose woolens shop in London had been destroyed by fire, left England in 1832 planning to settle in Louisville. His wife was stricken with cholera as their boat reached Cincinnati, and she died within a few days. With some experience in candle making in England, Procter saw a need for candles in the city and set up a shop on Main Street. He made the candles, packaged them, and delivered them personally to his customers. In 1833 he married Olivia Norris, sister of Elizabeth Ann.

After four years of carrying on their respective businesses, and upon the urging of their father-in-law, the two young men formed Procter & Gamble Company to make soap and candles. It was not the most propitious moment to go into business with a financial panic sweeping the country. But they were not expecting great things and worked long hours to put their business on a firm foundation. Gamble ran the "factory" while Procter minded the "office." Early every morning Gamble would make

Above: Procter & Gamble's Central Avenue factory in Cincinnati was situated next to the Miami and Erie Canal. Built in 1850, the factory was close to the city's slaughterhouses, which provided it with the necessary raw materials for candle and soap making. The Central Avenue building burned down in 1884, and Procter & Gamble relocated to St. Bernard, close to the railroad lines. Courtesy, Cincinnati Historical Society

A GOOD BAIT.

When hungry sharks pursue the ship,	They see it floating here and there
The sailors soon themselves equip	Upon the billows light and fair,
With fishing lines of halyard rope,	Without support or sign of aid,
And bait their hooks with IVORY SOAP.	And know of oil it must be made,
No cork they need upon the line,	From all impure ingredients free
Their bait will ride the foaming brine.	As pearls that lie beneath the sea;
The eager sharks soon fasten eyes	No further facts they wait to know,
Upon the white and tempting prize;	But seize the bait, and up they go.

If your grocer does not keep the Ivory Soap, send six two-cent stamps, to pay the postage, to Procter and Gamble, Cincinnati, and they will send you *free* a large cake of IVORY SOAP.

Left: This interesting ad for Ivory soap appeared in the September 1884 issue of Harper's Young People. Such a depiction of the Procter & Gamble product is quite different from the "Ivory Girl" image. Courtesy, the Procter & Gamble Company

Above: This is a typical Procter & Gamble advertisement for Ivory soap. This soap is said to be gentle and pure, appropriate for this beautiful woman and young girl. Courtesy, the Procter & Gamble Company

the rounds of the packing plants to collect meat scraps and fat essential for making soap. Expected or not, the company grew steadily. In 1850 the factory moved into a complex of buildings on Central Avenue and four years later the company offices were transferred to a five-story building on Second Street at the corner of Walnut. By 1859 it was one of the largest companies in Cincinnati with annual sales in excess of one million dollars.

By the 1880s the second generation—three Procter and three Gamble sons joined the firm—was in full control as the company continued to expand. It was now the recognized national leader among 432 soap manufacturers, with sales in the millions and profits in the half-millions. In 1890, in keeping with the popular new form of business organization, the company was incorporated.

Prior to reorganization, in 1881 Harley T. Procter had sold his brothers and cousins on the advan-

tages of large-scale advertising. He argued that notices in store windows, billboards, and newspapers were insufficient and urged that they get their message into nationally circulated magazines. Within a decade Procter & Gamble was advertising in *Ladies Home Journal, Good Housekeeping, Outlook,* and *Harper's Weekly.* One product, in particular, had become a household name through advertising and proved a turning point in the company's history. The successful promotion of Ivory soap, which had been submitted to professional chemists for testing and proven to be "99 and 44/100 per cent pure," substantially stimulated Procter & Gamble's reputation and revenues and marked a new stage in commercial advertising.

The Ivory soap ads implied that the product was not only useful but necessary in whatever job, business, or pastime in which one might be engaged. The new homemaker, the world traveler, the

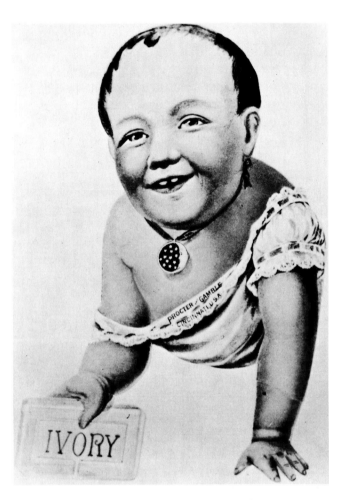

Above: The Procter & Gamble Company was a firm believer in the importance of advertising. Pictured here is the first Ivory baby, clutching a bar of Ivory soap and wearing the company's logo on a necklace. Courtesy, Cincinnati Historical Society

———

Right: This photo shows workers leaving the Ivorydale plant, so named because of the popular soap manufactured there. Production began in 1886 at the plant north of Cincinnati in St. Bernard. The company, known worldwide, became very important to the economy of the Cincinnati area. Courtesy, the Procter & Gamble Company

ostrich farmer, the new baby, and the factory worker all needed and used Ivory soap. One ad pictured a soldier in France tossing a cake of soap into a tub of water and as it rose to the surface an unbelieving mademoiselle shrieked in delight, "Il flotte!" Little ditties frequently accompanied an ad, such as this one in which a mother is tucking her tiny one in bed:

> *A bath in cleansing, sweet and mild*
> *As "Ivory" makes it, always seem*
> *To bring such comfort, that the child*
> *Drops fast asleep with happy dreams.*

When Procter & Gamble developed Crisco, its revolutionary vegetable shortening, in 1911, the product got a big send off in the advertising pages of major magazines.

While Cincinnati had no heavy industry, it was considered by some to be the most important manufacturing city in the state. It remained in the forefront of the machine tool industry, which had developed during the halcyon years of the river trade. As a major port on the Ohio River, Cincinnati possessed many shops to manufacture, replace, and repair steamboat boilers, engines, and gears. The city ranked sixth in the country in the manufacture of ladies' shoes and remained high on the list in its output of men's clothing. There were no more carriage makers, but Cincinnati was still a major furniture manufacturer. Globe-Wernicke was wellknown for its line of desks, filing cabinets, bookcases, and other office furniture. Hartwell Furniture specialized in chairs, rockers, and tables for the home. Peck-Williamson was noted for its warm-air furnaces and steam and hot-water boilers. And the "Queen City of the West" had the largest playing card factory in

The Procter & Gamble Company began marketing Ivory soap, "the pure soap that floated," in 1879. The men pictured here, with a wagon and Ivory soap signs, distributed free samples of the soap. Courtesy, Cincinnati Historical Society

Right: Pictured here is Barney Kroger's shiny red delivery wagon. The Kroger Grocery and Baking Company was incorporated in 1902, when the store became the first to bake its own bread. Soon after, Kroger began to sell meat in addition to bread, fruits, and vegetables. Courtesy, Cincinnati Historical Society

Right: Pictured here is Barney Kroger's shiny red delivery wagon. The Kroger Grocery and Baking Company was incorporated in 1902, when the store became the first to bake its own bread. Soon after, Kroger began to sell meat in addition to bread, fruits, and vegetables. Courtesy, Cincinnati Historical Society

Below: Cincinnati companies printed not only textbooks, religious books, and greeting cards, but also playing cards. The U.S. Playing Card Company was the nation's largest playing card factory. Pictured here is the printing of large sheets of cards not yet cut. Courtesy, Cincinnati Historical Society

the country, the United States Playing Card Company, founded in 1880.

The turn of the century saw many other Ohio cities prospering from the Industrial Revolution. Marion, fifty miles or so northwest of Columbus, never was a large town, but it produced Warren G. Harding and the Marion Steam Shovel Company. Marion shovels have been used worldwide for the most strenuous digging demanded by man. Founded in 1884, the company was instrumental in railroad construction throughout the American and Canadian West. Following the acquisition of the Panama Canal Zone in 1903, Marion shovels were used to dig the canal, and Marion became known as the "city that built the Panama Canal." Steam shovels gave way, as automobiles were doing, to electric and then gas-powered machinery. After World War I, Marion Shovel manufactured the largest shovel ever built and in the 1930s came out with an even bigger one. This weighed three million pounds and required forty-six freight cars to ship. Road building and strip mining were the major uses for these mammoth shovels between the wars. By this time several other Marion shovel companies were also doing a good business.

Springfield's Champion Machine Company was the major manufacturer of agricultural machinery at the turn of the century. Two thousand workers produced one reaper every four minutes. However, as the corn and wheat producing areas gravitated toward the Great Plains, the farm machinery business went with it and Springfield lost its lead. Yet it remained an important center for the industry well into the twentieth century.

Another industry in which Springfield was a leader was publishing. The Crowell-Collier Company was an outgrowth of the agricultural machinery business. John Crowell, a printer from Louisville, began publishing *Farm and Fireside* in 1877 to push the sale of cultivators. Later *Woman's Home Companion, Collier's Weekly, American Magazine,* and other national magazines were added to the list. Several thousand employees worked for Crowell-Collier during its most prosperous years.

Canton was part of the iron and steel complex of the northeastern part of the state. Republic Steel had a plant there. Among other things produced in Canton were auto bodies and roller bearings. The Timken Roller Bearing Company was founded there in 1900. The nationally known Hoover vacuum sweeper was made in North Canton. Safes and watches were also manufactured in Canton. After

the Deuber-Hampden Watch Works came to town in 1887, lured by $100,000 and free land, thousands of people also moved to Canton, hoping to work in the plant. By 1880 the population had jumped from 13,000 to 26,000. Deuber-Hampden boasted that its watches "were accurate to the second" and would not accidentally reset in one's pocket as the "common" ones did.

Columbus was not a major manufacturing city like Cleveland, Youngstown, Akron, or Toledo. It remained primarily a center for commerce and government. Among the industries for which Columbus was noted were paper making, publishing, and shoe manufacturing. One of the nation's major steel castings companies was also in Columbus. Buckeye Steel Castings began business on a small scale in 1881 making iron castings. Progress was slow until it began producing automatic couplers for railroads.

Left: The Dueber-Hampden Watch Works claimed to make extremely accurate watches. When the company moved to Canton, it lured potential workers to the city. Courtesy, Ohio Historical Society

Below left: Barney Kroger's first store, the Great Western Tea Company, opened in 1883. Within the year, Kroger bought out his partner and named the store after himself. Within ten years the first grocery chain had expanded to include seventeen stores. By 1912 the number of stores had grown to 157. Courtesy, Cincinnati Historical Society

Right: In 1857 the Ohio state government moved into the new capitol building which was under construction when the old State House burned down. Originally the new building was to cost $400,000 and take six years to construct; however, it took twenty-two years and some $1.6 million to complete this Greek Doric structure. Courtesy, Ohio Historical Society

Below right: Businesses of Columbus used motorized vehicles for making deliveries and often advertised their products on the sides of delivery trucks, as seen in this 1910 photo of Capital City Products. Courtesy, Ohio Historical Society and the Columbus Dispatch

Below: The Dueber-Hampden Watch Works was an important business in Canton for many years. This ad from an issue of The Outlook *in 1900 expounds the virtues of the Dueber-Hampden Watch, which is lever-set and will not "set in your pocket." Courtesy,* The Outlook

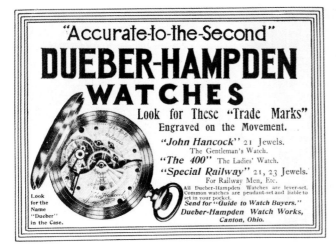

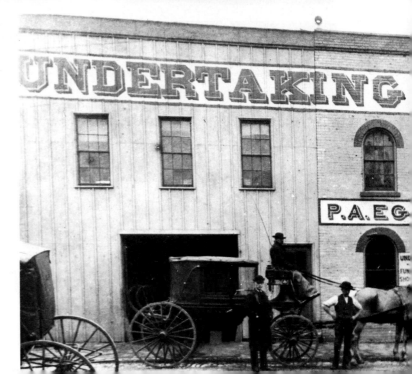

Above: In 1916 Buckeye Steel Castings Company claimed to have the world's largest steel foundry manufacturing steel casting for railroads. Located in Columbus, the company made automatic couplers which linked railroad cars together. Courtesy, Ohio Historical Society

Left: This Columbus business firm offered an interesting combination of services: undertaking and livery. Courtesy, Ohio Historical Society and the **Columbus Dispatch**

This collage shows production, from the drawing board to the factory, at the Sidney Machine Tool Company, established in 1904. Courtesy, Ohio Historical Society

As steel came in, Buckeye went to steel couplings. That was in 1902. A new factory was built in 1916 by which time the company was claiming that it was "the largest steel foundry in the world . . . devoted entirely to the manufacture of steel castings for railroad work." Two major reasons for the success of Buckeye Castings were its early utilization of the principles of "scientific management" and adoption of employee welfare programs.

Among the smaller towns, Sidney, Ohio, had a remarkable record of industrial success. In the late nineteenth century Sidney artisans made wooden parts for carriages and other products. The Wagner Company which made cast-iron parts and ventured into aluminum ware was also in Sidney. Sidney was noted for its community support of local firms. The most important industry in town was Monarch Machine Tool Company. Citizens of Sidney induced Monarch, then a small machine shop in Detroit, to move to their city in 1909. It prospered greatly during World War I with the huge demand for machine tools. The plant was enlarged after the war. In promoting home industry, Monarch purchased castings for its lathes from a neighbor firm next door.

An account of another world industrial leader will close this selective catalog of Ohio industry. The National Cash Register Company of Dayton was founded by John Patterson in 1884. A Dartmouth graduate, Patterson was a toll collector on the Miami and Erie Canal who was troubled by the inexact method of counting fares. When he and his brother opened a retail shop at Coalton in the late 1870s, dealing in coal and miner supplies, they had the same problems. John Patterson read about a cash register which did all the counting of all transactions and ordered two of them. The registers cut debts and saved money. In 1884 he bought controlling interest in the same cash register company, which had been failing, and the National Cash Register Company was born.

Patterson was a humorless, tough, single-minded man, determined to make the company succeed. He had little patience with inefficiency or insubordination. The people he fired or who left under pressure constitutes a "Who's Who" in American business leadership. Charles F. Kettering and Thomas Watson are two of the more memorable names. Between 1910 and 1930, "an estimated one-sixth of the top executives in the nation's companies were former NCR executives," proclaims a company brochure.

Patterson pushed his product with a driving intensity. His salesmen were carefully trained. They had to memorize a 450-word primer on selling techniques and were fired if they could not. Patterson made frequent "flying trips," unannounced, to check up on his people. He established a training school for the agents and converted annual conventions into instructional seminars. He believed strongly in advertising, but in contrast to Procter & Gamble which sold its product through national magazines, Patterson favored mailing his own publications, one of which was called the "Hustler," directly to potential buyers.

Patent fights and legal battles marked the first twenty-five years of NCR history, as they did with most other large corporations. In one case Patterson was fined and sentenced to jail, but the ruling was overturned on appeal. There was no stopping NCR's growth and eventual domination of the industry. Construction of a vast new complex of buildings was begun in 1906. The number of employees had increased from 13 in 1884 to 7,000 by the end of World War I, while cash register sales leaped from 359 to 1.5 million dollars.

One of the world's great paint companies was founded in Cleveland in the years following the Civil War. Henry Sherwin's career, to a point, paralleled that of John D. Rockefeller. Arriving in Cleveland as a teenager from Vermont in the 1850s, Sherwin avoided war service and got a grounding in business by working in a produce commission house. He was keenly aware of several new fields of business enterprise just opening, but where Rockefeller chose oil, Sherwin chose paint. In 1870, the same year Standard Oil was launched, the unschooled Sherwin and a Western Reserve Ph.D., Edgar P. Williams, formed the Sherwin-Williams Company.

In those days, paint manufacturers merely supplied the ingredients for the paint while buyers mixed the batch they wanted themselves. A few ready-mix paints appeared on the market in the 1870s, but Sherwin-Williams came out with the first quality ready-mix paint in 1880—Sherwin-Williams Paint. The acquisition of the Calumet Paint Company outside of Chicago in 1888 marked an important advance in the company's fortunes. Calumet's strategic location was well-suited to the growing paint market in Pullman and other railroad cars, farm equipment, and carriages. Over the years the com-

pany expanded into Canada, South America, and Europe. In 1905 it adopted its famous "Cover the Earth" logo, which well-reflected its rise to preeminence in the industry.

Without question Ohio made a major contribution to the Industrial Revolution which, between the Civil War and World War I, forever changed America. Many of the large business organizations which made the United States an industrial giant had some links with the Buckeye State. Great Ohio corporations, prominent Ohio "captains of industry," and well-known inventors played key roles in transforming the nation's rich resources into necessary goods and luxury items which significantly improved the way Americans lived. True, the Industrial Revolution had its negative side, but all things considered, as historian George Knepper put it, "these were good years for Ohio."

———

By 1895 Smith's European Hotel was beginning to enjoy its heyday in Columbus. The New York Oyster House, on the first floor of the hotel, was located near the corner of Broad and High. Courtesy, Ohio Historical Society

The 1939 strike at the Fisher Body plant in Cleveland erupted into violence during its final days. In response to management's refusal to negotiate, union leaders called for a walkout of selected skilled workers in strategically located plants. Thus, the plants were handicapped while other employees were able to work, draw their wages, and support their striking coworkers. Courtesy, Ohio Historical Society

Facing page: By 1930 a number of companies had merged into Republic Steel, strengthening Cleveland's position in the iron and steel industry. Problems arose in the summer of 1937, however, when a clash between strikers and nonunion workers at Republic's Corrigan-McKinney Plant left one man dead and sixty injured. In 1945 Republic was one of the largest single employers in the city, with 9,000 people on its payroll. Courtesy, Western Reserve Historical Society

The rise of big business transformed the United States in many ways. Although the standard of living was improved, wealth and power became concentrated in the hands of the very few. The exercise of this tremendous power was not always in the best interests of society. Exploitation of laborers and farmers and the disregard of the public welfare were commonplace. The *laissez-faire* philosophy had created a massive imbalance within the system. In 1900, according to one writer, one-half of the population possessed nothing, while one percent owned 54 percent of the national wealth. Fewer and fewer corporations controlled more and more of the country's industrial might. In 1897 the total capitalization of all one-million-dollar corporations totalled $170 million. In 1900 this figure had increased to five billion dollars; in 1904 it had escalated to twenty billion dollars.

This monopoly movement occurred, ironically, in the wake of passage of the Sherman Anti-Trust Act of 1890. This act was designed to prevent "trustification," yet within fifteen years huge monopolies had appeared, creating a national scandal. One reason for this was the ambiguous wording of the statute, which allowed federal courts, unsympathetic to antitrust regulation, to interpret the Sherman Act very narrowly. While monopoly provided efficiency, economy, and centralized control—desirable goals in business management—it also provided such unrestricted power that abuse was an inevitable consequence. The masters of the great corporations felt that they alone had the right to determine how their business should be managed and strongly opposed any attempts by legislative bodies to regulate them.

This arrogance excited the interest of a legion of investigative

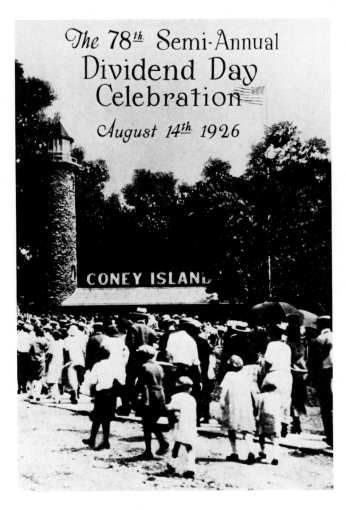

The 78ᵗʰ Semi-Annual
Dividend Day
Celebration
August 14ᵗʰ 1926

CONEY ISLAND

In April 1887 Procter & Gamble announced an agreement to share profits with its employees. To maintain the employees' enthusiasm, the company held Dividend Day Celebrations twice a year. Pictured here is the 1926 celebration at Cincinnati's amusement park, Coney Island. The tradition continued for many years. Courtesy, the Procter & Gamble Company

Facing page: Workers pose in front of the Xenia Machine Works factory. Wages were generally low and working conditions poor for the predominantly black female laborers, such as those pictured here. Courtesy, Ohio Historical Society

reporters, called "muckrakers." Beginning in 1903, articles began to appear in national magazines exposing abuses by the great railroads and corporations. These included bribery of legislators, price-fixing without reference to cost, forcing competitors out of business, blacklisting troublemakers among employees, and closing plants where unions had been formed. When these stories began to attract national attention, the most activist president in American history sat in the White House. Theodore Roosevelt, upset by the monopolization trend in business, gained fame as a "trustbuster." While he never "busted" too many trusts, he did focus attention on the situation.

But how should these "captains of industry"—or "robber barons"—be judged? Until the middle of the twentieth century historians dealt harshly with them. The classic view holds that they were men who devoured the nation's wealth, plundered its resources, and controlled its political institutions. They may have helped develop the economic system, but the road was strewn with the wreckage and waste of human and natural resources. More recently, however, this interpretation has been challenged. Allan Nevins, the famous Civil War scholar and biographer of Rockefeller and Ford, was one of the first historians to question the earlier judgement. While conceding that the behavior of many business leaders was indefensible, Nevins pointed out that the Industrial Revolution created an unprecedented economic environment for which no established code of ethics existed. Business leaders were fighting for survival in an atmosphere which demanded extreme measures to avoid destruction. Had they acted in a "moral" manner, they would have been eliminated and others, employing the ruthless tactics they had abjured, would have triumphed.

Moreover, these men created the mightiest industrial empire in the world. In addition, by the time this structure had been built, the great entrepreneurs had developed a social conscience, a recognition that perhaps they did have an obligation to society. Andrew Carnegie was the first of his generation to sense this. His "gospel of wealth" was not as well known as his libraries, but it marked new directions in corporate philanthropy. Establishing universities, cultural complexes, and foundations were other means by which robber barons/captains of industry bequeathed their fortunes for the betterment of mankind. In balance, holds the current view, the good they did outweighed the evil.

Along with the great entreprenuers appeared

great forces of laborers who manned the machines and plants. As large factories with their thousands of workers emerged, no particular thought was given to the workers' well-being or safety. Under hallowed *laissez-faire* doctrine, the worker was free to labor for an employer, or leave, if he so wished. The employer bore no responsibility for his welfare. As the system grew and as job competition intensified, the worker's freedom was restricted. Theoretically, he could still come and go as he pleased, but in reality this was not the case.

Working conditions were bad. Hours were long, work was hard, and the machinery was generally unsafe. During the famous strike at Carnegie's Homestead works near Pittsburgh in the summer of 1892, it came out that steelworkers were paid fourteen cents an hour for a twelve-hour day, six days a week. Since there was no lunch hour, food was eaten on the job. Some workers never went home, sleeping beside their machines. Because of the long hours and high noise level, the men's reaction time slowed down and they became prone to serious injury. Mutilation of hands and arms was common. Three hundred and eighty-one deaths occurred in Pittsburgh mills alone in 1891. Work in coal mines was also dangerous, not only because of cave-ins but because of the inhalation of bad air. Bad air was a problem also in the rubber plants, in Akron. Far more publicized were the miserable conditions in the packing houses, immortalized in Upton Sinclair's 1906 *The Jungle.*

Dissatisfaction with wages, hours, and working

Bottom: The United Mine Workers of America, founded in 1890, gathered in Columbus at its first convention. The union claimed to represent all workers in and around the mines. In 1898 a strike by the UMW won workers an eight-hour workday. After that grand victory, the number of union members doubled within two years. Courtesy, Ohio Historical Society

Below: On December 8, 1886, the Ohio State Journal announced the opening of the Columbus convention which led to the formation of the American Federation of Labor (AFL). The new organization, with Samuel Gompers as its leader, was basically a loose affiliation of autonomous craft unions, not a strong, centrally organized body. Courtesy, Ohio Historical Society

THE FEDERATED TRADES.

OPENING OF THE SIXTH CONGRESS.

The Relations of the Unions with the Knights of Labor — Preparing to Amalgamate with the Labor Union Conference.

The sixth annual Congress of the Federation of Organized Trades and Labor Unions of the United States and Canada was called to order by President Gompers in Druid's hall, South Fourth street, at noon yesterday. D. P. Boyer, chief organizer of the International Typographical union, introduced Grafton Pearce of this city who, as the representative of the Columbus Trades assembly, delivered an excellent address of welcome, in which he ably discussed the objects to be attained, urged harmony, deliberation, freedom from politics and the wisest course of procedure.

President Gompers returned the thanks of the congress for the cordial welcome, referred to the mistakes of organized labor in the past, the good it had done and the purposes for the future. He discussed the eight-hour law, the struggles of the past year, and urged harmony in all meetings and co operations.

conditions was responsible for the rise of trade unionism during the Industrial Revolution. Since Ohio was one of the most heavily industrialized states in the country, an active union movement developed there. The most powerful national labor organization, the American Federation of Labor, was founded in Columbus in 1886. Another important national union which was very prominent in Ohio labor matters was the United Mineworkers of America. Other active unions in the state were in steel, rubber, glass, and the skilled trades. Because of the continual struggle between employers and employees, hundreds of strikes broke out in Ohio between 1886 and 1905.

One of the most bitter strikes which occurred in Ohio involved the rubber industry. Serious trouble erupted early in 1913 at Firestone over the installation of laborsaving machinery. With a cut in the piece-rate wage the income for tire-finishers declined and a number of them stayed away from work. When Firestone fired the absentees, unrest spread to other departments in the plant and by mid-February engulfed other plants in the city. The strikers, who numbered almost 75 percent of the 22,000 Akron rubber workers, demanded an eight-hour day, a minimum hourly rate, and double pay for overtime. The companies rejected the demands. Refusing to negotiate with union representatives or impartial mediators, the employers built barricades, harassed picketers, imported strikebreakers, caused the arrest of strike leaders, and launched an extensive propaganda campaign to win over public opinion. This pressure, combined with developing internal conflict, weakened the strike front as February gave way to March. With their leaders either in jail or chased out of town, the strikers caved in by the end of the month. It came out later that most of the union leaders had been paid informers.

A good portion of the general public also believed that there was something un-American

about unions, but it was the "captains of industry" who had to deal with the issue. In their view, unions had no place in the factory. These men insisted that any improvements in working conditions that were made must be made on the company's terms and not dictated by workers or unions. Paternalistic "welfare capitalism," as this was called, characterized the new trend.

The subtitle of Samuel Crowther's 1923 biography of NCR's John Patterson is *Pioneer of Industrial Welfare.* Patterson had a good claim to the distinction. Like most successful businessmen, he personally went immediately to the source whenever serious problems arose. In 1894, $50,000 worth of equipment was returned to the company as unusa-

Above: Rubber workers at the B.F. Goodrich Company protested the plant manager's threat to move from Akron. These protestors were members of the Industrial Workers of the World, a radical strand of the American labor movement founded in 1905. Although these "Wobblies," as they were often called, advocated irradication of the capitalist system, most workers who joined the union were more interested in higher wages and improved working conditions. Courtesy, University of Akron Archives

ble. Patterson at once relocated his office to the factory floor. In addition to learning what had gone wrong with the returned cash registers, he found that working conditions for his employees were not satisfactory. This incident marked the beginning of a massive program directed to improve the workers' welfare.

The factory was cleaned up, bathrooms and restrooms were installed, and wages increased. Special privileges were extended to women. Workers were given a shorter work day, fifteen-minute breaks in the morning and afternoon for exercise, lunch at company expense in a special lunch room was provided, and a half-day holiday each week and a one-day holiday each month was granted. In addition, a new factory was built in 1894, which was equipped with "first class baths and locker rooms, and restrooms for the women, hospitals and first aid stations, medical inspections, and free, clean aprons

Left: Joseph and Feiss, one of the largest clothing concerns in the U.S., grew out of an earlier company, Kock and Loeb. Involved in the wholesale apparel field, Joseph and Feiss purchased, cut, and sent cloth to small contract shops to assemble. Pictured is a company library where Joseph and Feiss workers could go to read and check out books. Courtesy, Western Reserve Historical Society

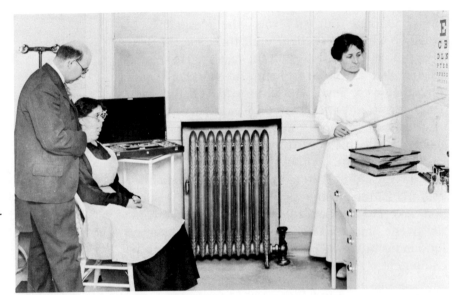

Right: Displaying an early interest in social welfare, Joseph and Feiss developed special services for its employees. Pictured are a doctor and nurse testing the eyesight of a clothing worker in 1915. Courtesy, Western Reserve Historical Society

Below right: Joseph and Feiss hired a large number of immigrants and offered educational classes for its employees. These women were enrolled in a 1916 English class. Courtesy, Western Reserve Historical Society

and sleevelets for the women."

NCR was located in a deteriorating neighborhood, called "Slidertown," which had an adverse impact on the company's image. Patterson saw the relationship between company and community and concluded that something should be done to improve the image of the former and the condition of the latter. A landscape architect was hired to improve the grounds and a young woman, Lena Harvey, was employed to win over the residents. Boys who had devoted most of their leisure hours to flinging rocks through NCR windows, were formed into clubs. The boys' clubs planted gardens and learned both technical and business skills. A number of them would later become valued employees at NCR.

Patterson's concern extended beyond the immediate environs of the factory. The women's Century Club set up coffeehouses for female workers throughout Dayton. The Men's Welfare Work League, founded in 1904, worked closely with local educators to upgrade the school system. None of Patterson's actions prevented the bitter strike of 1901. After putting down the strike, Patterson instituted changes in management and a program of welfare capitalism which would lead to a healthier work atmosphere in the future.

Procter & Gamble may have trailed NCR in several aspects of welfare capitalism, but in one particular area—profit sharing—it was well ahead. W. Cooper Procter, grandson of the cofounder, joined the firm, fresh out of Princeton, in 1883. He learned the business from the ground up and in 1907 became president of the company. In his first years young Procter labored side by side with the workers at a time when the Knights of Labor were recruiting members in the Cincinnati area. To blunt this campaign he proposed to his elders that all employees be given Saturday afternoons off with pay. A revolutionary idea for 1885, it was accepted by the company. This by no means resolved the labor unrest in the plant. Strikes broke out periodically and worker turnover averaged 50 percent annually.

In searching for an answer to the problem, Cooper Procter at length determined to experiment with profit sharing. The idea was not popular in business circles and he had no easy time convincing father, uncles, and cousins of its virtues. He contended that sharing company profits with the workers would give them a stake in the company's fortunes and lead to greater job satisfaction and improved performance. The plan was instituted in 1887. Dividends were paid from company profits twice a year to each worker. The first dividend day in October was celebrated with a party, entertainment, and a speech by Procter. He urged the employees to work as hard as they could, so the company would prosper and there would be more profits to share.

The plan did not work as intended. The workers came to view the dividends as simply a semiannual bonus unrelated to job performance. Procter

Above: William Cooper Procter, grandson of the co-founder of Procter & Gamble, was instrumental in the introduction of the profit-sharing system. This memorial to him is carved in stone outside the company building at Ivorydale: "William Cooper Procter, 1862-1934. He lived a life of noble simplicity believing in God and the inherent worthiness of his fellow men." Courtesy, the Procter & Gamble Company

---

Left: Sherwin-Williams, organized in 1870, has become the world's largest manufacturer of paints, lacquers, varnishes, insecticides, and other associated products. The company's trademark, "Cover the Earth," is included in the lower corners of this 1913 advertisement. Courtesy, **The Outlook**

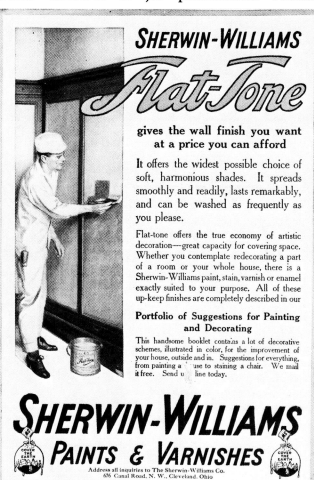

struggled with the plan for a number of years and at length arrived at a workable solution. In 1903 he revised the entire system by tying profit sharing to stock ownership in Procter & Gamble. To receive any profits an employee had to own company stock, and the amount he received was linked to the amount of stock he owned. Stock purchases were spread over a period of time and the company more than matched the employee's contribution. The plan worked. While not every employee bought company stock, well over half of them did.

The Cleveland Chamber of Commerce, organized in the 1890s, gave a boost to welfare capitalism in the big city. Under its leadership close to eighty companies, including several of the more important ones such as Cleveland Trust and Sherwin-Williams, had instituted welfare programs during

the first decade of the twentieth century. The chamber's purpose, like most companies which supported welfare capitalism, was to promote a healthier atmosphere within the industrial community and to avoid labor strife. M.A. Hanna Company, for example, adopted a life insurance program for its employees in 1914. The rubber companies were also active in promoting worker welfare. Paul W. Litchfield, a twenty-five-year-old MIT graduate, came to Goodyear in 1900 as factory superintendent. Instrumental in establishing Goodyear's employee welfare programs, Litchfield in 1909 helped create

Above: Goodyear provided buses to transport workers back and forth between Goodyear Heights and the Goodyear factories. To walk from the housing subdivision to the factories took about ten to fifteen minutes. Goodyear Heights covered 350 acres, with approximately 1,000 homes that were fifty feet by 115 feet. Courtesy, Summit County Historical Society

Left: This photograph shows the construction of company-sponsored housing for employees of Youngstown Sheet and Tube. This two-year project began in 1915 with a plan to build 500 dwellings; these would be sold to workers in an attempt to increase loyalty to the firm. At the same time, because of wartime shortages of labor and housing, the company was building a labor camp, complete with central dining hall and barracks, to house newly recruited workers. Courtesy, Ohio Historical Society

Above: Aside from condoning the nation's newly established welfare system and providing medical care for its employees, Buckeye Steel Castings Company took an interest in its employees' social and recreational lives. The Buckeye Steel baseball team, pictured here, played on a baseball field adjacent to its factory. Courtesy, Ohio Historical Society

the Goodyear Relief Association. This fund was designed for the benefit of injured or ill employees. In 1912 he founded the first employee publication, the *Wingfoot Clan*. The following year he established an employee development program, the "Flying Squadron," in which talented employees learned more of the company's total operations and enhanced their opportunities for advancement.

Frank Seiberling developed a unique employee housing plan for Goodyear workers in 1912. The idea was to reduce the commuting time to work and to allow employees to become homeowners at a moderate price. A large piece of property east of the plant—a ten-minute walk away—was acquired and the workers were given the option of purchasing three different types of structures: a single unit, double unit, or a bungalow. No down payment was required and modest monthly fees financed the purchase, which averaged about $3,500. All the services for a self-sustaining community were provided. By the spring of 1914 ninety homes were occupied and within two more years all lots were sold.

World War I stimulated company welfare programs because of the desire to increase production and keep workers happy. While it did not always achieve these goals, welfare capitalism became quite popular in the war years. Buckeye Steel Castings in Columbus, another pioneer in welfarism, set up a medical dispensary in 1903 within a year of the company's founding. By the time of World War I the dispensary had become a hospital, and the company had built washrooms, locker rooms, and a kitchen. Buckeye sponsored annual picnics, and a baseball field was laid out adjacent to the factory. An employee life insurance policy was instituted in 1917 and later the same year 108 acres of land were acquired and $143,000 appropriated for employee housing near the plant. Buckeye began cosponsoring technical courses with the Columbus YMCA

through which employees could improve their knowledge and skills. Athletic teams participated in YMCA leagues and social and recreational programs included musical performances, movies, and refreshments. Buckeye went out into the community and its officers provided financial assistance and leadership for Columbus' philanthropic endeavors.

. . .

For more than two and one-half years after war began in Europe in August 1914 the United States sat on the sidelines. Whatever the country's official stance, Americans were distinctly pro-Allies in sentiment and the industrial community began supplying France and Britain with the sinews of war. Exports to Europe jumped from one and one-half billion dollars at the time war began to four billion dollars in 1917 on the eve of America's entry into the conflict. Business, recovering from a pre-war decline, boomed, although it was a somewhat chaotic expansion. Planning came quickly following the declaration of war. The massive mobilization of manpower and resources required by the war effort could not be undertaken by an unregulated economy. Hence a host of national agencies were created to coordinate and maximize industrial, fuel, food, and transportation resources. Probably most central to the complicated network of agencies was the powerful War Industries Board, under the direction of the prominent Wall Street broker Bernard Baruch.

Coordinating American industry was not a simple task and countless problems and bottlenecks developed. Nevertheless the economy expanded and the job of winning the war was accomplished. Plant facilities of auto and steel companies grew at such a rate that they were well prepared for further expansion after the war. American steel production

The women's suffrage movement was important to Ohio women, many of whom contributed greatly to Ohio industries in World War I. Pictured here are women representing counties throughout the state at a 1914 rally in Columbus. Courtesy, Ohio Historical Society

attained forty million tons annually during the war years, far in excess of the output of all the Allies and Central Powers combined. Income in the manufacturing sector climbed from $8.7 billion in 1916, to $13 billion in 1918, to $16.8 billion in 1920. Profits skyrocketed in many industries.

Ohio, like most states, had its own wartime councils which worked with the national bodies. The Council of Defence was a branch of the War Industries Board, while state fuel, food, and employment agencies similarily were geared to their federal counterparts. A yeoman's task was the lot of Fred C. Croxton, who chaired both the defense council and food administration. The council's membership included leaders from both management and labor; the public and agricultural sectors were also represented. The council strove to coordinate the state's economy to minimize food and fuel shortages and to channel labor where it was most needed. With the demand for goods and services at a record peak and manpower mobilization in full swing, labor shortages continued throughout the war.

Not surprisingly, Ohio's contribution to the nation's industrial effort during the war was substantial. Steel for tanks, trucks, weapons, and munitions poured forth from the mills of the Mahoning and Cuyahoga valleys. Coal production reached an all-time high. Akron's rubber factories produced "hundreds of thousands of tires for the army, a tremendous number of gas masks, countless miscellaneous articles, and hundreds of blimps and observation balloons." Economically, this was Akron's greatest age of growth. Marion Steam Shovel produced tanks and shovels "that could crawl over marshy places." Machine tool makers throughout the state—especially in Cincinnati—were also busy. White Motor Company in Cleveland became famous in World War I for its trucks, and, as mentioned, earned the Croix de Guerre from the French government.

Operating a large industrial plant is never easy, but it is particularly difficult in wartime because of shortages of materials, labor, and transportation. George King, president of Marion Steam Shovel, reviewed these problems in his annual report of January, 23, 1917. While the country appeared to be prospering economically, he commented, difficulties caused by shortages had drained away most of the company's profits. "With few exceptions," he observed, "we are paying more for all materials than was necessary a year ago. Labor has not only been scarce and high-priced, but of very low competency. The floating laborer has hindered us a great deal because of his short period of employment."

Labor, indeed, was "feeling its oats" during World War I. Not since the movement had emerged as an influential force had labor been so in demand. Jobs were for the asking, wages were good, and the federal government generally supported the workers in disputes with employers. Good times usually find labor more aggressive than when the economy is on the downslide. From 1914 onward the strike spirit intensified. The outbreak of war initiated a wave of labor disputes across Ohio. Cary and Boryczka report that

> among those striking in 1914 were Portsmouth and Cincinnati shoe workers, Canton phone operators, retail clerks in Zanesville, buffers and polishers in Wooster, clay workers in Empire and Toronto, miners in Dillonvale. In 1915, the list of 115 strikes included paper makers in Middletown, molders in Hamilton, machinists in Cincinnati and Columbus, and munitions workers in Youngstown. The following year 276 strikes swept the state.

Among the latter number were violent disputes at Youngstown's steel plants. As grievances mounted some 16,000 workers finally lashed out in fury and frustration, leading to a million dollars in property damage and the summoning of 2,000 National Guard troops.

Once the United States entered the war, the workers' bargaining position improved dramatically as the national government pressed for a maximum production effort. The National Defence Council, which became the War Industries Board in 1918, included members from organized labor. As the eruption of strikes across the land escalated in 1917 a War Labor Policies Board was created. The board worked actively to nip labor disputes at their outset through mediation, although strikes continued to occur during the war. Union membership doubled under the favorable wartime conditions. The years following the Armistice, however, were marked by a backlash against unionism.

• • •

The decade following the end of the war was a gold mine for the social historian. With the

Pictured here are employees at the Crooksville China Company in 1919. Crooksville, like Roseville, East Liverpool, and areas in Perry County, is rich in clay deposits and therefore important to the thriving pottery industry. Courtesy, Ohio Historical Society

popularization of the automobile, the appearance of the radio, and improvements in movies and phonograph recordings, the lifestyle of millions of Americans was irreversibly changed. The 1920s is also a fascinating period for business historians to examine. Capitalism had matured with the quest for stability and systemized planning supplanting the prewar thirst for experimentation and innovation. Management tended more to mirror an impersonal bureaucracy than a daring wildcatter. The federal government was firmly in the hands of the friends of business and the *laissez-faire* spirit stimulated a period of economic growth. As an older textbook put it, "It was an age of unprecedented prosperity."

Before the arrival of prosperity, however, there was a sharp break in the economy in the summer of 1920. Conditions had been fairly good for over a year after the Armistice, but then the canceling of war contracts, the demobilization of more than two million men, and the loss of European grain markets made their impact. The rubber industry was hard hit at this time and before the dust had cleared one of the major figures in the business had been driven out of his own company. Frank Seiberling, who had founded Goodyear, though a fine engineer was not very good in the front office. The sudden break in the economy in 1920 found the company with a huge inventory, few buyers, and practically no cash. The work force was cut back from 34,000 to 8,000 and Seiberling went hat in hand to Wall Street.

Wall Street was not interested at this time, however, and Goodyear's crisis worsened. By the end of 1921 bankruptcy and receivership were imminent. Now Wall Street came to the rescue. Dillon and Read assumed the task of refinancing and reorganizing the company and were able to raise sufficient funds to restore Goodyear to a sound footing. However, both Frank and Charles Seiberling would have to go. Frank Seiberling with the help of friends was able to establish a new tire factory, under his own name, in Barberton, and within a few years was again one of the top tire manufacturers in the country.

In the early days of Standard Oil Company, horsedrawn tank wagons, built in the company's wagon works in the Cleveland Flats, made the rounds to farms, groceries, and hardware stores. The wagons, pictured here, were still in operation in the early 1920s, before the company began to use motorized tank trucks. Courtesy, Western Reserve Historical Society

Under new leadership and banker supervision, Goodyear slowly fought its way back. Ruthless cost-cutting practices prevailed for several months as the new managers were determined to eliminate the debt. Sales gradually picked up and furloughed employees began to come back. Litchfield, one of two top men to survive the shakeup, now moved full speed ahead to again make Goodyear competitive with its rivals. Meanwhile, the company's overseas operations had expanded. By 1928 the work force, at home and abroad, had climbed to 40,000. Goodyear was again the number-one tire manufacturer and the number-one rubber company in the world.

Goodyear was not the only rubber company to suffer in the postwar depression. Firestone, too, was in trouble. Prices for tires were cut drastically and employees were fired. Goodrich had good relations with New York financiers and was able to pull through the crisis with less discomfort than the others, although its entire advertising department was abolished.

Contributing to the refinement of corporate operations during the 1920s were both managerial and technical advances. Perhaps the wide adoption of the "scientific management" idea of Frederick W. Taylor was the most important of these. However, research and development divisions, standardization of products, and cost accounting methods all played an important role in increasing efficiency. Diversification of products and establishment of overseas plants were other new features of this maturation period. Mechanization of industry moved forward, unfortunately contributing to the rise in "technological unemployment." Installment buying—"buy now, pay later"—became popular, stimulating consumer purchases of a vast array of products. Statistics reveal that between 1920 and 1930 the value of Ohio's major manufacturers grew 18 percent. At the same time the national growth was 14 percent. The steel industry increased its production by 31 percent and production of motor vehicles and parts was up by 64 percent. The only major industry which experienced a loss in the 1920s was rubber, down 9 percent.

The automobile, plus installment buying, was the catalyst for the boom years of the 1920s. In 1921 one and one-half million cars were manufactured. By 1929 the output was up to four and one-half million, by which time there were some twenty-three million vehicles on the road. Automobile manufacturing, now the biggest industry in the land, comprised 12.7 percent of the total of all manufactures.

Significant improvements in the functioning of the automobile were the work of the famous inventor from Dayton, Charles F. Kettering. Graduating from Ohio State with an engineering degree early in the century, Kettering went to work for NCR. There he mastered the process of applying electrical power to the cash register, making obsolete the laborious hand crank. Later he established the Dayton Engineering Laboratories Company (DELCO). His major achievement took place in 1911 when he successfully operated a self-starter on a Cadillac. In 1916 Kettering's company was absorbed by General Motors and incorporated in its research division. His other contributions to the auto industry were the development of antiknock gasoline and refinements in the diesel engine.

Ohio's auto industry had declined with the rise of Detroit, although there were several plants in Toledo and Cleveland. The production of bodies, parts, tires, glass, and other car accessories was big business in the state. Among other Ohio industries which prospered during the decade were petroleum refining (up 58 percent), bread and bakery products (up 54 percent), paper and paperboard production (up 46 percent), chemicals (up 42 percent), and newspaper publishing and printing (up 126 percent). A more modest increase was scored by the machine tool industry (up 8 percent).

As has been mentioned, internationalization and diversification were prominent characteristics of the 1920s. NCR was an exponent of both. Actually, overseas plants had been built earlier, in Berlin, Germany, in the early 1900s and in Toronto, Canada, in 1918. Sales offices were established in the 1920s in South Africa, India, Colombia, and the Soviet Union. Its first effort at manufacturing something besides regular cash registers was in the early 1920s with the successful launching of the Class 2000 accounting machine. This was a "sophisticated cash register that printed data on inserted forms and provided 30 totals rather than half a dozen." The Statler Hotel chain adopted the Class 2000, but it was such a complicated machine with its 20,000 hand-assembled parts, that for awhile NCR had to have a repairman stationed at every Statler Hotel. In 1929 NCR acquired the Ellis Adding-Typewriter Company, and came out with its Class 3000 accounting machine, useful in "the preparation of payroll, stock records, billings for utilities and insurance companies, and in cost accounting operations."

NCR was one of the first large corporations anywhere to institute a personnel department for promoting better employee-employer relations. This was done shortly after the 1901 strike. Corporate personnel offices became quite common in the years after World War I. Marion Shovel joined the ranks in 1921 when it established a Department of Personnel Training, to provide training for workers in different aspects of the business. Announcing the new program, the company noted that the manufacture of sophisticated machinery had become increasingly complex. Employee training could no longer be permitted to take place on the job. I.B. Shoup was lured away from Westinghouse, where for four years he had been the director of vocational education, to head the new department.

Another feature of the economy of the 1920s was the shifting of production from industrial to consumer goods. With the industrial plant constructed, attention was focused on the wants and desires of the general public. The decade saw an outpouring of not only automobiles, but washing machines, refrigerators, vacuum cleaners, radios, tin cans, and a host of household conveniences. Many such machines and appliances were manufactured in Ohio and it took the genius of an Ohio inventor to make the consumerist revolution possible.

John Butler Tytus, born in 1875 near Middletown, took his Yale degree in English literature and returned home to work in the family paper mill. After the company was sold, Tytus sought a position with Middletown's new (founded in 1901) American Rolling Mill Company (ARMCO). No office jobs were available, so he worked in the sheet mill, "one of the lowest, hottest, and hardest jobs in steel making." He picked up the basics of steel work in a hurry and began to move up through the ranks.

As he observed the workers clumsily dragging heavy sheets of steel through the rollers, Tytus could not help but think of the big papermaking machines he once worked with which converted wood and pulp into one long continuous sheet of paper. If the principle could be applied to a sheet mill it would relieve workers of backbreaking drudgery while producing a much better and cheaper product. But steel was quite different from paper. United States Steel had already failed twice to construct continuous-sheet steel mills. Tytus confided his idea to several of his associates, but they doubted its feasibility. Yet he never lost hope and continued to study the matter. He examined carefully the steel sheets to determine what effects the rollers had on them. He made mathematical computations and collected scientific data. In a 1916 article he discussed the problem and concluded that the difficulty lay with the rollers which changed shape with each passage of the steel through them.

In 1921 ARMCO purchased the Ashland Iron and Mining Company in Ashland, Kentucky, for the purpose of constructing traditional sheet mills. Tytus recognized that this was the moment to proceed with the continuous mill. He and his supervisor, Charles Ruffin Hook, took the proposal to the board of directors. How much would it cost? Ten million dollars. If it failed, they were told, it might ruin the company and cost thousands of people their jobs. Would you recommend it, Hook was asked? "Yes." The directors gave Tytus the green light, recognizing full well the risk involved. But they had faith in the vision as well as the technical expertise of the English literature scholar from Yale.

Construction began in October 1922 and was completed about a year later. The special engineering office in Middletown was moved to Ashland and by late December 1923 all was ready for the first trial. Fourteen "stands of rolls" set in a straight line were prepared "to reduce red-hot, five-inch thick

Above: The American Rolling Mill Company was famous for its continuous hot strip mill. Shown here is an employee at work in the Zanesville plant. Courtesy, Ohio Historical Society

———

Right: This American Rolling Mill Company advertisement appeared in The Outlook, *a weekly magazine, in September 1914.*

The first controlled, powered flight took place at Kitty Hawk, North Carolina, on December 17, 1903. Victory thus came at last to the Wright brothers, the Ohio inventors who had been trying to fly at Kitty Hawk since late September. Courtesy, Department of Archives and Special Collections, Wright State University

slabs into thin steel sheets." On the first attempt one of the rollers broke down. Within the next few weeks other breakdowns occurred. But Tytus patiently corrected the flaws, and ordered bigger and stronger rollers, and the continuous mill began to work. Whereas the old rollers turned out 130 tons of steel weekly, the continuous mill within three years was producing 40,000 tons each month. By 1927 the experiment was over, the process perfected. Steel executives were invited to attend a demonstration of the mill that spring and went away in awe and admiration, having seen the smooth functioning of a plant they believed impossible to build.

ARMCO licensed its patents for the continuous mill to other companies, and it was not long before the revolutionary process was being used in all plants. The cost of sheet metal was cut in half just at the time consumer demand for cheap steel was rapidly increasing. The trade publication *Iron Age* observed that the "ARMCO continuous mill at Ashland is epoch-making . . . a monumental example of the scientific approach to a major manufacturing problem." When a critic complained to Tytus that

his machine had taken away men's jobs, the inventor quickly replied, "Did you ever try your hand at the kind of work it eliminated?"

One of the great industries of the twentieth century—aviation—came of age in the 1920s and 1930s. Again Ohioans were central figures. By tradition aviation history began on the sand dunes at Kitty Hawk, North Carolina, on December 17, 1903, when the brothers from Dayton, Orville and Wilbur Wright, made the "world's first sustained, controlled power flight." It lasted twelve seconds and the plane traveled 120 feet. Work on improving the speed, load, and altitude of aircraft progressed over the next few years. In February 1908 the brothers contracted for their first military plane with the United States government. During 1909, 1910, and 1911, they conducted numerous aerial exhibitions which brought increasing recognition to the novel form of transportation.

The first successful commercial flight, as with many "firsts," was not spectacular by modern standards, yet it marked a milestone in aviation history. In November 1910 Philip O. Parmalee, one of the Wrights' exhibition pilots, flew two packages of Salome Silk, weighing 200 pounds, from Dayton to Columbus, a distance of about seventy miles. Flying at 2,000 feet, the wind cutting him to the bone, Parmalee made the trip without incident in about an hour. He nonchalantly debarked, commenting, "Well, that was going some." The popularization of commercial aviation, however, would have to await further advances in the field.

Military aviation progressed slowly after the army's purchase of its first plane from the Wrights in 1908. With the outbreak of war in Europe, the aircraft industries of England, Germany, and France were forced to grow; thus the United States lagged behind when it entered the war in 1917. A facility was developed at McCook Field in Dayton, where an engineering force was assembled and buildings and runways were constructed. There was little time to produce planes, however, and most of McCook's efforts were devoted to the redesigning of British planes for American use. More importantly, McCook became a center for testing and experimentation. Even though the end of the war slowed down operations, the engineering division continued functioning, developing and refining aircraft design. Numerous records for speed and maneuverability were set there during the 1920s. The celebrated Jimmy Doolittle was one of the record setters.

By the mid-1920s over thirteen million dollars

Above: The Wright brothers participated in a number of aerial exhibitions, drawing many eager and curious spectators. The inventors were frequent guests of European nobility, as seen in this pictures taken at Pau, France, in 1909. Courtesy, Department of Archives and Special Collections, Wright State University

Left: The Wright brothers made several attempts to fly before they finally succeeded on December 17, 1903. Wilbur Wright is seen here at the controls. Courtesy, Department of Archives and Special Collections, Wright State University

Above: The Dayton Wright Airplane Company built this plane, ready to take off for France in 1918, during World War I. Courtesy, Department of Archives and Special Collections, Wright State University

Right: Orville Wright is seen here flying a single propeller pusher plane over his hometown, Dayton, in 1912. Courtesy, Ohio Historical Society

Left: Wilbur Wright and his wife Katherine are pictured here in Pau, France. Although Katherine tied down her skirt to keep it from billowing up during flight, the look became fashionable and the "hobble skirt" was born. Courtesy, Department of Archives and Special Collections, Wright State University

Below: To give the city a lift from the worries of the Depression, the Women's Art League of Akron hosted a Rubber Ball. Everyone who attended was required to wear a costume made of rubber. C.W. Seiberling, of the Goodyear Company, was crowned king of the First Rubber Ball. His queen was an elevator operator from a local department store. Courtesy, University of Akron Archives

had been invested in McCook Field. However, by then the aircraft industry had outgrown the field's capabilities and the government was seriously considering relocating the plant to Langley Field in Virginia. But aware of its rich aviation history, the people of Dayton raised sufficient funds to acquire land east of the city which was then donated to the government for a new facility. Construction began in 1926 and in October 1927 Wright Field was dedicated. In ten years McCook Field had, in the view of one historian, "helped lay the foundation for the aircraft industry and had aided in the development of civil aviation in the United States." Wright Field continued this work and contributed substantially to the aircraft industry's future military and civilian growth.

While the nascent aviation industry was prospering, one ancient industry was not. The problem had little to do with the economy, but much to do with a band of militant crusaders. The temperance movement had a long history, predating the Civil War. Its ultimate triumph was hastened by World War I when it was concluded that drinking was harmful to military personnel. Resulting from the massive propaganda efforts of the Woman's Christian Temperance Union and the Westerville-based Anti-Saloon League, the politicians finally surrendered. Congress approved the Eighteenth Amendment, by which the "manufacture, sale, or transportation of intoxicating liquor . . . within

the United States . . . is hereby prohibited." It was ratified in 1920. The Volstead Act, passed in 1919, barred the manufacture or sale of any beverage with more than one-half of one percent alcoholic content.

Naturally, this was a blow to brewery interests and Cincinnati, long one of the nation's best beer towns, suffered accordingly. It had over twenty breweries before Prohibition. When repeal came in 1933, Bruckmann's was the only one remaining. However, plenty of people experimented with "bathtub gin" and "home brew," and frequented speakeasies. By the late 1920s, 3,000 beer parlors were doing business in the city. Bootlegging was big business, too. In 1929, the busiest year, 490 bootleggers were jailed. But enforcement proved

Right: Originally situated in an old German neighborhood, the Wolf Ledge Brewery became the property of Wilhelm Burkhardt in 1879. After his death, his wife changed the brewery's name to Burkhardt, and the business remained in the family until the 1950s. Burkhardt, in the center of the first row, posed for this photograph with his employees. Courtesy, Summit County Historical Society

Below right: The men in this photo were cutting tobacco, which would later be hung to dry and then stripped. Tobacco was an Ohio industry that gradually diminished over the years. Courtesy, Ohio Historical Society

impossible, not only in Cincinnati but every place else, and the cry for "repeal" became more strident. Repeal came with the New Deal in 1933. Cincinnati's brewery industry recovered slowly, however, and it was not until 1940 that sales regained the 1918 level.

Farmers, like brewers, did not do well in the 1920s. They had enjoyed plush times during the war. With European farmland ravaged, a premium was put on American grain, particularly wheat. Anything that could be grown could be sold—and at good prices. With greater income, farmers invested in new homes, machinery, equipment, and blooded animals, and began living a life of "unnatural ease." Then the war ended. The European market evaporated and prices began a sharp decline which was not arrested until the New Deal era.

If breweries went out of business and farmers had their backs to the wall, the decade of the 1920s was still considered one of "unprecedented prosperity." But was it really? In the fall of 1929, soon after the stock market collapse but before the Depression had set in, writer Stuart Chase published an economic study of the previous decade. It was a period of only limited prosperity, he argued, and to illustrate his point he used an onion to represent "the total economic life of the United States." He began peeling off one layer after another, each one signifying a weak spot, a sick industry, in the economy. After stripping away eleven layers of the onion, including farmers, a portion of the middle and professional classes, the unemployed, coal miners, shoemakers, and shipbuilders, the core still remained, but it was not as big and healthy looking as it had once been. Illustrating Chase's argument, in Ohio coal production dropped over 10 percent during the decade, one out of every four miners was discharged, and for those who retained their jobs, yearly earnings declined by 21 percent.

The decade following the First World War was a mixed one, economically speaking, for organized labor. In an effort to retain wartime gains in the face of the country's desire to cut back, a wave of bitter strikes broke out in 1919 and 1920, which resulted in a series of setbacks for labor. Business, while not opposed to what it considered labor's legitimate rights, remained steadfast in its opposition to collective bargaining and the closed shop. Welfare capitalism expanded and company unions were instituted in many plants. As the "prosperity" of the 1920s spread into more sectors of the economy, working classes began to share a bit in the bounty. The combination of employer pressure, adverse court rulings, and spreading affluence had a debilitating effect on militant unionism. Union membership declined.

These shadows were cast by men standing in line for jobs during the Great Depression. The sign overhead warns that "dirty men will not be sent out." Scenes like this one from Cincinnati were repeated all over the state of Ohio. Photo by Paul Briol. Courtesy, Cincinnati Historical Society

The story of the Great Depression has filled many books. Looking back one can readily see that much was amiss with the economy in the years before the collapse. Rather than reducing prices of goods or raising workers' wages, corporations either plowed their huge profits back into plant expansion or gambled them away in the skyrocketing stock market. Between 1922 and 1929 profits rose by 83 percent, while the real income of the laboring man rose only about 20 percent. In the words of one economist, "the future was oversold." Far more was being produced than could be consumed.

One of the most cruel ironies of American history is that the man in the White House when the capitalist bubble burst was an exemplary product of that very system. Herbert Hoover had risen from humble origins to fame, fortune, and political favor by virtue of his intelligence, energy, business skill, and engineering talent in a society which richly rewarded such qualities. A more perfect specimen

of the American success story would be difficult to find. Now Hoover had to preside over the collapse of the system to which he was indebted for his success. It is not surprising that he had problems accepting the fact that the free enterprise system had failed.

Slightly over a year after Hoover had said, "We in America are nearer to the final triumph over poverty than ever before," the stock market collapsed. "Black Tuesday," October 29, 1929, witnessed the worst percentage drop in market history and the decline which set in would continue uninterrupted for over three years. The supply of investment funds dried up, business confidence was shaken, production was cut back, and unemployment spread rapidly. By the winter of 1932-1933, when the nation's economy was practically at a standstill, the value of all stocks traded on the New York Stock Exchange had dropped from their 1929 high of eighty-seven billion dollars to only nineteen billion dollars.

Hoover's response was to encourage voluntary help for the needy and to urge the hard-pressed to help themselves. Times were hard, he conceded, but the system was basically sound and would bounce back. He continued to support budget balancing and other deflationary policies when what

Women often ran machines at the Williams' shoe company, while men worked in other parts of the company, such as the cutting room. Courtesy, Ohio Historical Society

was needed was massive federal spending. In 1931, under pressure from Democrats who gained control of the House of Representatives in 1930, he signed into law spending measures for public works projects, but they were hardly adequate to deal with the crisis. Unemployment grew, local welfare resources became exhausted, and the country settled into an abyss of gloom and hopelessness. An estimated fifteen to seventeen million were on relief by 1932.

While no state escaped the harshness and horror of those Depression years, Ohio suffered unduly because of its large population and industrial character. Production dropped 24 percent in the 1930s, while nationally the figure was 19 percent. As a consequence, the state's factory work force declined 20 percent. The number of industrial workers unemployed statewide in 1930 was 307,000; in 1931, 576,000; and in 1932, 869,000, over 37 percent of all Ohio workers. The large industrial centers suffered the most. By the time the economy struck rock bottom in 1932 Cleveland's unemployment figure had reached 50 percent, Akron 60 percent, and Toledo 80 percent. As for particular industries, construction was hit the hardest with a 67 percent decline, with manufacturing next, down 44 percent.

Statistics cannot convey the degree of human suffering visited on millions of workers without jobs. People starved to death; families evicted from their homes moved in with overcrowded relatives or set up in ramshackle lean-tos; miners gained "sustenance" from blackberries and dandelions; former millionaires subsisted by selling apples on street corners; furniture was burned for fuel; the hungry grubbed through garbage cans like alley cats; children could not learn in school because they were hungry, cold, and ill-clad; thousands rode the rails and suffered in shantytowns, or "Hoovervilles," along railroad sidings.

Most large corporations weathered the Depression. The Cincinnati Milling Machine Company (since 1970 Cincinnati Milacron) exemplifies how one of them pulled through. Cincinnati Milling, founded in 1884, had become one of the nation's foremost machine tool manufacturers. The demands of World War I greatly stimulated demand for its milling machines, but the end of the war meant a sharp cutback. The work force dropped from 1,223 to 922 within a year of the Armistice. The burgeoning auto industry, however, picked up some of the slack. But another setback came with the 1920-1921 recession. Sales

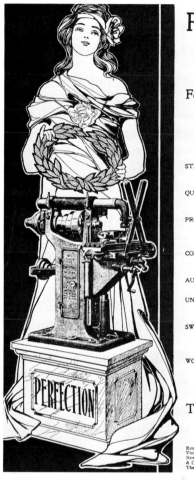

The Cincinnati Screw and Tap Company became the Cincinnati Milling Machine Company in 1889. The company kept that name until 1970, when it changed its name again, to Cincinnati Milacron. It has long been an important employer in the Cincinnati area. Courtesy, Cincinnati Milacron

dropped 70 percent and employment fell off 75 percent. Management salaries were reduced, stock holdings in other firms were sold, and cash reserves were depleted. Recovery was slow. As late as 1926 the work force was only about 50 percent of its wartime high. Then, spurred by an order from the Ford Motor Company for ten "centerless" grinding machines, the company by 1927 had secured title to all American patents for the centerless grinding process. Because of this and other new machines, new markets opened up and by the late 1920s Cincinnati Milling had become the largest machine tool producer in the country. In 1929 sales exceeded ten million, while the work force numbered 2,300.

Oddly, 1929, the year of the stock market crash, was the company's best year and there were great hopes for 1930. Sales reached $2.3 million in the first quarter of 1930, but then the cancellations began coming in and only $3.6 million sales were recorded during the remainder of the year, a 42 percent drop from 1929. By 1933 sales had declined to only 20 percent of the pre-Depression figures. Occasional large orders assisted in the difficult years. Such an order came from Ford at Christmas time in 1932. "I can keep 100 men on for three more months with that order," cried a happy Frederick A. Geir, company president. To help the unemployed, the Mutual Aid Committee, an employees' assistance organization set up in 1916, was transformed into a relief agency. The committee purchased food and clothing, which was distributed without charge. It helped out in paying rent and utility bills. Fringe benefits were continued by the company.

Cincinnati Milling instituted a number of innovations during the bleak years, which would serve it well when better times returned. In 1931 it began sending its own salesmen into the field, abandoning the use of manufacturers' representatives. It also adopted the "scientific management" plan. In 1934, by which time business had begun to pick up, a branch plant was opened in Birmingham, England. Thanks to overseas and export operations, sales improved, surpassing the ten million mark in 1936. The work force now numbered more than 200 over the 1929 figure. Sales improved to $13.6 billion in 1937.

It did not work out the same way with the Van Sweringen brothers, Oris Paxton and Mantis James. Their rise and fall was as meteoric as any in the annals of American history. Born in rural Wooster in 1879 and 1881, the boys moved with their family to Geneva, Ohio, in the early 1880s and after their father's death in 1886 relocated on Cleveland's east side. Dropping out of school in the middle grades, they held various jobs and displayed an obvious flair for business. The boys, who never married, had a closer personal relationship than most brothers and conducted all of their affairs as a unit.

One of the trademarks of the Van Sweringens was the purchase of property without the investment of their own funds. They used this tactic first in the real estate business in the early 1900s. In 1905 they took an option on a small lot southeast of Cleveland, where the Shaker society had once built a communal farm. They continued to buy up additional lots over the next ten years and by 1916

had developed a beautiful suburban community called Shaker Heights replete with broad boulevards, landscaped lots, lakes, and a golf course. Shaker Heights, remote from downtown Cleveland, needed a transportation system to connect it with the metropolitan area.

The Van Sweringens planned a "rapid transit" street railway line to the Public Square in downtown Cleveland, where they had already purchased land for a railroad terminal. However, they still needed five miles of right-of-way, on which to bring their line into the center of town. At this very time, in 1916, the New York Central had been ordered by the Interstate Commerce Commission to divest itself of the Nickel Plate Railroad. Its right-of-way ran along the route needed by the Van Sweringens to complete their rapid transit system. On July 15, 1916, they bought the entire Nickel Plate line to get that five-mile stretch.

Once in control of the Nickel Plate, the brothers got the itch to buy more rail lines. They studied railroad maps avidly as they plotted their moves. Oris Paxton once said that his favorite book was the Rand-McNally atlas. In 1922 they acquired the Lake Erie and Western, and the following year, the Toledo, St. Louis and Western, both of which were merged with the Nickel Plate. Later in 1923 they bought the Chesapeake and Ohio, while in 1924 they added the Erie and Pere Marquette.

By the late 1920s, while the Van Sweringens had amassed a railroad empire covering 9,000 miles and valued at more than three billion dollars, they had also amassed a huge debt. It grew larger with each new purchase. A Morgan bank loan of forty million dollars in 1926 was the first of several such transactions, but it barely scratched the surface of the debt. However, the financial mood of the country was a bullish one in the late 1920s. The general feeling was that the old cycle of boom and bust was over and that economic conditions would continue to improve without end. As long as business prospered the brothers would be all right.

The beginning of the end arrived with their purchase of the Missouri Pacific in 1928 and 1929. The brothers' plan was to extend their railroad holdings into the Southwest and to the West Coast. By the spring of 1929 they had control of the Missouri Pacific but it was to be their last purchase. The stock market crash that October hit them very hard. Prices of their holdings dropped sharply, earnings fell off, and creditors demanded repayment of loans. They managed to secure another forty-million-dollar loan in 1930, but this was totally inadequate to

The Ohio Relief Production Units provided jobs for Ohioans during the Depression. The Cleveland Unit made suits, pants, and hosiery for men and women. The girls shown in this photo are working at "looping" machines, sewing up the toes of hosiery. Courtesy, Cleveland Public Library: Newspaper Enterprise Association

ward off disaster. When that loan fell due in 1935 the brothers were unable to redeem it and on September 30, 1935, their assets were auctioned off—what was left of their assets, that is, for they had already lost a great deal and were having difficulty meeting their annual living expenses of $150,000. Worn out from work, stress, and disillusionment, the brothers died in quick order—Mantis James on December 13, 1935, aged fifty-four, and Oris Paxton on November 23, 1936, aged fifty-seven. The Van Sweringens never did anything illegal, they never stole from their companies, and they stayed at their desks through the worst of times to salvage something from the disaster which had struck They had simply gotten in too far over their heads.

American Greetings Corporation represents a happy fulfillment of the "American Dream" which even the Depression could not erase. Jacob Sapirstein emigrated from Russian-controlled Poland in 1905 to avoid becoming cannon fodder for Tsar Nicholas II's armies then engaged in war with Japan. Although he arrived in this country penniless and unable to speak English, by 1906, at age twenty-two, he was in business for himself. He sold postcards, imported from Germany, to drugstores and candy shops. Studying the market closely, Sapirstein gradually expanded his business, operating out of his own home. Driving a horse and wagon he called personally on all of his customers. One day a woman driving a Buick ran into the wagon, but Sapirstein was now able to buy a brand new

Model-T Ford in which to make his visits.

World War I stopped the importation of German cards, but, oddly, the war gave birth to the greeting card business. American manufacturers began to produce specialty cards which recognized birthdays, holidays, and other such events. The market was ripe for this innovation and Sapirstein cashed in. He was able to move his business out of his home and into a regular office, although it was only a garage on East 95th Street. When the Depression struck, the greeting card business continued to thrive, simply because people who were no longer able to give presents on special occasions could still give greeting cards. In 1932, during the depths of the Depression, Sapirstein and his three sons, who had entered fully into the business, decided to break with the past and manufacture their own greeting cards. They were immediately successful in this new departure; more office space and more employees were soon needed. In 1938 the Sapirstein Greeting Card Company became American Greeting Publishers. It went public in 1952 and is one of the largest greeting card corporations in the world. (It ranked 296th on the *Fortune 500* 1986 list.)

A new approach toward the problems of the Depression was apparent when Franklin D. Roosevelt took office as president on March 4, 1933. Abandoning the deflationary philosophy of the Hoover administration, the New Deal plan was to spend as much money as necessary for the relief of the unemployed and the recovery and reform of

This photo taken by a WPA photographer shows employees running a calendar stacker at the Champion Paper and Fiber Company in Hamilton during the Depression. Thanks to the efforts of the WPA, valuable documentation of life during the 1930s is available. Courtesy, Ohio Historical Society

the economic system. Relief was the immediate concern and through the numerous alphabet agencies funds were parcelled out through the states to those in need. Relief funds were expended in two forms: direct relief, or the "dole;" and work relief where the recipients were employed on public works projects.

Ohio made a brave effort to bring unemployed workers and idle industrial plants together when it organized the Ohio Relief Production Unit in the spring and summer of 1934. Between July 2 and November 19, twelve empty factories were reopened employing about 1,000 persons. The largest companies were Sun-Glo Industries of Mansfield (furniture), Toledo Garment (clothing), Moore Shirt in New Philadelphia (work shirts), and Comer Manufacturing in Dayton (coats and windbreakers). The plan did not work. Too many clothes and not enough other necessities were produced. Payment was in scrip which could not be used to buy most things the workers needed. The shortcomings of the plan became apparent within a year or so and all the plants were closed in May 1935.

The most massive of all federal relief programs—the Works Progress Administration, or WPA— was launched in the spring of 1935. It lasted until 1942 when World War II made it no longer necessary. All projects were screened and approved and workers were certified as relief recipients. From the time the program began until World War II between 200,000 and 300,000 Ohioans were on WPA. Up until October 1938, federal funds spent in the state amounted to fifty-five million dollars. In that month Ohio had the largest number of people on WPA among all states.

It is no doubt an understatement to say that the business community was not happy with the New Deal. Its spending and deficit financing policies, for one thing, violated all that had been sacred to the "masters of capital." More offensive, however, was its attitude toward labor. The National Industrial Recovery Act (NIRA), passed in 1933, was intended to bring about a maximum cooperative effort from industry to revive the economy. As a price for the suspension of antitrust laws, business had to recognize the legitimacy of trade unions. This was a bitter pill and numerous companies would not swallow it. The Supreme Court invalidated the NIRA in 1935, but Section 7a of that act, which authorized and encouraged trade unions, was salvaged and elaborated in the Wagner Act, which was adopted shortly after the NIRA was thrown out. Not only did the Wagner Act recognize the right of unions to organize and bargain collectively with employers, it also created a National Labor Relations Board to conduct elections and investigate charges of unfair employment practices.

Encouraged by this legislation, labor went on an organizing orgy. The main body of the conservative AFL was not much interested in this, but the militant industrial arm of the AFL, the Committee for Industrial Organization, was. Led by the outspoken head of the United Mineworkers, the bushy-browed John L. Lewis, the committee broke away from the AFL in 1936 and founded the Congress of Industrial Organizations, or CIO, for the purpose of recruiting hundreds of thousands of industrial workers shunned by the AFL. The CIO's membership crusade led to repeated clashes with corporations which were dead set opposed to outside control of their workers.

A bitter strike broke out at the Autolite plant in Toledo in 1934, where the new local of the United Auto Workers demanded recognition. Violence erupted in May as thousands of unionists and allies reacted angrily to the use of strike-breakers, tear gas, and the efforts of company and municipal police to rout the picket lines. Federal

mediators finally were able to bring the two sides together and tensions eased. Concessions were made to the union, but it did not gain the bargaining rights it had demanded. Workers in the rubber industry contributed the sit-down strike to the arsenal of union pressure tactics. In February 1936 a series of sit-downs at the major plants in Akron halted all production. The United Rubber Workers won a partial victory and union membership rose.

The sit-down strike at Cleveland's Fisher Body plant of General Motors in December 1936 initiated the most memorable confrontation between labor and management during the New Deal era. The strike spread to other GM plants and soon the entire organization was at war with the auto workers. The main combat zone was at the Fisher Body plant in Flint, Michigan. Having made no progress in the negotiations, the company turned off the heat in the plant and ordered police to storm the building. They were beaten back by the strikers. Eventually, due to the intervention of Michigan Governor Frank Murphy, GM agreed to recognize the union. The forty-four-day strike of 44,000 workers, which had tied up sixty plants in fourteen states, was labor's greatest victory in history. In the wake of this success, Lewis and the CIO turned next to the steel industry. To the amazement of everyone, United States Steel surrendered without a whimper and the rest of "Big Steel" went along, recognizing the steelworkers' union as the bargaining agent for their employees.

It was not the same with "Little Steel," however,

The Nickle Plate Railroad, organized in 1881 to run from Buffalo to Chicago, brought its first passenger train through Cleveland in August 1882. Pictured is the Nickle Plate under construction at Broadway Avenue. Courtesy, Western Reserve Historical Society

represented by Inland Steel, Youngstown Sheet and Tube, Republic Steel, and Bethlehem. These companies, which had plants in six Ohio cities —Cleveland, Youngstown, Massillon, Canton, Warren, and Niles—refused to follow the example of U.S. Steel. Union organizing attempts in May and June 1937 were met with bitter resistance, as policemen and National Guard troops struggled with strikers. A battle at Massillon led to the death of one man and the wounding of twelve others. At the Warren plant of Republic Steel 1,000 strikers clashed with 250 policemen; one striker was killed and fourteen injured. Little Steel won out and the CIO was defeated in these unionization efforts. However, four years later, in a calmer atmosphere, and under National Labor Relations Board auspices, the steelworkers won elections in all of the plants where they had suffered defeats just a few years before. Militant unionism subsided after 1938. Major victories had been achieved and a time for consolidation of the gains was necessary.

. . .

The period of boom and bust, the 1920s and 1930s,

closed out on an up note. Despite the recession of 1937-1938, business was reviving. Conservative critics denounced the New Deal for its massive spending without having ended the Depression, since ten million were still unemployed in 1940. Yet the economy had improved. In most industries sales were much better and workers were going back on the job. Although business was not pleased with the new role of government in the lives of Americans or with the maturing of the labor movement, it was reluctantly adjusting to the new dispensation. But now more pressing matters were at hand. With the outbreak of war in Europe in September 1939 and with eventual American involvement, industry and labor needed to work together to provide the materials of war to bring down the Axis powers.

———

Pictured here is the Republic Steel plant in Cleveland. By 1930, after merging with several companies, Republic Steel Corporation had greatly strengthened its position in the iron and steel industry. Courtesy, Cleveland Public Library: Newspaper Enterprise Association

Road and mileage signs give clues to the location of this small Ohio town. Urbana, in Champaign County, looks serene as the country emerges from the throes of the Depression. Courtesy, Ohio Historical Society

VII
WAR AND PEACE

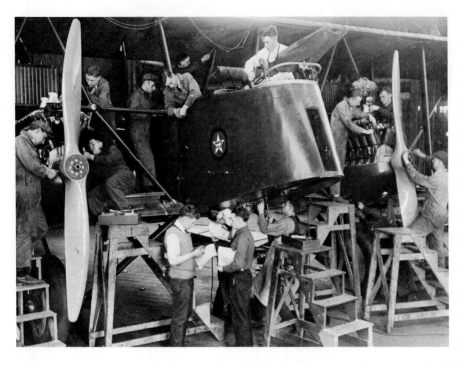

The Glenn L. Martin Company of Cleveland received a government contract in January of 1918 to build six Martin bombers to accommodate the famous Liberty Motor. Pictured is the final assembly of the MB-2, a plane designed to hold 2,000 pounds of bombs carried by a special bomb-dropping device, in addition to a 1,700-pound Mark VII navy torpedo. Courtesy, Western Reserve Historical Society

Facing page: The Hoover Company, the oldest and most widely known manufacturer of vacuum cleaners in the world, ceased producing vacuum cleaners in order to concentrate its manufacturing capabilities on the war effort. Advertisements such as this one appeared nationwide during World War II, urging women to share their Hoover cleaners with those who did not have one. Courtesy, the Hoover Company

I t took America well over a year after the Japanese bombed Pearl Harbor on December 7, 1941, to get its war machine in full running order. Once operating, it turned out an incredible number of tanks, aircraft, ships, artillery pieces, guns, grenades, bombs, and all the other needed instruments of war. Twenty-five thousand planes a year were being produced by 1943 and early the following year the production of American war plants was double the amount of the Axis countries. As a major industrial state, Ohio was expected to contribute substantially to the war effort. It did. From the outbreak of war until V-E Day in May 1945, eighteen billion dollars in war contracts were let to Ohio companies. The most important contracts were in aircraft, ordnance, and shipbuilding. Cleveland, Cincinnati, Akron, and Dayton were the busiest cities. The number of workers in Ohio manufacturing plants during the war jumped from 755,000 to almost twice that number. Wages went up by 65 percent.

But while war stimulated the economy and eliminated unemployment, all was not happy in the work place. To maximize production and reduce labor-management friction, the government created the War Labor Board in 1942. The WLB proposed a plan whereby, on the one hand, wages would be frozen except for cost-of-living increases and labor would agree not to strike. On the other hand, in order to conciliate labor leadership, the government would guarantee that union members could not withdraw from their unions. Hardly an equitable arrangement, but it was sufficient to secure national union approval. The rank and file, however, did not approve. Their dissatisfaction surfaced in countless work stoppages, which made

The Neighborly Spirit of Sharing

These are days when many good, old-fashioned virtues are coming back into their own—Neighborliness . . . Sharing what we have.

The common enemy has given us a new appreciation of our homes, our friends, our country and the way we live.

We are giving each other many little "lifts."

A great cause has made America a nation of neighbors again.

HOW TO MAKE YOUR HOOVER SERVE LONGER

Empty bag after each cleaning. A clean bag will help keep your cleaner operating at top efficiency and prolong its life.

Do not wind the cord tightly. Coil it loosely around the cord clips. *Pull* out *plug*—never *jerk* cord —to disconnect cleaner. When using cleaner, avoid running over the cord.

Do not try to pick up pins, hairpins, tacks, pebbles or other hard objects with cleaner. These may damage belt or other moving parts.

Have your Hoover inspected once a year. To be sure of obtaining genuine Hoover parts and service, register your cleaner with your Hoover Factory Branch Service Station (*consult classified telephone directory*) or dealer. If you cannot locate either, write: The Hoover Company, North Canton, Ohio.

Remember, do not discard any worn or broken parts. They must be turned in to secure replacements.

The Hoover Company is no longer making cleaners; it is completely engaged in making precision products for America's fighting forces.

If you are fortunate enough to have a modern Hoover Cleaner, your cleaning problem is answered for many years to come.

But there are times when all of us must be interested in the other fellow, too; when we want to spread our blessings and give the lifts in our power to give. The woman who wants clean clothes for her family can't get the washing machine she needs. Her next door neighbor has a washing machine and uses it only once a week. Other appliances, other needs, other friends. Why not share?

Some relative of yours, some near-by neighbor or some close friend down the street or across the hall may have been unable to get a cleaner. Your Hoover Cleaner is husky enough to clean for you and her too. Why not share? Incidentally, she may have some household appliance that you have been unable to get.

You can help her, she can help you. That's how sharing works. That's how America is looking at things these days —one for all—and all for our country!

THE HOOVER

IT BEATS : . . . AS IT SWEEPS . . . AS IT CLEANS

a farce of the "no-strike" pledge. In 1943, 300,000 Ohio workers were involved in 467 wildcat strikes and although in 1944 the number of strikers dropped to 216,000, work stoppages increased to 549. In 1943 a massive coal strike so disrupted the operations of Hanna and other coal companies that the federal government took over management of the mines.

Local union officials were caught between the militant demands of the workers and the insistence of their national leaders that discipline be maintained. Factional disputes erupted within many unions such as at the General Tire and Rubber plant at Akron over wildcat walkouts in 1943 and 1944. At the Willys-Overland factory in Toledo, workers belonged to four different unions and jurisdictional

——

A riot broke out during a strike at the Goodyear Tire and Rubber Company in Akron. Police are shown here advancing on a throng that surrounded the plant's main gate. More than 100 persons were injured in the clash between 200 officers and strikers. Courtesy, Acme Photo and the Ohio Historical Society

fights repeatedly broke out. Disputes also developed between locals of the same union, such as among electrical workers in Dayton. Bitter union wrangling reached all the way to the top, particularly between John L. Lewis' United Mineworkers and the Ohio CIO.

One significant breakthrough on the labor front brought about by World War II was the infusion of large numbers of women into the work force. Because of the heavy demands on manpower for the military, the need for laborers in war plants grew proportionately. Millions of homemakers donned slacks and caps and went into the factories. "Rosie the Riveter," the title of a popular song of the day, symbolized the American woman during wartime. (Cincinnati Milling claimed it had a "Millie the Machinist" before there was a "Rosie the Riveter.") From May 1942 until late 1943, the number of female war workers increased almost fourfold. As the war progressed, the number continued to grow until over one-third of all workers in war plants were women. The Ohio state legislature abolished age and occupation restrictions on women working in industry. In time not only were many single women working in war plants, but many married women including some grandmothers had also

entered the work force. Female workers were discriminated against in wage and seniority matters, which caused occasional wildcat stoppages, such as at Libbey-Owens-Ford in 1943.

But despite the labor unrest throughout war plants, production of the necessary material accelerated and Ohio industry played an important role in the ultimate Allied victory. One of the remarkable aspects of industry during the war, and Ohio's industries were no exception, was the speed and relative ease with which companies retooled their plants for war production. Firms which specialized in nonmilitary products already had the physical plants, engineering expertise, and labor skills that could be adapted to the needs of the moment. But quite a few companies did not have to retool, as they were already manufacturing products needed in war.

Cincinnati Milling Machine, a producer of machine tools, was in a particularly advantageous position. As with other machine tool plants, it did not need to retool. It simply had to produce more machines which could make the tools of war. Well

Before there was Rosie the Riveter, the Cincinnati Milling Machine Company had "Millie the Machinist." This company, as well as others, depended on women to work in its plants during World War II. There was a seven-day standard work week during the war that consisted of eleven-hour days. More than 2,000 Cincinnati Milling Machine employees entered the military, with thirty-one losing their lives. Courtesy, Cincinnati Milacron

before Pearl Harbor, the company's management anticipated that war would come and began expanding its facilities and increasing its labor force. This head start proved vital as the orders for machine tools began pouring in following America's entry into the war. Not that Cincinnati Milling alone tooled the country for war; the entire industry turned out more machines between 1940 and 1943 than in the previous forty years. Yet by 1942, when the demand for machine tools peaked, Cincinnati Milling had manufactured 17,511 machines, one-twelfth of the national output.

By 1942 and 1943 the demand for machine tools had abated, the job of supplying war plants with the needed machinery having been accomplished. In the last year of the war only 40 percent of Cincinnati Milling's capacity was devoted to machine tools. Hence it was necessary to produce specific war goods if it was to keep its inflated work force occupied. Among a number of such products that the company manufactured were parts of B-29 landing gears, parts for tractors, transmissions for amphibious landing craft, radar components, dies for ammunition makers, and artillery fuse setters.

Thompson Products in Cleveland also did not need to retool as it was already into aircraft parts and products which were readily adapted for tanks, trucks, and tractors. Existing plant capacity was increased to meet the demands of the American as well as the British military. The federal government, even before Pearl Harbor, subsidized the construction and operation of a new plant known as the Thompson Aircraft Products Company, or TAPCO, in the Cleveland suburb of Euclid. By 1943 the factory, which operated seven days a week, twenty-four hours a day, had 16,000 employees. Engine parts for airplanes remained a much more important component in Thompson's product line after the war than it had been before. In addition to helping the country arm for war, the company enjoyed a profit boom as sales skyrocketed by 700 percent by 1945.

Another company which was not required to retool for war was the Austin Company of Cleveland, builders of big buildings around the world. Austin specialized in aircraft plants, but as company historian Martin Greif reports, Austin also constructed "numerous shipbuilding facilities, machine tool factories, two major penicillin plants, an air base in Alaska, several factories for the manufacture of electronic instruments and devices . . . the design of special Naval facilities, and America's largest wind tunnel . . ." However, perhaps Austin's greatest contribution was the design and construction of "con-

Above: Ohio's lake ports buzzed with activity as the demand for iron and steel grew, resulting from U.S. involvement in World War II. Here, an ore boat is towed up the Cuyahoga River in the early 1940s. Courtesy, Ohio Historical Society

Facing page, bottom: The Hanna Coal Company was a major coal producer in Ohio. Although coal mining was quite successul throughout the years, the industry had its share of strikes. A massive strike in 1934 brought the federal government in to manage the mines. Courtesy, Ohio Historical Society

trolled condition" plants, which were windowless, insulated, and under constant temperature controls. The buildings also met wartime blackout needs. In 1939 the company built such a plant for General Motors for the manufacture of Allison liquid-cooled aircraft engines. This led to contracts for controlled-conditions factories for Grumman Aircraft's fighter and torpedo planes. During the war Austin built eleven blackout plants for the aircraft industry as well as many traditional aircraft factories.

The company was proudest of three controlled-conditions plants. At Fort Worth, Texas, and Tulsa, Oklahoma, it built twin-bomber assembly facilities for Consolidated-Vultee and Douglas Aircraft. The insulated fiberglass and steel-panel walls and the light-reflecting white concrete floors made these plants unique. These features provided advanced and improved air-conditioning and lighting conditions. The Fort Worth building was later expanded and became, next to the Pentagon, the largest air-conditioned structure in the world. In 1943, when steel was in short supply, Austin designed a "breathing" masonry wall for its Oklahoma City Douglas Aircraft plant. Seventeen and a half million bricks were substituted for the steel walls.

One concern which had to retool was Hoover Company of North Canton. Vacuum sweepers were of little use in winning the war, so their production ceased shortly after Pearl Harbor. Machines for manufacturing vacuum sweepers were removed from the plant and machines for war production were installed. According to a company brochure, Hoover

Right: The Austin Company of Cleveland had an interest in the quality of its work environment. Pictured here are men working under fluorescent lighting, in an air-conditioned room, to help reduce the strain of their work. Courtesy, Cleveland Public Library

Below right: The Hoover Company became an active participant in the war effort. The company ceased manufacture of new vacuum cleaners in order to devote its facility to the production of helmet liners, parachutes for fragmentation bombs, parts for the variable time fuse, and turret motors. The War Department ordered Hoover to remove its name from their buildings to prevent the company from becoming a target during an air raid. Pictured here are women working in the parachute department. Courtesy, the Hoover Company

secured war contracts for the production of "helmet liners, parachutes for fragmentation bombs, propeller pitch control motors, turret motors, and amplidynes for bombers." Most important, perhaps, was its production of the variable time or "proximity" fuse, critical in the detonation of artillery shells and bombs.

National Cash Register was in a somewhat similar position as Hoover. The manufacture of cash registers also ceased soon after Pearl Harbor, by which time the conversion to war production was well advanced. Military items made by NCR included bomb fuses, parts of artillery shells, rocket motors for five-inch antiaircraft rockets, carburetors for B-29s, and "analog computer gunsights" for aircraft defense systems. During the war years, government contracts paid the company's overhead costs, while the rebuilding of old machines brought in a little profit.

The fact that NCR had extensive overseas oper-

ations led to strange and amusing wartime incidents. NCR personnel, men and women, served in the armed forces of their native countries in Great Britain, Europe, Africa, the Middle East, and the Far East. They served on both sides in the conflict and some, including a future president of the company, spent time in prison camps. As German forces entered Paris in 1940, a tank thundered to a halt outside the NCR office on the Champs Elysees. An officer dismounted and knocked on the door, which was opened tentatively by an apprehensive employee. "Hello," said the smiling German. "I am from National Cash Register in Berlin and I am wondering if you made your quota last year? We made ours." Five years later an American tank rumbled by the ruins of the NCR office in Berlin where employees were digging through the rubble. A grinning GI called out: "Hi, I'm from NCR-Omaha. Did you guys make your quota last month?"

Goodyear by no means abandoned tire production during the war, but it devoted more attention to aircraft production. It entered the aircraft business before Pearl Harbor when on December 5, 1939, it contracted with the Glenn L. Martin Company to manufacture parts for the B-26 Marauder. Goodyear Aircraft Corporation was incorporated at that time to handle the aircraft parts business and the Goodyear Airdock, idle since the collapse of the dirigible industry, was reactivated for a production facility. In the fall of 1940 Grumman and Curtiss-Wright contracted with Goodyear for the Avenger torpedo bomber and the P-40 Warhawk fighter. The navy ordered patrol and training blimps. Orders for additional airplane parts in 1941 led to the construction of two new plants near the airdock and a third in Litchfield Park in Arizona. Sales ran to $330 million for 1941, 52 percent over the previous year.

With American entry into the war, Goodyear built on the solid base already established for the manufacture of aircraft parts. In February 1942 it

signed an agreement to produce the navy Corsair fighter plane, the one complete plane to be built by the company. It subcontracted 40 percent of the job to plants large and small throughout the country and the first Corsair taxied out of the factory one year later, in February 1943. Before the war's end, over 4,000 Corsairs went into naval service. In addition to the Corsair, the navy ordered a large number of blimps from Goodyear to patrol both Atlantic and Pacific coastal waters. One hundred sixty-eight blimps had been manufactured by the spring of 1944 when, because of the decline in need, production was halted.

With the loss of natural rubber sources from Southeast Asia by 1941 it was imperative to develop a synthetic substitute. The federal government called on the major rubber companies to expedite their research so that something would be available when the stockpile of natural rubber gave out. By 1943 the formula had been developed and produc-

Goodyear Aircraft produced this Corsair fighter plane for the navy during World War II. The navy also used Goodyear blimps to patrol the Atlantic and Pacific coastal waters. Courtesy, Goodyear Tire and Rubber Company Archives

Above: Ohio industries, such as Akron's General Tire and Rubber Company, were active in the war effort. Pictured here are tires of all shapes and sizes being manufactured for the military. Courtesy, Ohio Historical Society

Above right: World War II rubber manufacturing focused on products for use in the war effort. With the cut-off of rubber shipments from Southeast Asia, the development of synthetic rubber was a top priority. By the end of the war, rubber companies reverted to civilian tire manufacturing. Courtesy, University of Akron Archives

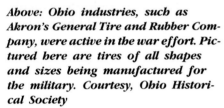

tion of synthetic rubber was well underway. Goodyear produced the first synthetic rubber tire early in 1943, but all of the tire companies were soon in the business. Firestone, Goodrich, Goodyear, and General Tire each had three or four plants scattered from Akron to Texas. Tires for military vehicles were the primary products in the early war years, but later on the companies began to shift back to civilian production. Goodyear's Jackson, Michigan, plant stopped tire manufacturing when the war began, retooled, and by late 1942 was turning out antitank cannons. Within another year or so it had re-retooled and was back to manufacturing tires.

Marion Shovel did not need to retool as it was called upon to dig and excavate all across the country. Its powerful cranes were employed to handle

materials for the Austin Company in the erection of the twin bomber plants at Fort Worth and Tulsa. It played an important role in the excavation and construction of ordnance plants. Marion Shovels moved two million cubic yards of dirt and rock prefatory to the building of an electrical power facility for the Aluminum Company of America in the Tennessee Valley. In Idaho men using four Marion cranes, the company proudly proclaimed, "poured 24 concrete igloos in a 24-hour period," which were used to store explosives. Marion shovels dug coal, copper, and iron ore from the nation's mineral beds. Its huge stripping shovel had a thirty-five-cubic-yard capacity with a monthly output figure of over one million yards, which helped increase Ohio's wartime coal production by 82 percent.

Perhaps the greatest American hero of World War II was not a man but a machine. Willys-Overland in 1938 hired Delmar G. "Barney" Roos, an engineer with long experience in various automobile factories, to work on improving a light, four-cylinder car. Roos determined to develop a more powerful, more durable, and more long-lasting engine for the car. Beginning with a forty-eight horsepower engine at 3,400 rpm's, which ran for only four hours, Roos in two years' time had increased the engine's performance to sixty-five horsepower at 4,400 rpm's with a continuous running time of 150 hours. Numerous other refinements lessened the weight and increased the strength of the car.

At this same time, the United States Army was searching for a tough, light, all-purpose vehicle; a machine with four-wheel drive, capable of speeds as low as three miles per hour, with substantial pulling power, and not weighing over 1,600 pounds. Bids were requested by the army but only

Willys and American Bantam responded. In tests the Willys car outperformed the Bantam, but it was too heavy, weighing 2,400 pounds. Revised specifications increased the weight limit to 2,175 pounds. Roos either had to scrap his engine or streamline his vehicle. He went for streamlining and the modified machine won army approval. Thus was born the famous "jeep."

Willys produced over 650,000 jeeps during the war and their achievements were legendary. They could climb steep grades and cross sandy deserts. They could accelerate quickly up to sixty miles an hour. The jeep was a multipurpose machine as well. With mounted machine guns it became a tank, with stretchers it became an ambulance, with a radio it became a command post, and with flanged wheels it became a locomotive. It became the subject of Bill Mauldin cartoons and soldier anecdotes: A corporal was in tears in his bombed out jeep. "Don't worry, you'll get another one," he was comforted. "But you don't understand," was the tearful reply. "I loved *this* one."

Sherwin-Williams continued to manufacture paint in World War II, but it also manufactured shells and bombs. The company built a munitions plant in Carbondale, Illinois, which at one time employed 15,000 workers. More than ten million artillery shells, millions of antitank mines, and a million 500-pound aerial bombs were turned out at this facility without rejects, and more important, without any fatalities. Along its traditional product line, Sherwin-Williams also manufactured camouflage paints for the military. One story has it that the Allied invasion of North Africa in November 1942 was delayed because of the late arrival of camouflage paints.

Although Cincinnati was no longer the pork-packing center that it once was, the industry continued in the city. Pictured here are women working at the Kahn's Company, the city's largest packing plant. Courtesy, Ohio Historical Society

Many Ohio companies other than those mentioned played their part in the Allied victory in World War II. It is not possible to name them all or to catalog their contributions. By looking at a few of the major ones, however, one can sense the ferment and pulsating beat of wartime America in one of the most important industrial states in the Union.

War ended in Europe in May 1945 as the Allied noose finally strangled Hitlerite Germany. A few months later in August, Ohio's Colonel Paul Tibbetts piloted the *Enola Gay* over Japan, dropped the atom bomb, and the war in the Pacific came to an end. Now the massive task of demobilization and reconversion was at hand, a challenge hardly less formidable than the original one of gearing up for war.

Despite the joy and relief when the guns stopped firing and the bombs stopped dropping, the future state of the economy generated considerable concern. The abrupt termination of billions of dollars worth of war contracts and the labor glut prompted by the return of millions of service men and women to the work force, led to predictions of a massive depression. Yet countervailing forces were at work, which blunted the impact of the expected economic decline.

The two factors most responsible for this unexpected turn of events were the large pent-up buying power of Americans, and the continued high level of government spending. Because of price controls, high wages (due to overtime work), and shortages of consumer goods, potential spending resources of private persons and corporations had climbed to $200 billion toward the end of 1944. With the end of the war the sudden pouring of these funds into the economy had a stimulating effect on peacetime production. Moreover, federal budgets continued to rise after the war as more and more public monies found their way into social and economic programs begun under the New Deal and continued under the Fair Deal of President Harry Truman. While serious problems of reconversion did occur and while a number of violent labor disputes broke out, there was no postwar depression.

As the country rushed onward, it became apparent that conditions were going to be quite different from what they had been before 1940. New technology, new processes, and new products marked what was coming to be called the "postindustrial society." Basic industries of the Industrial Revolution were giving way to a service-oriented economy. The standard of living of Americans would rise to unanticipated heights in this new "Age of Affluence." American life in the 1950s and 1960s displayed a new face. It featured plastics and Pampers, suburbs and supermarkets, environmentalism and ecology, aerobics and robotics. It was an age of interstate highways and fast food restaurants, motels and discount houses, television and computers, nuclear power and aerospace exploration, shopping centers and health spas. The scientific research upon which this new society was built received a major impetus from World War II. Two good examples of this are nuclear power and numerical controls, or computer systems. Prior to the war, research and development was confined chiefly to the electrical, chemical, rubber, petroleum, and automotive industries. After the war, research and development divisions became key departments in all industrial plants. Expenditures on research and development jumped dramatically between 1947 and 1968. And whereas industry had shouldered most of the financial burden for research and development in earlier times, the federal government steadily increased its contribution in this area. The following figures reflect the increase in and sources of research and development funds for the different years in millions of dollars:

	1947	1955	1960	1968
Federal Government	500	3.490	8.720	14.972
Industry	1.515	2.510	4.510	8.941
Other	85	270	480	1.170
Total	2.100	6.270	13.710	25.083

Diversification, decentralization, and internationalization were other characteristics of postwar industry. None of these were new departures, but their degree of acceleration was far greater than before. Shifting markets, population migrations, changing consumer appetites, and labor difficulties all were prominent factors in causing companies to diversify, relocate, and internationalize.

Diversification was accomplished in two ways, either by creating new divisions within the corporate structure or by acquiring businesses producing other products. This generally led to the decentralization of manufacturing centers and the appointment of autonomous heads to manage the new operations.

Particularly by acquiring other plants, diversification led to the "age of the conglomerate" in the 1950s, 1960s, and 1970s. By applying sophisticated management techniques, a parent company could transform an undervalued business concern into a real money-maker. Gulf and Western and ITT were among the more successful early large-scale conglomerates. Two big Ohio steel companies, Republic and Youngstown Sheet and Tube, were absorbed by Ling-Temco-Vought (LTV) in the 1970s and 1980s. LTV began as Ling Electric in 1958 with about seven million dollars in sales. By 1968, after acquiring twenty-five or so companies, its sales were over three billion dollars.

Meanwhile the image of the corporate manager was changing. No longer was the highly visible "captain of industry/robber baron" dominant on the business scene. Instead one began reading more of "organization men" and "men in gray flannel suits." An antiseptic sameness characterized the new industrial leader and his middle-management underlings. Rather than coming up through the "school of hard knocks," the new executive had his MBA from a distinguished university, lived in a prosperous suburban community, and played the corporate game. Those who would rise to the top usually had to accept transfers from plant to plant with the inconveniences that such frequent moves entailed, as they mastered all phases of the business. It was not as glamorous a life as it seemed to outsiders, but for those who paid the price the rewards were ample.

Dana Corporation of Toledo illustrates several of the trends noted above, although Dana is not a conglomerate. Founded in 1904 as the Spicer Company in Plainfield, New Jersey, the organization specialized in manufacturing universal parts for the burgeoning automobile industry. World War I gave a big boost to its business with the sharp increase in truck production. Charles A. Dana, related to the famous newspaperman, poured a large amount of needed capital into the company in 1914 at a time when it was in difficulty. Dana played a growing role in the company in the 1920s and 1930s, buying up companies producing universals, axles, and auto and truck frames. In 1929, to be closer to the heart of the auto industry, Dana relocated the Spicer Company to Toledo. The company name was changed to the Dana Corporation in 1948. Fifty years after its founding, Dana had become dominant in its field as a supplier of automotive components with annual sales of $153 million.

A new regime headed by Jack Martin took over the company at this time. A tough, demanding executive, Martin had a solid grounding in industrial management in steel, ordnance, and rubber-tire plants. He came to Dana in the late 1940s as executive vice-president and was named president in 1953. Martin opposed diversification but favored the acquisition of companies producing automotive parts, and moved heavily into the replacement-parts business. Perfect Circle and Aluminum Industries were added in 1963, giving Dana a strong foothold in the automotive "aftermarket." Three years later Victor Manufacturing and Gasket Company were acquired to further strengthen the company in this field. In the twenty years following his elevation to chief executive officer at Dana, Martin had increased the company's replacement parts sales from a few million to $309 million.

Following the acquisition of Perfect Circle, Dana went to decentralized control. Starting with five divisions, each maintaining its own manufacturing, engineering, finance, and sales force, the company expanded to twenty-one divisions by 1975. Martin also pressed actively for internationalization. In 1958 auto manufacturing outside the United States for the first time exceeded that within the country, so it was essential to develop overseas affiliates. By 1975 the network embraced 166 facilities managed by forty-five affiliated corporations in twenty-one countries in Europe, Asia, Africa, and South America. Dana owned from 33 percent to 49 percent of the stock in the affiliates, which were managed by nationals of the particular country. International operations were carried on before Martin's time, but between 1965 and 1975 investment abroad grew from $175 million to $430 million.

Austin Company was in the international market as early as 1914 and gained widespread recognition with its construction of the automobile plant in Nizhni Novgorod (Gorky) in the Soviet Union in the early 1930s. It built airplane plants in China in 1933 and opened its London office in 1938. Following the Second World War its international operations expanded greatly with subsidiaries located throughout Europe, in Asia, and in South America. Each subsidiary was a completely integrated and autonomous operating unit. As with its American offices, the subsidiaries were staffed with their own planners, architects, engineers, accountants, supervisors, and field workers.

Austin played a significant role in changing the face of America in the postwar world by building research laboratories, shopping centers, banks, computer facilities, television studios, college dormitories, hospitals, food-processing plants, department stores, and much more. In doing this, the company's engineers were in the national forefront in the suburbanization of industry. With superhighways and suburbs, corporations began relocating their plants from congested and deteriorating downtown quarters to spacious, attractive grounds in the city's outskirts. In this new setting came the adoption of the single-story, straight line, controlled-conditions plant, developed and popularized by Austin.

An example of the company's contribution to the suburbanizing of industry was the Northlake, Illinois, factory of Automatic Electric, a division of General Telephone Corporation. Business had increased so rapidly in the 1950s at Automatic Electric, which manufactured equipment for the telephone industry, that new quarters were a must. The company's facilities occupied seventeen different buildings in the Chicago "loop." Austin was commissioned by Automatic Electric to survey Chicago's outlying areas and recommend a new site. In addition it was authorized to design a new plant layout which would provide for maximum efficiency. Austin engineers selected the Northlake site and eighteen months after ground was broken the 1,520,000-square-foot, integrated, single-story, straight line plant went into operation. The ideal for a unified office and manufacturing facility had been attained.

Timken Company in Canton extended its international operations after the war, but did not diversify in the traditional way. It preferred to expand its own operations into related fields of steel manufacturing. Founded in 1899 in St. Louis by Henry Timken as the Timken Roller Bearing Axle Company, the concern produced a new kind of tapered roller bearing to eliminate friction in the carriage and infant automobile industries. In 1909 Timken moved operations to Canton for the same reason as Dana moved to Toledo, to be near the heart of the auto industry. To insure a high quality of steel, Timken built a plant in Canton in 1916, becoming the only bearing company to operate its own steel facility. In 1932 it expanded its operations by developing a percussion rock bit for mining, quarrying, and blasting operations. Before World War II new plants had been located in Columbus and Wooster as well as in Canada, Great Britain, and France.

Following the war, rock bit operations were centralized in a new plant at Colorado Springs and an automated bearing facility was opened in Bucyrus. Other bearing factories were built in nearby New Philadelphia and in faraway South Africa, Australia, and Brazil. Research was a top priority at Timken in the 1960s and considerable effort was devoted to improving the company's steelmaking capacity. With growing national concern over pollution and the environment, improvements were undertaken to eliminate the noxious gasses and wastes, normal byproducts of large manufacturing concerns. Since roller bearings had not been the company's sole product for over half a century, the name was changed in 1970 to simply the Timken Company.

Mead Corporation, the venerable Ohio paper and paper products company in Dayton, practiced internationalization and diversification, but also engaged in some de-diversification. Founded in 1846 by Daniel Mead, the company almost went broke in the years following Colonel Mead's death in 1891. After reorganization, it grew steadily in the first half of the twentieth century. Prior to World War II, Mead had acquired and built paper mills in Kingsport, Tennessee, Brunswick, Georgia, and Escanaba, Michigan. It also began to diversify, before the war, by getting into paperboard manufacturing, but these operations were greatly expanded in the decade after the war. By the late 1960s Mead had

acquired several recycling plants which turned out "specialty boards" for a number of industries.

Mead began its move toward the "billion dollar club" in the 1950s and 1960s by extensive diversification. Corrugated shipping containers, multiple-packaging systems, and specialty papers were related to the company's basic product. But in 1958 Mead acquired Data Corporation, which put it in the electronic storage and retrieval business. Mead Data Control developed systems known as Lexis and Nexis, which have become, according to a company brochure, the "world's leading computer-assisted legal research service" and "leading full-text search and retrieval service for news and business information," respectively. In 1968 Mead also bought the Woodward Company which manufactured iron castings and rubber products, and mined metallurgical coal. In 1977 it purchased a pipe, valve, fittings, and electrical supply company, Gulf Consolidated Services.

But bad times lay ahead. In the late 1970s a five-year $1.5-billion modernization plan was instituted to replace obsolete and worn-out machinery. Close upon this came the economic decline of the early 1980s, leading to an $86-million loss for Mead in 1982. Retrenchment was a necessity and the corporation began unloading several of its non-forest companies, such as Gulf Consolidated, a portion of the Woodward holdings, and a good chunk of the container operations. Twenty percent of Mead's assets were unloaded in 1982 alone. Confining itself to paper, paperboard, pulp, and electronic retrieval, the company made a solid comeback in the next few years.

Hoover got right back into the vacuum sweeper business as soon as World War II ended and has largely confined its domestic operations to that product. However, new buildings have been constructed in the industrial park north of North Canton and the latest technical advances have been employed in the plants. Efficiency and productivity have been improved by the use of computer terminals, robotics, lasers, and microprocessor technology. Self-operating cleaners, portable cleaners, and rug and floor conditioners have been marketed around the world. Hoover also manufactures refrigerators, freezers, dishwashers, and washing machines in its overseas factories. It has plants in Wales, England, Scotland, Australia, South Africa, Colombia, Portugal, and Canada.

Cincinnati Milling established a "Committee of Five," composed of its top executives, to plan postwar readjustment. It was well that it did because

This 1947 photograph shows new auto-mobiles being transported on the Ohio River. Today, Cincinnati still uses the Ohio for river transportation, as well as for recreation. Courtesy, Cincinnati Historical Society

---

there was a slump in the milling business when the guns stopped firing. The Committee of Five insisted that Cincinnati Milling must diversify if it was to survive. Cincinnati Milling acquired a lathe company in 1945 and got into the chemical business when it purchased the Carlisle Chemical Company in 1948. Its work in chemicals opened the door to the field of reinforced plastics in the 1950s. Between 1945 and 1950 other ideas for diversification were experimented with—zippers, brushless shaving cream, automatic telegram recorders—most of which were abandoned. Among new products which worked out well were Cimcool (a synthetic cutting fluid), abrasive grinding machines, and centerless grinders for making bearings.

The computer revolution of the 1950s and 1960s impacted heavily on industry. Although the origins of the computer have been disputed, it is immaterial to enter the debate or to become involved in the technical aspects of the computer revolution. Suffice it to say that in 1946 a 150-man team of scientists at the University of Pennsylvania produced ENIAC, a mammoth thirty-ton computer which carried out mathematical calculations thousands of times faster than any existing mechanical device. The early computer consisted of large banks of vacuum tubes and mechanical switches that filled three normal-sized rooms. Advances in the next ten to fifteen years brought about a steady reduction in the size of the component parts and with it a greater efficiency in output. The biggest breakthrough came in the 1960s with the development of miniaturized integrated circuits. Further improvements brought greater miniaturization of controls, more accurate control, and greater memory, all at reduced cost.

Cincinnati Milling welcomed the computer. In 1955 it was one of several companies awarded Air

Force contracts for the manufacture of computerized machines. The technology for developing a method of numerical controls for milling machines was available, but Cincinnati Milling proceeded to develop its own. In 1958 it shipped its first machine to the Air Force. In another year it was applying the technology to other machines. Engineers at the company were also groundbreakers in the field of software production and CINAP was among the first numerical control packages available on the commercial market. The company developed a "machining center," which had the capability of changing tools for different cutting operations by computer control.

The advent of miniaturized circuits in the 1960s, as noted, signaled a major step forward in computer technology. Until this time Cincinnati Milling, although it had been making some progress, appeared to be falling behind in the field. However, it now pressed ahead and in 1966 came out with Acramatic IV. The idea had originally been developed for use in the government's Minuteman Guidance system; however, the company adapted it to commercial use and stole a march on its competition. It boasted that "each tiny IC (integrated circuit) in the Acramatic IV replaced as many as 90 discrete components. IC's made it possible to increase control reliability by a factor of ten while shrinking the size of the control unit itself."

In 1968, after three years of research, Cincinnati Milling engineers developed a computerized system to automate the production of machine parts. Called a "flexible manufacturing system" (FMS), it incorporated a central computer which controlled the routing of workpieces to individual numerical control machines. While it was slow to catch on, the flexible manufacturing system might be viewed as the initial step in designing the "factory of the future." Thus through diversification and computer technology Cincinnati Milling had broken sharply with its prewar history. In fact, its name no longer suited its product and processes. In January 1970 the Cincinnati Milling Machine Company became Cincinnati Milacron.

It was a different story up in Dayton at National Cash Register. In the early 1950s the company's president, Stanley C. Allyn, acknowledged that NCR was at a fork in the road with the advent of computers. It could either stay with its original mechanical products with the prospect of only limited growth, or it could forget the past and move fully into computers and risk the financial dangers common to any uncharted field. Not everyone in the company believed that the future was necessarily wedded to computers. Business with the mechanical machines had been so good in the twenty years since the war that it was not easy to let go. Therein lay the dilemma. NCR tried to combine the new with the old and got into trouble.

NCR did go into computers, all right, and may have even recorded a few "firsts." As early as 1952 the company acquired a young California firm, Computer Research Corporation, which became NCR's Electronics Division. In 1957 the company came out with the NCR 304 data processing system, which was installed at the Marine Corps base at Camp Pendleton, California, and later at Marine headquarters in Washington, D.C. A smaller system, the 390, announced in 1960, became widely used for payroll processing by the Air Force and Navy. To accommodate medium-to-small present and potential customers, NCR installed data processing centers at half a dozen cities both in this country and abroad. In 1962 NCR was among the first companies to use the Telstar satellite for data transmission. A year later it introduced the 315, a full on-line system for banking operations. NCR took its most important step into the computer market in 1968, with its two-part Century Series.

However, throughout the 1950s and 1960s NCR never gave computers a very high priority. Demand for mechanical registers, accounting machines, and other traditional products remained high during this period and most of the company's attention was focused upon them. Plant facilities were expanded and sales offices were added. In 1960 NCR employment throughout the world totaled 52,000 and revenues were close to $500 million. New products were introduced regularly, in addition to cash registers and accounting machines. Kits were prepared to help workmen modify older machines in India, Pakistan, and South Africa, then shifting to the decimal system. The prosperity which the traditional machines were bringing the company apparently clouded management's view of the broader picture. Robert Oelman, who became president in 1960, continued the policies of his predecessor. That is, while expanding computer production, the chief emphasis remained on the manufacture and marketing of mechanical business machines. The bulk of NCR's income was derived, by a substantial margin, from the traditional market throughout the 1960s.

But problems began to emerge during that decade, which would soon bring the company to the brink of extinction. One was the escalating costs of its computer rental service. Another was the difficult position company salesmen found themselves in as they attempted to peddle both computers and mechanical machines, the one competing with the other. Moreover, as noted, management preferred improving the mechanical machines rather than developing new ideas. As an example, as late as 1967 NCR brought out a brand new mechanical register, the Class 5. It could do all kinds of things, but not as many as a computerized machine could do more economically. As the Class 5 contained thousands of parts it was an expensive machine to manufacture. So it was with most of the mechanical machines: they sold well, but costs were eating up profits. Revenues doubled from $458 million in 1958 to $1.1 billion in 1968, but profits did not go up accordingly. NCR was eighty-ninth in revenue in *Fortune* 500's 1968 list, but 334th in profits. Even the company's biggest plunge into computers, the Century Series, had been costly to produce and developed performance problems.

The cumulative effect of rising manufacturing costs for old products, marketing difficulties with new products, inflation, recession, and higher unemployment led to a drop in sales in 1970 and 1971. Orders were cancelled and NCR was forced to cut back production and to fire workers. While 1970 revenues were 12 percent above those of 1969, earn-ings dropped from forty-six million dollars to thirty million. The worst was yet to come. In 1971 earnings dropped to $1.3 million. A bitter strike of 8,500 workers idled the Dayton plant from October 1971 through January 1972 and contributed to the poor earnings report for 1971.

Summoned to the rescue was a man who had headed up NCR's successful Japanese operation. William R. Anderson had joined NCR in 1945, soon after his release from a Japanese prison camp, where he had spent the previous four years. After service with the Hong Kong branch he took over the Japanese office in 1960. It was the number-one overseas facility when in 1972 Anderson was called to Dayton. He was in his early fifties at the time. The new president stated quite clearly that the company's future depended on its total commitment to the computer. He eliminated old mechanical machine operations and began converting the various plants to the new mode. In addition, he decentralized manufacturing and instituted vocational marketing. Although recovery was slow, NCR eventually got back on the road to economic health. When Anderson retired in 1984, NCR was among the world leaders in electronic and computer systems.

One Cleveland-based firm which rose to the front ranks of major industrial concerns after World War II was TRW Inc., formerly known as Thompson Products. Founded in 1902 as a manufacturer of valves for automobiles, the company grew up with the auto industry. It benefited handsomely from an early agreement with the Winton Company and improved its condition during World War I. In the 1920s it developed the Silcrome valve which was important for the aircraft, as well as the automotive, industry. In 1926 it became Thompson Products Inc., honoring the man who had nursed the company from infancy to maturity, Charles E. Thompson.

The Depression hurt Thompson Products, but the company returned to health in the late 1930s under the leadership of its new president, Frederick C. Crawford. World War II boosted the fortunes of the organization as most of its products were easily adapted to military usage. Reconversion to peacetime presented no problem for the company as sales rose steadily from $64 million in 1946 to $125 million in 1950. During the Korean War the figure more than doubled to $327 million.

The "quantum leap" forward came in 1953 when Thompson, poised to press on to new frontiers, backed an infant California company, the Ramo-Wooldridge Corporation. Dean Wooldridge and Simon Ramo, brilliant Cal Tech Ph.Ds., specialized in ballistic missile design at a time when the United States was deeply immersed in competition with the Soviet Union in this new field. In 1955 their company became the technical advisor for a $17-billion ballistic missile program for the Air Force. Within two years this program grew to such dimensions that it involved 220 major contractors and thousands of subcontractors. The work force exceeded 3,000 and revenues were over twenty-eight million dollars. In 1958 Thompson absorbed Ramo-Wooldridge thereby forming Thompson Ramo Wooldridge. In 1965 the name was changed to TRW Inc.

In the 1950s and 1960s TRW began to diversify heavily and expand its overseas operations. It acquired auto parts, oil field equipment, and electronic companies. It pushed into markets throughout Europe, Asia, and South America. By the mid '80s international sales brought in 30 percent of all revenues. Its three main divisions were Car and Truck, Electronics and Space Systems, and Industrial and Energy. For research and development, the company built its Space Park in Redondo Beach, California. Of the 17,000 scientists employed there, 750 had Ph.D. degrees. By 1977 sales cleared the $3.2-billion figure. In 1985 TRW ranked fifty-ninth on the *Fortune* list with revenues in excess of six billion dollars.

In Canton another company, somewhat unique, adjusted well to the economic climate of postwar America. Perhaps its uniqueness was a factor. Diebold Incorporated, founded in Cincinnati in 1859, manufactures industrial security systems. These include bank safes and vaults, alarm systems, cash and record protection equipment, and information retrieval and material handling systems. Diebold had no second thoughts about computerizing its diverse product lines as soon as the technology was available.

The terrible Chicago fire of October 8, 1871, the year before Diebold moved to Canton, gave a big assist to the company's fortunes. Diebold had 878 safes installed in banks and other buildings in the Windy City. Despite the awesome destruction wrought by Mrs. O'Leary's thoughtless cow, all 878 safes survived the holocaust with contents intact. The free publicity afforded by this led to a flood of orders for Diebold safes and vaults. And the company has built some big ones. In 1874 Wells Fargo ordered the largest vault ever built up until that time. It required forty-seven railroad freight cars to ship the monster to San Francisco. The Detroit National Bank ordered the biggest vault for a commercial bank in 1921, only to be outdone by one commissioned by the Union Trust Company in Cleveland three years later.

From the company's inception, Diebold's engineers have had a running battle with resourceful bank robbers. To frustrate burglars who possessed duplicate keys, combination locks were devised. To foil kidnappers of bank cashiers who knew the combinations, the automatic time-lock came into being. When burglars started using TNT to blow up time-lock vault doors, Diebold pioneered in the manufacture of manganese steel doors which withstood TNT. Decades of experience with bank robbers have caused Diebold engineers to develop sufficient knowledge and expertise to design vaults which are virtually impregnable today.

Postwar architectural trends in business and industrial design stressed cleanliness, spaciousness, and style. Diebold caught the spirit with its Basic Vault Door in 1951. Without compromising security, the vault, whether it was open or shut, blended in nicely with the building's decor and became the interior showcase of the bank. A revolutionary wedge-lock door introduced in 1956, which was installed in many banks, similarly was designed to be architecturally harmonious with the

The Armco plant in Hamilton, a city in the lower Miami Valley, was described in The Ohio Guide *in 1940 as follows: "Here amid a welter of long buildings, giant smokestacks, tracks, and large cranes, are the furnaces and pits in which iron ore is changed into all types of steel." Courtesy, Western Reserve Historical Society*

environment.

Diebold began diversifying in 1938 when it made its first tentative step into information retrieval. Work in this area was intensified after World War II and the engineers developed highly sophisticated processes for easy storage and quick recovery of vast amounts of data. With the acquisition of the Herring-Hall-Marvin Safe Company of Hamilton, Ohio, in 1959, Diebold moved into the bankteller counter equipment field. Drive-in banking caught on in the early 1950s, but many of the early systems were not practical. Diebold devised a plan whereby closed circuit television and an inter-com network brought customer and teller close together. The company even manufactured a drive-in unit which extended itself outward to meet the reach of a customer who had parked too far away.

Unlike Diebold, Parker Hannifin Corporation of Cleveland, one of the leaders in the manufacture of fluid drive systems, had a bumpy postwar adjust-ment. Arthur Parker founded the Parker Appliance Company in 1918, but it failed in 1919. He started it up again in 1924 and, by linking the firm closely to the nascent aviation industry, was able to carry it through the Depression. With the outbreak of World War II, Parker Appliance was well-fixed to secure government contracts. During those years it became the world's largest manufacturer of hydrau-lic connecting and flow control devices.

The problem with this was that all of Parker's business was with the federal government and once the war ended, all contracts were cancelled. Employ-ment dropped from 5,000 to 300 within a few months of the war's close. The plant was idle and the family—Arthur Parker had just died—was ready to abandon the business. Stubborn Mrs. Helen Parker, however, said "no," and resolved to rebuild. New but experienced corporate managers were brought in and under their guidance the company's condition improved. Fluid power technology was the basis for the company's successful return to industrial respectability. Parker's position was enhanced in 1957 with the acquisition of the Han-nifin Manufacturing Company of Des Plaines, Illi-nois. The corporate name was changed at this time to Parker Hannifin.

Goodyear enjoyed many good years in postwar America. The new age was marked by advanced product lines and stepped-up emphasis in marketing and public relations. But perhaps the company's out-standing achievement was the globalization of its operations. By 1955 Goodyear production facilities had been expanded to include seventeen countries in Europe, Asia, and South America. In 1957 Good-year International Corporation was created as an umbrella management organization for overseas facil-ities. That same year, the Goodyear Technical Cen-ter-Europe was opened at Colmar-Berg in Luxem-bourg, which in time became a mammoth center of research and development and the second largest employer in the country. Within the next ten years, European operations were accelerated with the opening of new plants in France, Italy, and West Ger-many. In the early 1970s the company opened the first tire-making factory in Zaire.

Following the war, rubber consumption in the United States was divided between the natural and synthetic varieties, although in Europe natural rubber had a commanding lead. While Goodyear pos-sessed large sources for natural rubber, it remained the biggest American producer of synthetic rubber throughout the 1950s. In 1954 Goodyear produced its first tubeless tire. But the most important break-through in tire construction came from France with Michelin's radial in 1948. The radial caught on quickly in Europe in the next two decades, but was resisted in the United States. Goodyear developed what was called a "transitional" tire in the 1960s, something halfway between the traditional and the radial, but the future was obviously with the radial. Following Michelin's all-out invasion of the Ameri-can tire market by 1970, Goodyear and the others recognized that they had better regroup and go to the radial.

Through its experience in aviation, Goodyear early entered into the aerospace business. In 1963 the Goodyear Aircraft Corporation was renamed the Goodyear Aerospace Corporation. The company pro-duced parts for missile, guidance, and radar systems, ground support equipment, flight simulators, and space satellites. Air-conditioning and heating sys-tems were installed in the Apollo 11 and Apollo 12 spaceships, which carried out the first two moon landings. The two-wheeled rickshaw which astro-nauts Alan Shepard and Ed Mitchell piloted over the moon's surface on Apollo 14 was equipped with Goodyear tires. Flotation bags used to flip over upside-down spaceships as they landed in the ocean were also made by Goodyear.

Goodyear had sponsored racing cars as a promo-tional tool in its early years, but had dropped the practice after World War I. However, following World War II sports car sponsorship became an important advertising weapon. The increase in auto racing as a spectator sport and the great success Fire-stone and Dunlop were enjoying in promoting their tires could not be ignored. A prestige factor was involved as well. The manufacturers of tires of win-ning cars had a big advantage over other tire com-panies. Goodyear inconspicuously began sponsoring entrants in major races in the mid-1950s and within a decade had attained parity with other companies. The first Goodyear driver to win the Indianapolis 500 was A.J. Foyt in 1967.

Goodyear began advertising on television even before it got back into racing, sponsoring "The Paul Whiteman Revue" in 1949. "TV Playhouse" was another program sponsored by the company during television's first decade. An important promotional project was the widespread use of the Goodyear blimp at sporting and ceremonial functions around the country. In 1958 only one blimp was in service and it was about to be mothballed when a new and enterprising public relations man, Robert H. Lane, recognized its advertising possibilities. By the midsixties a number of new blimps had been built and were in great demand, particularly by television networks, to serve as aerial camera platforms for football and baseball games, yacht races, golf matches, auto races, and world fairs. Television audiences came to expect to see the "Goodyear of goodwill" at sporting events.

Goodyear faced some problems in this era of growth and globalization. First, there was an upsurge in tire imports from abroad in the last half of the 1960s. Foreign auto and truck imports jumped from 3 percent of the American market in 1965 to 9 percent five years later. Cheaper labor costs, differential tariffs, and government subsidies all contributed to the less expensive foreign products. The growing demands from environmentalists for pollution controls led to a battery of rules and regulations, with which all industries had to comply. The threat of the radial hung overhead, while the company delayed entering the competition. The energy crisis of 1973-1974 sparked by the sharp rise in oil prices impacted on the entire economy, but especially on auto-related industries, such as tire manufacturers. Finally, labor unrest, which developed during the "age of protest" in the late 1960s and early 1970s, led to massive strikes.

Despite these difficulties, Goodyear's sales and earnings proceeded steadily upward. In 1952 it was the first tire company to exceed $1 billion in annual sales. By 1958 sales were up to $1.3 billion and in the mid-1960s broke through the $2-billion barrier. In 1969 Goodyear was the first rubber company to pass the $3-billion mark in sales. Strikes in the auto, rubber, and trucking industries in 1970 caused a drop that year, but from 1971 through 1982 there were regular increases in both sales and earnings. Foreign subsidiaries showed a similar steady growth during the same period.

Like other "smokestack" states, Ohio's heyday of industrial glory had passed. Heavy industry, as spawned by the Industrial Revolution, was giving way to a new type of business activity, one which supplied the consuming public with the countless goods and services its enhanced economic con-

dition demanded. The nation's industrial plant, you might say, had been built. What was now needed were the refinements, the frills, and the luxuries that an affluent society could afford. Thus there emerged sometime after World War II the "post-industrial age," a time when "service" industries moved to the forefront, rivaling, if not surpassing, the once vaunted industrial giants that had made the United States a formidable economic power.

———

The American Ship Building Company, formed through the merger of the Cleveland Shipbuilding Company, Globe Iron Works Company, and the Shipowners Dry Dock Company, is shown here celebrating its 50th anniversary. Within five years of the company's formation, it had constructed 181 vessels and was involved in the construction of more ships for the Allied effort during WWI and WWII. Courtesy, Western Reserve Historical Society

VIII
THE POST-INDUSTRIAL AGE

As in the past, the Ohio River remains the major artery for an economically thriving state. Photo by Deborah E. Sarabia

Facing page: This ad for Procter & Gamble's new washing product was placed in newspapers in 1946. At first only available in six U.S. cities, Tide was a great success for the Cincinnati-based company. Courtesy, the Procter & Gamble Company

The later postwar era has become associated with the rise of "service" industries. *Fortune* initiated this new classification in 1983, although the distinction had been commonly recognized for many years with the development of the "postindustrial" society. A service company is a nonindustrial concern, with 50 percent or more of its revenues derived from nonmanufacturing. The chief subcategories of service organizations are diversified financial, diversified service, commercial banking, insurance, retailing, transportation, and utilities. As the years passed, many of Ohio's leading companies transformed into different entities but in the mid-1980s Ohio ranked fifth nationally in headquarters for service corporations with twenty-five, being surpassed by California, New York, Texas, and Illinois. As for cities, Cleveland was eleventh nationally, Columbus tied for eighteenth, and Cincinnati tied for twenty-second.

Statewide, Kroger was by far the largest company in retailing, while Roadway lead in transportation, Ohio Casualty in diversified financial, Nationwide in insurance, American Electric Power in utilities, Super Food Services in diversified service, and National City Corp. in banking. What is intriguing about this list of service leaders is that four of the seven—Kroger, Ohio Casualty, Nationwide, and American Electric Power—were located in Cincinnati and Columbus, cities which lagged behind during the glory days of heavy industry. They appeared to symbolize the postindustrial era.

Burger King, McDonald's, Hardee's, Taco Bell, Long John Silver's—all became familiar names along the "fast food freeways" of most American cities. Although a later development in the changing postwar American scene, the fast food restaurant is now such a part of the lives of Americans that we sometimes wonder how

we ever got along without them. Indeed, by the year 2000, Americans were eating the greater proportion of their meals outside of the home.

One of the most famous fast food restaurants is Columbus-based Wendy's International Inc., founded in 1969. R. David Thomas, born in Atlantic City, New Jersey, in 1932, always "wanted to be in the hamburger business." Orphaned at an early age, he traveled about the Midwest as a teenager with his adopted father, a construction worker. He worked in several restaurants during World War II, entering military service in 1949. Still a teenager, he was the youngest soldier to manage an NCO club. In the mid-1950s, a civilian again, Thomas worked at the Hobby House Restaurant in Fort Wayne, Indiana, which held an early Kentucky Fried Chicken franchise. He worked with and learned much from Colonel Harland Sanders. In 1962 he took over the operations of four failing Kentucky Fried Chicken restaurants in Columbus and turned them around. But he still wanted to get into hamburgers.

On November 15, 1969, the first Wendy's Old-Fashioned Hamburgers restaurant was opened in Columbus. The name was taken from Thomas' eight-year-old daughter, Melinda, called "Wendy" by her brother and sisters. In charge of his own place, Thomas was now able to apply a few of the ideas he had gathered in the fifteen years or so of his apprenticeship in the business. He insisted on the use of "100 percent pure American beef," served

fresh daily rather than being prepackaged and heated by a lamp. He also offered customers a broad array of condiments to season their hamburgers. Made-to-order hamburgers and the novel pick-up window, in the view of the company historian, "revolutionized the fast service restaurant industry and sparked Wendy's rapid growth across the nation in the early to mid-1970s."

It was one full year later, in November of 1970, before the second Wendy's restaurant was opened. This was also in Columbus. From that point onward the chain expanded rapidly throughout the Midwest. On June 25, 1975, the 100th restaurant was opened in Louisville, Kentucky. One and one-half years later the 500th restaurant opened in Toronto, Canada. At the end of 1985, 3,442 restaurants were scattered throughout all fifty states and eighteen foreign countries. In just over fifteen years, R. David Thomas' brainchild had become the world's fourth-largest restaurant chain, with annual sales well over $2.5 billion.

Wendy's rapid growth and success were linked to its energetic television advertising campaign. Beginning in 1973 the company ran ads on local radio and television stations. In April 1977 it went national with a "Hot N' Juicy" ad. The commercial ran for three years and, according to a marketing official, "put Wendy's on the map." It ran on breaks during *Monday Night Football* and the *Tonight Show*, and earned the Clio Award for creativity. In 1980 the company introduced both its salad bar and

Bob Evans shows a grill cook the proper procedure for frying sausage. Evans began making his own sausage in the late 1940s because he couldn't obtain sausage of comparable quality in the Midwest. Bob Evans Farms employs more than 12,000 workers and sells its sausage in nineteen states. Courtesy, Bob Evans Farms, Inc.

chicken sandwich, which were featured in its "Wendy's Has the Taste" ad. In 1984 Clara Peller's 'Where's the Beef?" query perhaps more than anything made Wendy's a household name.

Although not as well-known nationally in the food business as Wendy's, but perhaps more "Ohioan," is Bob Evans Farms Inc. Born on a farm in rural northeastern Ohio in 1918, Bob Evans began putting together his "sausage empire" in 1946, soon after his return from military service. That year he opened the twenty-four-hour Bob Evans Steak House just outside Gallipolis. The breakfasts were popular, especially with truck drivers, but there were complaints about the sausages. Bob Evans decided to make sausages using hogs from his own farm in nearby Bidwell. The sausage was sold in retail stores in southeastern Ohio as well as at the Steak House. So well-received were Bob Evans' sausage products that in 1953 a second plant was established near Xenia. Later, additional plants were opened in Hillsdale, Michigan, Galva, Illinois, and Gallipolis.

Evans bought another farm at Rio Grande, about twelve miles west of Gallipolis, in the early 1950s, which over the years has become a tourist attraction and showcase for many activities. People began visiting the farm in such numbers that in 1962 a small restaurant was opened to accommodate them.

Above: Bob Evans is pictured here at his Rio Grande farm, posing with his mare and colt. Built in 1824, his home was once used as a stagecoach stop and inn. Courtesy, Bob Evans Farms, Inc.

Left: Bob Evans' 1,100-acre Rio Grande farm in southeastern Ohio has become a tourist attraction, hosting special events from April through October. Courtesy, Bob Evans Farms, Inc.

David Frisch bought the first Big Boy franchise in the 1920s and opened his first restaurant in Norwood. This picture shows the thirteen original Frisch's Big Boy Restaurants. Courtesy, Cincinnati Historical Society

In 1969 a third restaurant was opened in Chillocothe, the first of the standardized "Red-and White" design. The number of restaurants grew steadily, although the total never reached that of Wendy's chain. In the mid-1980s over 165 "family" restaurants had been spawned from Michigan to Florida, from Pennsylvania to Missouri. In addition, the five pork-packing plants were delivering fresh pork regularly to 7,600 retail outlets in nineteen states throughout most of the eastern part of the country.

People kept coming to the farm. In 1970 it was decided to hold a farm festival and 10,000 visitors arrived. The festivals became so popular that twenty were held each summer—including an International Chicken Flying Meet, a Country Music Convention, Homesteading Days, and a 4-H Fall Round-up—which culminated in a kind of Oktoberfest every autumn. Various outdoor activities—horseback riding, canoeing, and hiking—were available to guests at the 1,100-acre plantation. Cattle were bred, horses are raised, and tobacco, sugarcane, corn, and wheat are grown. Bob Evans, his sausages, and his restaurants became an Ohio institution.

Although Wendy's was the largest fast food company headquartered in Ohio, it was not the only one. A Columbus competitor was Rax Restaurants, whichmade its first appearance in *The Ohio Roster* in 1986. Other major Ohio restaurant systems were Ponderosa, based in Dayton, and Frisch's in Cincinnati. The largest Ohio corporation according to earnings was Kroger Company of Cincinnati. The revenue figures for the multistate super-market chain exceeded seventeen billion dollars. It ranked fourth nationally in *Fortune's* list of retail organizations and first in *Business Week's* list of food retailers. Other large

Ohio supermarket chains, no longer in business now gone, were Big Bear (based in Columbus), Fisher Foods (Cleveland), and Seaway Food Town (Toledo). Others were Super Food Services of Dayton a large food wholesaler with sales close to $1.4 billion; and J.M. Smucker, a more diversified food manufacturer in Orrville.

Rubbermaid, now known as Newell Rubbermaid and located in Georgia, originally began as the Wooster Rubber Company in 1920, a manufacturer of toy balloons. Rubber dustpans first appeared in 1934, a central turning point in the company's history. From then on, as a major producer of rubber and plastic products for household use, Rubbermaid began the growth which has placed it in a commanding position in the field. The name Rubbermaid was adopted in 1937. The coinpany had never gone in much for diversification, staying primarily with rubber and plastic goods. In those areas it did well, despite being a relatively small organization. Employees manned Rubbermaid facilities throughout the United States, Canada, and Europe, manufacturing many vari-eties of sinkware, bathware, food containers, "roughneck" containers, and microwave cookware.

The coming of age of the automobile in the 1930s, 1940s, and 1950s not only led to the decline of the railroad, but contributed directly to the rise of a major postwar industry—trucking. And one of the top trucking companies in the country was headquartered in Akron. It was in 1930 that a young Akron attorney, Galen J. Roush, formed Roadway Express. He recognized the need for a direct means of transport between his hometown tire center, the auto center in Detroit, and other major cities. Within a couple of years Roadway terminals dotted

"Look, Mom—no cavities!"

Crest Toothpaste stops soft spots from turning into cavities—means far less decay for grownups and children. And Crest freshens your mouth—sweetens your breath.

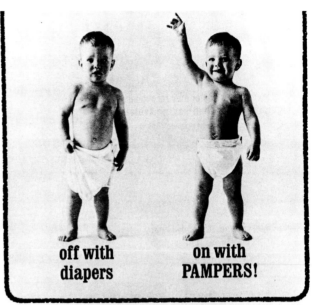

off with diapers

on with PAMPERS!

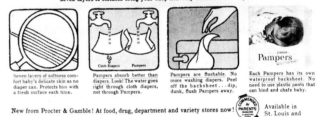

Pampers®—the discovery that makes diapers old-fashioned!

Seven layers of softness bring your baby heavenly comfort as no diaper can!

Seven layers of softness comfort baby's delicate skin as no diaper can. Protects him with a fresh surface each time.

Pampers absorb better than diapers. Look! The water goes right through cloth diapers, not through Pampers.

Pampers are flushable. No more washing diapers. Peel off the backsheet...dip, dunk, flush Pampers away.

Each Pampers has its own waterproof backsheet. No need to use plastic pants that can bind and chafe baby.

New from Procter & Gamble! At food, drug, department and variety stores now!

Available in St. Louis and eastern Missouri

the map throughout the East and South. Originally, the drivers operated their own trucks under a franchise arrangement with Roadway. In 1945, however, the company acquired its own trucks and equipment.

At the end of the war Roadway introduced a novel distribution system, beneficial to small communities. The company's trucks would carry less-than-full loads from tiny towns to large central "break-bulk" terminals for consolidation and distribution. Similarly, less-than-full loads would be transferred from the break-bulk centers to satellite terminals in small places. Over 500 Roadway terminals are scattered across the country today, mostly in the Midwest, East, and South. Break-bulk terminals are to be found in places like Chicago, Kansas City, St. Louis, Toledo, Cincinnati, Columbus, Memphis, Nashville, Winston-Salem, Atlanta, Buffalo, and Phoenix. Forty-two thousand communities are served in this fashion.

The importance of trucking in postwar America is readily seen from an examination of Roadway's growth. In 1951 the company had only fifty-two terminals. This figure increased to 178 in 1971 and to 506 in 1982. For these same years revenue grew from about $50 million to $400 million to $1.2 bil-

Above: Pampers disposable diapers has been a successful product from the time it was first marketed by Procter & Gamble in the 1960s. Courtesy, the Procter & Gamble Company

Above left: Norman Rockwell painted this 1957 advertisement for Crest toothpaste. When Procter & Gamble finally obtained the American Dental Association's endorsement of Crest, the toothpaste became the best-selling brand in the country. Courtesy, the Procter & Gamble Company

lion. Income followed a similar path upward. Today, Roadway operating within YRC National Transportation, is headquartered in Overland Park, Kansas. It is classed as an international corporation since it ships across the borders into both Mexico and Canada.

An old familiar name, Procter & Gamble, made important contributions to consumer-oriented, post-World War II America. Within fourteen years the soapmaking company came out with three products which forever changed the lives of housewives and consumers, to say nothing of brand new babies. In 1947 it was Tide, in 1955 it was Crest, and in 1961 it was Pampers. Interestingly, only one of these three products had anything to do with soap.

Research advances during the 1930s and World War II led to the development of a heavy, multiduty laundry detergent. However, test-marketing had to be delayed until the war was over. But when Tide was put on trial it was a smashing success. Nothing before had ever been able to wash clothes cleaner, leave colors brighter, make better suds, make clothes whiter, and eliminate hardwater problems all at the same time, as did Tide. The new product overwhelmed all other soap products. Along with the advent of the automatic washing machine, it immeasurably eased the burden of homemakers. Ironically, it destroyed almost half of the company's market for traditional soap products and made obsolete a sizable bulk of its soap-manufacturing equipment.

Procter & Gamble had some experience in toiletries as early as 1933, but it was not until after the war that we heard about Prell Concentrate, Lilt-Home Permanents, and Gleem Toothpaste. Soon the company was into therapeutics. Working closely with researchers at Indiana University, the company developed a fluoride compound which became the basis for an anticavity toothpaste. Crest was successfully test-marketed in 1955, but was not the instant success that Tide had been. It was more difficult to quickly demonstrate the benefits of a dentifrice than it was with a detergent.

To give its new product credibility, Procter & Gamble went to the American Dental Association, which had made a practice of not endorsing tooth-pastes. For five years ADA scientists tested and eval-uated Crest. In August 1960 it reported that "Crest has been shown to be an effective anticaries [tooth decay preventive] dentifrice that can be of significant value when used in a . . . program of oral hygiene and regular professional care." This was the recognition the company needed and within two years Crest was by far the best-selling toothpaste in the country.

Building on the success of Crest, Procter & Gam-ble moved further into the health-care field and by the mid-1980s had become the largest manufacturer of over-the-counter drugs in the United States.

But what put young mothers into the company's debt was Pampers. Developing a highly absorbent pad that could be encased in a plastic wrapper was not only unpleasant, but complicated. 'We had to design the entire production line from the ground up," said one of the engineers. At length the problems were overcome and test-marketing began in Peoria, Illinois, in late 1961. One of the early users of the disposable diaper was Beverly Greenhall of Peoria. She first used Pampers on her daughter, Vickie, who was born December 10, 1961. In 1986 Procter & Gamble held a twenty-fifth anniversary party in Peoria, and twenty-four-year-old Vickie, now Mrs. Williams, was one of the honored guests. Her eighteen-month-old son Andrew naturally was equipped with Pampers.

Three other Ohio companies illustrate the range of service industries and further emphasize the significant role Cincinnati and Columbus play in the consumer-oriented economy of the modern day. In fact, many well-known national retail stores are actually parts of Federated Department Stores and United States Shoe Corporation, both of Cincinnati, and The Limited of Columbus.

Federated, one of the largest department stores in the country, was founded in the late 1920s when five independent stores—Lazarus, Shillito's, Filene's, Abraham and Straus, and Bloomingdales—were brought together under one large umbrella. Fred Lazarus assumed control of the combine in 1945 and commenced an acquisition policy by which he built an empire of fifteen "divisions" by 1970. Among the acquisitions were Foley's (Houston), Bullock's (Los Angeles), I. Magnin (San Francisco), Rike's (Milwaukee), Goldsmith (Memphis), and Burdine's (Miami). Pursuing a strategy of strong divisional autonomy in which "upside-down" or buyer management plays a significant role, Federated rose to its preeminent position in the retail field. In the mid-1980s *Fortune* listed it eighth among all retail stores by sales and fifth by income.

United States Shoe is a good example of a company which came into being to do one thing, but which over the years evolved into a service industry. It was founded at a most unlikely time, 1931, by the merger of two small Cincinnati shoe manufacturers. Growth was slow but steady. Expansion

resulted largely from acquisitions of other shoe companies, but also from the construction of several new factories. Until 1962 United Shoe was strictly a manufacturer of footwear, but that year, with the purchase of Wm. Hahn and Co., it entered the retailing field. Then in 1970 it acquired Casual Corner, a retailing chain specializing in women's apparel. Other specialty shops were added, catering to young women, "misses," "petite misses," and young men. Lenscrafter optical was another addition, marking United States Shoe's entry into the healthcare field. By the mid-1980s the company has 2,267 retail stores, while only 373 handle footwear. Luxottica Group an eyewear company later purchased the firm.

The Limited of Columbus, a retailer specializing in women's clothing, is another billion-dollar-plus corporation. Leslie H. Wexner, the owner, ranks in *Forbes'* collection of billionaires. The employees of the company man such stores as Victoria's Secret, Bath & Body Works, and Henri Bendel. Wexner started out with one store, but by acquiring failing chain groups he built an empire. He also opened up a number of men's apparel shops.

A common feature of American suburbia from the 1950s forward has been the shopping center—that mammoth aggregation of retail outlets, grouped together, which sell almost anything anyone would ever want to buy. The founder of the shopping center was Youngstown billionaire Edward J. DeBartolo, Sr. A graduate of Notre Dame and a World War II veteran, DeBartolo first worked for his father, a paving contractor. He thought of building shopping malls in 1949 and plunged boldly ahead with the untested idea. It was a great success and in the next decade he built over 100 shopping centers. Seeking new fields, DeBartolo sold most of the plazas and turned his attention to enclosed shopping malls in the 1960s. DeBartolo became the largest mall developer in the country.

From what has been written to this point, the postwar economic picture would appear to be a prosperous one. Many companies expanded, diversified, globalized, and made a lot of money. Numerous new enterprises also did very well. Ohio continued to rank among the top states in the country in manufacturing, services, and financial institutions. It has had its share of corporations among *Fortune's* elite 500. The state's location is still a good one, serviced as it is by interstates and airports. Its natural resources are not as plentiful as they once were, but they remain an important component in the industrial scene. Still many things have changed, which, to a degree, have blunted Ohio's industrial progress.

From the end of the war until the 1960s, the

state's economic growth continued unabated. Yet there was an uneasiness about this growth. The decline in manufacturing jobs had proceeded steadily despite increased production. Automation was beginning to take its toll. In the late 1960s, for the first time in Ohio's history, the number of workers engaged in services exceeded those in manufacturing. By 1970 the figures were 54 percent in services and 46 percent in manufacturing. The postindustrial age was at hand.

Because of liberal concessions to trade unions, workers' wages and benefits increased steadily. These high labor costs led to developments that

Like its neighboring state, Kentucky, Ohio recently attracted foreign car manufacturers. A Honda of America Manfacturing facility is headquartered in Marysville and abides by the company's motto, "Accept no bad parts, make no bad parts, and pass no bad parts." Pictured here is a quality assurance inspection. Courtesy, Honda of America Manufacturing, Inc.

were not good for either labor or the state. For one thing, strikes accelerated the trend toward automating plant facilities. For another, where unions proved intransigent to making changes or concessions, plants were sometimes closed down. For still another, companies with labor difficulties found it simpler to move to the "Sun Belt," where unions were less strong than in the northern "Rust Belt." As a corollary to this, when stories about the militancy of Ohio labor got out—not that such reports were new—the natural tendency was for companies to look elsewhere when planning to build a new plant. Moreover, excessive labor costs led directly to a flood of foreign imports, particularly automobiles, which could be produced more cheaply than the American product. "Buy American" has a noble ring, but in an age of heavy inflation, Americans will shop for lower-priced goods.

Honda of Japan was one of the first foreign companies to "invade" the American auto market with a cheaper product. At the time of the 1973 oil embargo Honda introduced into the United States its fuel-efficient Civic. Honda expanded its offerings in the next several years and the response was so good that in 1977 it decided to build an American

assembly plant. It chose Marysville, Ohio, about twenty-five miles northwest of Columbus, as the site. Honda already had a prosperous motorcycle factory in Marysville and the auto plant was to be built next to it. The first automobile rolled off the assembly line in 1982 in time to circumvent the quota on imported Japanese cars. So successful was this operation that Honda constructed an engine plant in Marysville.

The Marysville facility is unlike the typical American automobile factory. The workers are not unionized, although they are paid well and receive fringe benefits. They also operate under a "democratic discipline" that the United Automobile Workers would have difficulty living with. Other Japanese automakers have been quick to follow Honda's example in building American plants—Nissan built a facility at Smyrna, Tennessee, and Toyota at Georgetown, Kentucky.

But other factors contributed to the malaise of Ohio business in the 1960s and 1970s. Industrially speaking, Ohio was an out-of-date state. It was deep

The Honda of America Manufacturing auto plant in Marysville has all manufacturing operations located under one roof. Here in the welding department, the body of a Civic sedan is checked, cleaned, and inspected prior to painting. Only three years after beginning production at Marysville, Honda of America became the fourth largest auto manufacturer in the United States. Courtesy, Honda of America Manufacturing, Inc.

Right: This Honda employee is using a computer-aided probe system to check quality before the blocks are passed to assembly. This engine plant, located in Anna, can turn out 90,000 engines per year. Courtesy, Honda of America Manufacturing, Inc.

Below right: Honda's 260,000-square-foot plant in Marysville was the company's first motorcycle facility in the United States. Opened in 1979, with a production capacity of 60,000 cycles per year, the plant adheres to the philosophy that "Honda quality is built in, not inspected in later." Pictured here is a step along the assembly line of the Gold Wing motorcycle. Courtesy, Honda of America Manufacturing, Inc.

into heavy industry, particularly steel and autos, which was not the wave of the future in the post-industrial age. Though steel and autos were still important, technological change had significantly altered American thinking as to what should be manufactured and how it should be manufactured. The new "hi-tech" engineering had centered itself in the newer states of the South and West. Old-fashioned Ohio had little appeal in this regard. Many Ohio industries were still operating their original plants, which were becoming obsolete.

But even new plants built in Ohio by American companies were not always the answer to the problem. A case in point is the Lordstown "state-of-the-art" factory, built by General Motors west of Youngstown in the mid-1960s. Rather than labor's traditional "gut" issues of wages, hours, and conditions, the problems at Lordstown were psychological. Management's tough policy toward absenteeism and union arrogance, and its determination to maintain maximum production levels, generated a rising resentment among the workers over the humdrum routine of the assembly line. "Alienation" and "depersonalization," new words for work place conditions, characterized the "blue-collar blues." A long strike in 1972 received national attention, as the "new worker"—young, antiauthoritarian, assertive —challenged the traditional management. The workers did win minor concessions, but Ohio's struggling economic image had been struck another blow.

Two other related problems which have plagued industry, not only in Ohio but across the land, are in-plant health hazards and environmental pollution. A strike broke out at the Columbus Coated Fabric plant in February 1974 which lasted well into the summer. Whereas alienation was a factor, as at Lordstown, health safety was perhaps more important. Environmental pollution can only be dealt with by extensive renovation of old plants and the installation of costly antipollution equipment. It was not unusual for some factories to budget over one-third of their resources to clean up the facility. Even the modern Bruce-Mansfield plant devotes nearly half of its annual operational budget to pollution control.

Unemployment figures suggest the ups and downs of the Ohio industrial work force in recent times. Between 1969 and 1977, particularly following the oil crisis of 1973-1974, the eight most industrialized counties lost on the average over 15 percent of their jobs in manufacturing. Dayton (Montgomery County), Youngstown (Mahoning County), and Cleveland (Cuyahoga County)

suffered job losses well above the 15 percent figure. Something like 140,000 jobs in all were eliminated. The crisis in steel and rubber brought the problem into sharp focus. Two of the oldest and most hallowed industries in the state were dealt near-lethal blows because of plant obsolescence, technological advances, labor costs, and foreign imports.

Steel appeared in good shape until 1959, although there had been some slippage in employment. But a 110-day industry-wide strike that year was a turning point. Plant closings marked the

—

This steam engine provides a nostalgic glimpse into Ohio's past, when lifestyles were slower and less complicated. Although no longer running, in the '80s the Cuyahoga Valley Train Line introduced a twenty-two-mile excursion between Cleveland and Akron through the Cuyahoga Valley National Recreation Area. A 1918 Mikado Steam locomotive pulls the train and its passengers along on a trip into yesterday. Courtesy, Western Reserve Historical Society

1960s and 1970s, culminating in the shocking shutdown of Youngstown Sheet and Tube's massive works in the late 1970s, which cost thousands of steelworkers their jobs. Conditions were no better in Akron. The oil embargo hit the auto industry hard with a rippling effect on tire manufacturing. The United Rubber Workers, fearful of losing hard-fought gains, conducted their longest strike in history, 141 days, in 1976. While gaining substantial wage and cost-of-living increases, the union really won only a "pyrrhic victory." In four years' time the major tire producers closed their Akron plants and transferred manufacturing operations elsewhere. Incredible as it may seem, no automobile tires are manufactured in Akron today.

• • •

The Central Trust Building in downtown Cincinnati stands over a thriving city of industry. Photo by Andrey Gibson

For some years now Ohio has been the object of abuse and ridicule for its supposed economic decline and other shortcomings. It is not an easy matter to sort out the assets and liabilities on such a nebulous balance sheet. Certainly, unemployment has been high and companies have left the state. It is true that the Cuyahoga River caught fire and that Cleveland went bankrupt. Of course, New York City practically went bankrupt at one point and unemployment in Detroit has been high with the slump in automobile production. Many communities across the country have been visited by economic hardship.

Yet when all is said and done, Ohio was the fourth-ranking manufacturing state in the Union in the '80s, a position it has maintained throughout most of the 100 years since the beginning of the Industrial Revolution and the top ten in the 2000s. It was sixth in population and possessed seven major market regions with populations in excess of 500,000. Its central location puts it within a day's motor reach of all of the Midwest and most of the East and South. Ohio is among the top-five states in volume of freight trucked over its numerous interstate highways. Early in the book, Ohio was described as the "Gateway State," the gateway to the West. Today it might well be called the "Gateway to all of the United States."

Corporate industry likes doing business in Ohio, whatever the state's detractors might say. Roughly forty Ohio industries regularly appeared on the *Fortune 500* list through the '90s, a number reduced to about twenty-six by the new millennium, caused in part by mergers and consolidations. The October 1986 edition of *The Ohio Roster* reported that business has recovered substantially from the recession of the early 1980s. "This continued strong performance confirms that Ohio businesses are holding their own in a highly competitive business environment and a low inflation economy," says Gary Pildner, author of *The Ohio Roster*.

The origin, growth, and maturation of industry in Ohio, one of the most important states in the Union, has contributed significantly to America's rise to industrial greatness. It is a story which must ignite a spark of pride in those who call themselves "buckeyes."

Compliments of the STANDARD Sewing Machine Co Cleveland, O.

Previous page: This advertisement was for one of Standard Sewing Machine Company's biggest selling item, the Rotary Shuttle.

Right: Cincinnati became famous in 1811 for the production of beer. With the arrival of more German immigrants to the city, the brewing industry thrived in the 1840s and 1850s. The first lager beer was produced in 1853 by Christian Moerlein, and by 1892 Cincinnati exported 600,000 barrels of lager beer. Pictured here is the Bellevue Brewing Company, formed in 1878, which met its end during Prohibition. Courtesy, Cincinnati Historical Society

Above: Ohio's agricultural resources and industry still contribute significantly to the state's economy. Photo by Tom O'Grady

—

Below: Many of Ohio's historic downtowns are being appreciated for their unique environments and are undergoing revitalization efforts. Photo by Nancy Recchie

Top: The cap built over I-670 in downtown Columbus illustrates how creative planning and development can reestablish the connection between downtown and its surrounding historic neighborhoods. Photo by Nancy Recchie

—

Above: The historic downtown of Granville, Ohio encourages a sense of community through both planned and chance social interaction. Photo by Nancy Recchie

Above: The McIntire Terrace Historic District in Zanesville, is an example of one of Ohio's many historic districts that have been designated and protected with design review. Photo by Jeffrey Darbee

Top: Ohio has many small towns and villages like Granville that retain their pedestrian scale and orientation. Photo by Nancy Recchie

———

Above: Mariemont is a historic planned community near Cincinnati. It has been designated as a National Historic Landmark for its design significance. Courtesy, Mariemont Preservation Foundation.

———

Right: New Albany, located near Columbus, Ohio, started as a small village and is expanding into a planned suburban community. Photo by Nancy Recchie

Aerial view of Put-In-Bay, a popular summer tourist site on Lake Erie. It played a significant role in the War of 1812 as the location of the squadron of U.S. naval Commander Oliver Hazard Perry. Ferry service connects it with Catawba Island, Kelleys Island, Port Clinton, and Sandusky, Ohio. Photo by John E. Rees

Known as a "museum of conscience," The National Underground Railroad Freedom Center is located in Cincinnati, where thousands of slaves once escaped to freedom via the Ohio River. Opened to the public in 2004, the Center challenges visitors to contemplate the meaning of freedom in their own lives. Courtesy, National Underground Railroad Freedom Center

Thousands of acres of both wild and developed land, as well as numerous historical sites, have been preserved in the Cuyahoga Valley National Park, located between Cleveland and Akron. Courtesy, Columbus Metropolitan Library

Geauga Lake first opened in 1888. Courtesy, Geauga Lake & Wildwater and Cedar Fair Entertainment Company

Left: Located in Licking County, The Dawes Arboretum is dedicated to increasing the love and knowledge of trees and nature in general. Founded in 1929 by Beman and Bertie Dawes, The Arboretum houses The Japanese Garden, the Bald-cypress swamps, The Dutch Fork Wetlands, and many plants, ponds and walking trails. Photo by Laura Kaparoff

Below: Hocking Hills State Park, a popular camping and lodging site, is known for its cliffs, gorges, rock shelters and waterfalls. It houses Old Man's Cave, Rockhouse, Ash Cave and Cedar Falls. Photo by Andrew H. Hochheimer

*Cars coming off turn four
at Lake Erie Speedway.
Photo by Mark Bell*

Inset and above: Located on the Ohio River, Riverfront Stadium, later known as Cinergy Field, was the home of the Cincinnati Reds National League baseball team and the Cincinnati Bengals National Football League team. The stadium was demolished by implosion in 2002. Photo by Steve Hudson

The amusement park and resort at Cedar Point, on Lake Erie at Sandusky, has drawn generations of visitors for well over a century. Its many roller coasters are admired worldwide by coaster enthusiasts. *Courtesy, Cedar Fair Entertainment Company.*

The Rock and Roll Hall of Fame and Museum in Cleveland was designed by Chinese architect I. M. Pei and opened in June 1993. It is dedicated to recording the history of some of the best-known and most creative people who have influenced the music industry. Cleveland was not the only city to be considered to house the Hall. Other cities considered included Memphis, Cincinnati and New York. Courtesy, The MetroHealth System. Photo by Rebecca Collins

The amusement park at the Columbus Zoo and Aquarium has one of only a few historic carousels in Ohio. Courtesy, Joseph M. Knapp

Reflecting the efficiency of modern railroads, dozens of container "stack" trains cross Ohio daily, carrying as many as 300 shipping containers on each train. Courtesy, Rickenbacker Port Authority, Columbus, Ohio

IX

A NEW LEGACY FOR A NEW MILLENNIUM

Ohio's Historic West brochure cover. Ohio's official heritage areas are increasinly important contributions to the state's huge tourism industry. Courtesy, Ohio's Historic West Heritage Area

Opposite page: Tower City Center transformed Cleveland Union Terminal into a shopping, entertainment and transportation complex, spurring other economic development in downtown Cleveland. Photo by Eric Gregoire

Ohio enterprise since the late 1980s is a story of the same spirit of innovation, creativity, and risk-taking that characterized the state's rise to prominence during the twentieth century. Facing wrenching changes in the heavy industries that long powered the economy—steel-making, coal mining, railroading, automobile production—Ohioans found new ways to work. When central cities suffered decline due to continued dispersal of people and businesses out into suburban areas, city dwellers undertook downtown revitalization projects. When Ohio's rich natural and cultural heritage became threatened, its citizens found new tools to preserve important natural resources and historic places.

Scholars and pundits often talk of the United States as having a "postindustrial economy," as though there is no more industrial base and everyone works in some service industry rather than making things. In fact, Americans still manufacture an astounding array of products, from toys to raw steel, and industrial production remains a vital part of the national economy.

At the same time, there have been significant changes. Much production has shifted overseas to take advantage of lower labor costs. Labor unions have steadily lost membership and bargaining power. Computer technology and innovations on the factory floor have greatly increased productivity, permitting job reductions with no loss in output.

In a heavily industrialized state such as Ohio, these changes have been very disruptive. It is certainly true, for example, that Ohio remains a

Ohio has seen the growth of businesses such as micro-breweries that target specific niches in the consumer market. Great Lakes Brewing Company Brewhouse. Courtesy, Great Lakes Brewing Company

——

major steel producer, with large mills in operation in Middletown, Lorain, Cleveland, and in the Ohio Valley near Pittsburgh. However, a steel mill on the Ohio River in Mingo Junction today can produce as much or more steel with 500 workers as it did with 5,000 just a few years ago. Glass and fabric-making plants in Columbus have closed entirely. Tires are no longer made in Akron, and the glass industry of Toledo is much smaller than in the recent past. Buyouts of manufacturing firms have led to consolidation of production facilities and large job losses.

From change, however, often comes opportunity, and entrepreneurial Ohioans have created whole new kinds of economic development to replace jobs, businesses, and industries that have disappeared. More than anything else, these efforts have been characterized by a difference in scale: large new enterprises employing hundreds of people still make the news every so often, but much of recent job creation and economic development has been by much smaller firms. Sometimes employing only a few people, niche industries and small businesses have found Ohio to

be fertile ground in a bewildering variety of economic pursuits. It has been known for a long time that most job creation in the nation's economy is the result of hiring by small businesses, and this has certainly been true in the Buckeye State.

The systemic change and job losses across Ohio's industrial landscape have spurred thoughtful and creative people to find new ways to make a living, and the Ohio economy is the better for it. To be sure, the failure rate of small businesses tends to be higher than for larger firms, but the rate of business creation is higher among smaller enterprises, too, so there always are new opportunities. Smaller businesses often are not able to offer the same employment benefits as larger companies—pensions and healthcare come to mind—but increasing numbers of large firms also are cutting or entirely eliminating these same benefits. Consequently, and in lockstep with national trends, Ohioans are rising to the challenge of securing their own economic futures.

A good portion of economic activity and growth in Ohio in the late twentieth and early twenty-first centuries has revolved around development of specific consumer products and innovative marketing of those products. The growth of micro-breweries is a case in point. By the 1970s the emergence of large national brewing companies had nearly put an end to the locally-made beers and ales that often were the pride and identity of their communities, particularly in industrial towns. Since then, however, custom-crafted local brews have been reborn in response to the perception of sameness and lack of distinctive taste in the offerings of the big brewers. Sometimes well-remembered brands of the past have been resurrected, as is the case with the Hoster brewery in Columbus. Other brewers are entirely new, one example being the Great Lakes Brewing Company of Cleveland. Equipped to brew relatively small batches of unusual, flavorful, and seasonal offerings, enterprises such as these at first served only local markets, with several later seeking regional distribution. Some have become known nationally. Usually, however, due to limited production capacity—and also to the preference of their owners—the micro-breweries have stayed largely local in scope. They market their brews with distinctive names and packaging, often incorporating local history and a good sense of humor; Great Lakes Brewing Company's popular "Burning River Pale Ale" is one example. Over about a twenty-year period, numerous successful small brew-

Many of Ohio's distinctive historic downtowns are being rediscovered and revitalized. Athens, Main Street. Photo by Tom O'Grady

ers have become a significant force in the Ohio marketplace and seem destined to stay.

In the area of retail sales, the globalization of trade and the emergence of the "big box" chains has had a strong negative impact upon the small merchants and businesses that typically were located in the downtown areas of both large and small communities; this has been most pronounced since about the mid-1970s. The roots of this change, however, go back farther. In the immediate post-World War II period, expansion of the highway network and widespread automobile ownership encouraged development of rural land outside established communities. There was a resultant outward migration of jobs, retail stores, and professional offices; decline and disinvestment in the older downtown area was the immediate result. This trend was further strengthened by completion of outerbelt freeways around both large and small cities, which opened up huge new rural areas to commercial and residential development.

For a long time, downtown businesses and property owners did not know how to respond. Some efforts to counter the new shopping and strip malls were self-defeating: demolition of downtown buildings to create more parking; covering up of historic buildings with new materials to make them look more modern; blocking off traffic to create pedestrian malls. None of this seemed to help, until finally a new approach was pioneered in the late 1970s by the Chicago regional office of the National Trust for Historic Preservation. The National Trust, a nonprofit organization based in Washington, D.C., realized that achieving its goal of preserving historic buildings could not be achieved unless there were sound economic uses for those buildings. In addition, the Trust learned that attacking the problem one building at a time could not address the core issues of why downtowns were in decline. Something new and innovative was needed.

The result was the Main Street program, a comprehensive approach to revitalization of traditional downtown areas. Suitable for both large cities and small towns, the program has grown from a test effort in three Midwestern cities to many hundreds of communities in every state of the Union. Its comprehensive approach stresses four areas: creation of a permanent organizational structure; careful design of building rehabilitations and of new buildings; ongoing, effective promotion of the downtown as a viable component of the community's economy; and restructuring of the economic base of the downtown, in recognition that its former role as the community's retail center is usually a thing of the past.

Many Ohio communities have embraced the Main Street concept with nearly universal success. A key concept has been that, while there is a role in the program for local governments, Main Street is driven primarily by the local business community, based on making good economic decisions about investments. Sometimes it is necessary to provide incentives, such as facade improvement grants or tax abatement, in order to balance the subsidies so readily granted to spur suburban development. Even modest subsidies in traditional downtown areas have triggered significant economic activity: building rehabilitation, temporary and permanent job creation, and development of new businesses.

The impact of the Main Street approach has been measured in various ways. Ohio's official program, which is managed by Heritage Ohio, Inc., a nonprofit organization based in Columbus, counted nearly three dozen participating communities in a five-year period starting in 2000. Cumulatively the participants had invested almost $300 million in downtown revitaliza-

The Longaberger® Basket is both an office building and a tourist attraction, reflecting the widespread interest in the company's hand-crafted products. Courtesy, The Longaberger® Basket Company

---

tion, gaining 315 net new businesses and nearly 3,000 full- or part-time net new jobs. Efforts in these communities resulted in more than 1,100 downtown building rehabilitation projects. Counting communities that follow the Main Street program but which are not formal participants in the statewide program, these figures are multiplied even more, and participation in Main Street grows each year.

Main Street calls for new, creative approaches to solving the problem of neglected downtowns. Ohio business owners, property owners, and entrepreneurs have responded: new businesses and expansion of existing enterprises have been the key to the most successful Main Street efforts; a willingness to take risks and try new ideas has paid off. As a result, the downtown areas of many communities—large and small—are home to many new, small enterprises.

Ohio's many micro-breweries are just one example of this new economic spirit. They are ideal businesses for traditional downtown areas, because they tend to draw a clientele looking for places with authentic character. Many of the breweries have full-service restaurants as part of their operations. These enterprises alone have been important contributors to their local economies, but there are many others. They range from coffee shops to computer consultants to dog

groomers and are part of their communities' new economic base that bodes well for the future.

Some innovative Ohio enterprises started small and became known nationally. Dave Longaberger's baskets are a good example. From a small custom shop producing hand-crafted baskets, the Longaberger Company has grown to have a national and international presence in the field of basket collectibles. The firm is known for several things: as an excellent employer that has had a major economic impact in Muskingum County and the surrounding area; for having revitalized the village of Dresden and made it a major tourist destination; for extensive philanthropic undertakings in eastern Ohio; and as the builder of a unique headquarters building in the form of a huge basket (located on State Route 16 just east of Newark).

The story is similar for the Rothschild's line of fruit spreads and other products, which began as a berry farm near Urbana in Champaign County and has grown to have a national presence; and for Rossi Pasta, which began as a small pasta maker in Athens and then later moved to Marietta; it is known for the good flavors and high quality of its pasta products.

Other people have pioneered businesses that have stayed small and provide either full-time or part-time work for their owners. These include purveyors of non-timber forest products such as ginseng and mush-

---

Ohio's public markets and seasonal farmers' markets provide entrepreneurial opportunities for small businesses and have increased the public's appreciation for locally-grown and produced foods. Black Swamp Arts Fest, Bowling Green. Photo by Susan P. Clanton

*While the old Municipal Stadium is fondly remembered.
Browns fans look to the new facility, Cleveland Browns
Stadium. Photo by John Reid III.*

rooms, and also bakers, farmers, flower growers, and others that sell either seasonally or year-round at Ohio's many public and farmer's markets. Such markets have become extremely popular as people have sought alternatives to supermarket shopping and as appreciation has grown for the quality and taste of locally-grown and -produced foods such as fruits, vegetables, meats, sausage, eggs, cheese, and baked goods. In Columbus, the North Market, last of the city's public markets, relocated from a run-down Quonset hut to a newly renovated historic building in the 1990s and continues to thrive; and in Cleveland the historic West Side Market draws customers from all over the metropolitan area. Farmer's markets pop up on side streets and in downtown areas all over the state during warmer weather.

Taken together, all these different kinds of businesses—small, distinctive, run by risk-taking, creative entrepreneurs, have added variety to the quality of life in their communities, becoming important components of the Ohio economy. Parallel to these developments, the field of information technology—computers and the Internet—has worked a transformation in businesses large and small. It has enabled better education through distance learning; cut inventory costs for manufacturers and retailers; facilitated growth of small home-based businesses; extended the marketing reach of existing businesses; and cut the cost of business administration and overhead. As with any new technology, this has

caused some disruption—travel agents, for example, have found that their business has changed radically—but the IT age has, overall, been a huge plus for Ohio businesses and continues to grow and evolve. The State of Ohio has taken steps to aid these efforts through promotion of the state's high-tech capacity to aid business development. The Ohio Third Frontier Project kicked off in 2002 with a goal of building top-drawer research capability; supporting early-stage business capital formation; supporting new product development; and improving manufacturing productivity with advanced technologies. Initial funding, allocated by the Third Frontier Commission established by the General Assembly, was set at $1.6 billion.

Ohio's sports teams have played their own role in the state's economic life. The Cleveland Browns had played in Cleveland's Municipal Stadium since the team was formed in 1946, a vital thread in the fabric of the city's life. When the team's owner, Art Modell, decamped to Baltimore in 1995 (despite twenty years of sold-out home games), Cleveland was bereft of football for several years, until the triumphant return of the Browns as a new team in 1999. The team moved into a new Cleveland Browns Stadium, which seated more than 73,000 and stood on the original lakefront site of the old Municipal Stadium. The Cleveland Indians, which played baseball in the old dual-purpose stadium, moved to their new home, Jacobs Field, in 1994. Located adjacent to the city's downtown core, Jacobs Field has spurred significant commercial investment nearby, no doubt encouraged by the Indians' Major League record of 455 sellout games between 1995 and 2001. Nearby, the city's basketball Cavaliers moved into Gund Arena in 1994; it has since been renamed Quicken Loans Arena.

Cincinnati, too, undertook major investment in sports facilities for its professional teams. The circular Riverfront Stadium had served both the Reds and the Bengals since 1970. It was replaced by two side-by-side facilities on the city's riverfront, Paul Brown Stadium for the football Bengals in 2000 and, to the east, the Great American Ballpark for the Reds, baseball's first professional team, in 2003.

Professional sports in Columbus took a different course. The city's residents have long been loyal supporters of the minor league baseball Clippers, but in 2000, Columbus landed a National Hockey League franchise, the Blue Jackets, along with a new downtown arena as the team's home. Major investment in office, retail, restaurant, and residential developments in the district around the arena has accompanied a general downtown renaissance. However, as is generally well known, Columbus is a football town—college football, specifically Ohio State University Football—and still savors the 2002 national title won by the OSU Buckeyes. They play in the historic, rehabilitated, and expanded (in 2001) Ohio Stadium on the university campus.

Two other minor league baseball teams, the venerable Toledo Mudhens (dating from 1896) and the younger Akron Aeros (which began as a team in Massachusetts in 1980 and moved to Akron in 1997), gained new prominence in their cities with completion of modern ballparks—Fifth Third Field in Toledo and Canal Park in Akron. Both are located downtown and have brought new life to their cities.

Ohio's state government undertook a number of other initiatives in the late 1990s and early 2000s intended to bolster statewide economic activity. Many of the new sports venues in the larger cities have received state support. Creation of the Ohio Cultural Facilities Commission has helped establish both large and small facilities for museums, galleries, theaters, and performing arts centers through the state's biennial capital budget.

To encourage alternatives to reliance on the automobile, the Ohio Department of Transportation has administered numerous federal Transportation Enhancement grants for bikeways and associated facilities. The Ohio Scenic Byways program encourages designation and management of public roads of scenic, historical, natural, and recreational character.

Regional economic development has received state support through the Governor's Office of Appalachia, and programs of the Ohio Arts Council, a state agency, which has resulted in a long-term effort to integrate the arts into Ohio's economic life. Establishment of state heritage areas, as well as grants to smaller downtowns for revitalization efforts have also had a significant impact.

In the late 1990s, the Ohio Farmland Preservation Task Force, created at the request of Governor George Voinovich, tackled the issue of loss of prime farmland to continued suburban sprawl. The task force made numerous recommendations, a principal one being that Ohio must do more to make its existing cities and villages desirable places to live and work. This will reduce the pressure to develop farmland for residential and commercial uses. Although farmland loss continues, communities are responding to the state's initiative by making greater investment in existing developed areas.

Ohio is a state of drivers: nearly all passenger travel among the state's cities is by automobile. Public transportation options are fairly limited. They include bus service between major cities and middle-of-the night Amtrak train service through Cincinnati on one route and Bryan, Toledo, Sandusky, Elyria, Cleveland, and Alliance on two other routes. However, the automobile handles the vast majority of people traveling between Ohio cities.

Freight traffic is another matter. Until development of the Interstate Highway System, which began in the 1950s and 1960s, most of the nation's freight—raw materials, intermediate products, finished goods of all types—was transported by rail. Even before the Interstate era, trucks had begun nibbling away at this traffic, particularly high-value and time-sensitive shipments. This trend only accelerated as the Interstate system facilitated the movement of manufacturing, warehousing, and distribution of goods out from traditional city centers to new facilities in suburban locations easily accessible by truck.

The nation's railroads, especially those in Ohio, which had a very dense rail network and was served by railroads intimately tied to the Midwest's older industrial districts, entered a period of decline that began in the 1950s and accelerated rapidly in the 1960s and

The former Rickenbacker Air Force Base, south of Columbus, has been transformed into a multi-modal transportation, warehousing, and distribution hub. Courtesy, Rickenbacker Port Authority, Columbus, Ohio

1970s. Bulk shipments of commodities such as coal, coke, ore, and gravel stayed with the railroads, but these produced lower revenues than the finished goods that had shifted to trucks. Coupled with high terminal costs and labor agreements that seemed out of touch with the realities of modern railroading, company after company entered bankruptcy. At one time, a good percentage of Ohio's rail mileage (the state once had over 9,000 route-miles), owned by companies such as Penn Central Transportation and the Erie-Lackawanna Railway, were operating in bankruptcy and had at best a dim future. However, two important events took place that changed the rail industry for the better and put it back on a paying basis. The first was the creation of Conrail in 1976 to take over several bankrupt lines; with federal assistance similar to that already provided to competing transportation modes, the new company was able to slim down the outmoded predecessor systems and in a fairly short time create an aggressive, profitable transportation company serving the northeastern part of the nation. Ohio was a prime beneficiary of Conrail's success,

since so much of the state was served by the system.

The second and even more important step was the deregulation of the railroads in the early 1980s. For a century, the nation's railroads had been heavily regulated by the Interstate Commerce Commission, which dictated which lines had to have service and how much the railroads could charge. This regulation was well-meaning and effective at protecting the shipping public when railroads had a monopoly on land transportation. However, by the mid-twentieth century it had become so onerous and inflexible that the very existence of the nation's rail system, especially in the northeast, was in doubt.

Federal deregulation legislation in 1980 enabled railroads to negotiate rates at whatever level could be agreed upon between shipper and carrier, and abandonment of unprofitable branch lines was made much easier. Over time, this new environment enabled the railroads to provide better, faster, and more reliable service at rates that reflected the value of the service, and it resulted in a much smaller national rail network. Ohio eventually declined to just over 5,000 route-miles of track, on which the total tonnage hauled annually is higher than ever, thanks to efficiency improvements.

As in other parts of the state's economy, this new era in transportation resulted in disruptive change and loss of jobs, but it also presented opportunities. As the major carriers shed many of their branch lines, entrepreneurs formed new short-line and regional railroad companies to take over the abandoned routes and continue service. Today a long list of local and regional rail lines—Ohio Central, Ohio and Indiana, and Great Miami are just a few—serve all kinds of businesses in places that long ago would have been abandoned by the major carriers. This trend is continuous: every so often, as the large railroads continue to "rationalize" their systems, small carriers step forward to acquire unwanted lines. Ohio today has fewer railroad jobs than in the past, but those jobs are far more secure than in the old pre-deregulation days.

New trends in freight transportation in Ohio and nationally also have integrated the railroads with other modes, resulting is vast improvements in efficiency. The move to shipping containers for products of all kinds has resulted in true "intermodal" shipping, since containers can be carried by ship, rail, and truck. Growing globalization of the economy has spurred the "container revolution" through a massive increase of imported goods, particularly from Asia. This still-developing pattern sees thousands of daily container "landings" at numerous U.S. seaports that have been specially re-built to handle container traffic. Containers are immediately transferred to custom-built railcars, and the country's four major railroads provide line-haul service, often a thousand or two thousand miles, to inland terminals, where another transfer takes place and trucks take the containers on the final leg—often in the range of 300 to 500 miles—to their destinations. Ohio's ideal location astride major transport routes and within a day's travel of a majority of the U.S. population has made it a significant distribution center for goods of all kinds. As result, it is no longer a novelty to see "Hapag-Lloyd" or "China Shipping" on the sides of rail- or highway-borne containers. Just one example of this trend is the conversion of the former Rickenbacker Air Force Base south of Columbus into a major "inland port" that handles billions of dollars' worth of goods each year. A good portion of its traffic

decades. The Ohio Historical Society has long operated a collection of State Memorials such as Serpent Mound in Adams County and Zoar Village and Tuscarawas County, all of which regularly draw visitors.

Students of the tourism industry have realized, however, that there is a significant sub-set of tourism with characteristics all its own. Known as cultural heritage tourism, it includes travelers and tourists looking beyond just fun or entertainment and has its own definition. Cultural heritage tourism is traveling to experience the places, artifacts, and activities that authentically represent the stories and people of the past and present. It includes cultural, historic, and natural resources. This definition was developed by the Travel Industry Association (TIA), the trade group for the tourism industry. In a 2003 study the TIA

Cultural and heritage tourism has been recognized as a significant and growing segment of the state's multi-billion dollar tourism industry. Photo by Tom O'Grady

is air freight, which tends to be used for high-value goods and for overnight and express services, but truck-to-rail and rail-to-truck traffic is a growing portion as well.

It might seem strange to think of the arts, heritage and culture as elements of a vital and lively economy, but they definitely are, and Ohio has done much to prove this fact. One of the most intriguing developments in the state's economy since the late twentieth century has been the increasing recognition of the importance of tourism, particularly the segment known as "heritage tourism."

Tourism has been an economic force in Ohio for a long time. Both Lake Erie and the Ohio River—the natural features marking the Buckeye State's north and south boundaries—long have drawn boaters, anglers, and tourists. Major amusement parks such as Cedar Point on Lake Erie and King's Island near Cincinnati have been significant engines of Ohio tourism for many

summarized what it had learned to that point about cultural heritage tourism in America:

More than two-thirds of adult travelers include culture or heritage on their trips.

Twenty-five percent of cultural heritage travelers take three or more trips a year.

A third of cultural heritage travel is by households with children.

Cultural heritage travelers stay longer and spend more than other travelers.

Shopping is part of the experience for 44 percent of cultural heritage travelers, compared to 33 percent of all travelers.

Cultural heritage travelers are more likely to stay in a hotel, motel, or bed and breakfast than other travelers.

Forty percent of cultural heritage travelers extend their trips because of heritage and cultural activities.

There is an increasing recognition of the economic impact of heritage cultural travelers and of how creating appropriate destinations and activities for such travelers can give a community or even a region a whole new base for economic development. This development is nonindustrial, small in scale, and service- and experience-oriented. Careful packaging of cultural and heritage attractions, together with high-quality advertising and promotion, is essential.

Here it is worth remembering the principles of the Main Street program, which stresses using a community's architectural heritage as the focus of economic development. A well-run Main Street program has a strong emphasis on good design and creative promotion, and Main Street efforts, in Ohio as elsewhere, has done much to create real, authentic heritage-oriented places that people want to visit.

The idea of identifying, documenting, celebrating, and promoting a community or a region's heritage has led to the concept of heritage corridors and heritage areas. Heritage corridors are typically linear in nature, while heritage areas are broader in geographic coverage. The concept for each, however, is the same: they are physical landscapes that are linked historically or thematically and contain substantial numbers of authentic historic buildings, districts, structures, or sites. Establishment of a heritage corridor or area provides the opportunity for diverse communities, businesses, attractions, and other stakeholders to work together on promotion, development, advertising, tour routes, and tourism packages that can benefit everyone.

One of Ohio's major heritage areas is in the northeastern part of the state: the Ohio and Erie Canal National Heritage Area. With the former canal as its spine, part of the heritage area is in the Cuyahoga Valley National Park, but it also extends beyond the park to Roscoe Village in Coshocton. At numerous locations visitors can learn about the canal's importance in Ohio's transportation history, ride a reproduction canal boat, and visit historic houses and commercial districts in several communities.

In the Appalachian region of the state, Ohio's Hill Country Heritage Area has helped forge its own regional identity and has provided a means for disparate artists, craftspeople, food producers, retailers, hotels, B&B's, and others to work together in a network to promote the region's many natural, historical and cultural assets. The Ohio River and areas such as the Hocking Hills already were major destinations before creation of the heritage area, as were historic cities such as Marietta and State Memorials like the John Rankin House in Ripley. Creation of the heritage area, which began as an effort by the Ohio Arts Council to use the arts as a basis for regional economic development,

facilitated cooperation among the thirty-one participating counties, pooling of funding for printed materials and promotional efforts, and networking activities to try out new ideas. The Hill Country heritage area evolved into a self-supporting nonprofit organization offering educational programs, a website with thematic heritage tour routes, and an annual conference known as The Gathering to keep its members in touch with each other.

One part of Ohio's Hill Country in particular had suffered significant economic decline during much of the twentieth century. Adopting the heritage area concept on a local basis, the portions of Athens, Hocking and Perry counties that were the center of the Ohio coal industry in the late nineteenth and early twentieth centuries have embraced their sometimes tumultuous history as the basis for new economic development. Before World War I, the roughly fifty small towns in the region were dubbed the Little Cities of Black Diamonds by a newspaper, and in the period up to about 1920 they prospered along with the coal industry. From then on, however, the small scale of the industry in that region, together with the high costs of underground mining, resulted in significant reduction in mining activity. Decline through the 1920s and economic dislocations of the Depression period could not be made up by higher demand during World War II, and the Little Cities region saw a continuing loss of jobs, people, and businesses. Coal mining did not disappear entirely, but over time a relatively high sulfur level in the coal and new mining technology have resulted in ever fewer mining jobs. Many of the Little Cities became virtual (and some actual) ghost towns, and many disappeared entirely. The ones that remained seemed suspended in time, particularly the Perry County village of Shawnee, which looks as though it was ordered up for a Hollywood backlot as the archetype of a mining boom town.

Working together in groups such as the nonprofit Little Cities of Black Diamonds Council, these small former mining towns are organizing both guided and self-conducted tours, food and cooking demonstrations, historic building preservation projects, promotional efforts, and even social and youth programs. These all benefit local citizens in addition to attracting cultural heritage tourists. Local museums celebrate the area's heritage, and summer chautauquas feature local artists and writers. Through small, incremental steps taken over a long period and against sometimes forbidding odds such as destructive fires and occasional floods, the Little Cities of Black Diamonds are building a new economic life on the foundation of their history, culture, and architecture.

The story is the same in other parts of the state. Economic conditions, as well as the physical and cultural setting, vary widely around Ohio, but each region has a story worth telling. In addition to the nationally-designated Ohio and Erie Canal Heritage Area and the state-designated Ohio's Hill Country (which runs from Columbiana County in the northeast to Clermont County in the southwest), the state's rich heritage is inspiring efforts elsewhere. The areas include Ohio's Historic West (seven counties between the Indiana line and Logan and Champaign counties; the Lake Erie Heritage Area (all the lakeshore counties); the Miami and Erie Canal Heritage Area; and the Maumee Valley Heritage Area. Some of these are state-designated and some are not, but all are working toward the same goals and expect to welcome other areas into their network in the future.

Another approach, related to, but run separately from the heritage area program, is the state's system

Above: One of Ohio's many scenic byways, in Holmes County, provides an oppor-tunity to learn about the area's Amish heritage. Photo by Tom O'Grady

Left: The historic Headley Inn is located on the National Road Scenic Byway in Muskingum County. Photo by Nancy Recchie

of scenic byways. Based on the idea that long-established transportation routes often have valuable intrinsic qualities—scenic attributes, historic properties, historical associations, natural features—the program uses both state and national designation of scenic byways to encourage both preservation of those attributes and use of the byways for tourism and recreational activities. Nationally-designated byways include the old National Road (U.S. Route 40) across the mid-section of the state, and the Ohio River Scenic Route, which covers the entire 462-mile path of the river and was Ohio's first nationally-designated byway. State-designated byways include, among others, the Welsh Scenic Byway in Jackson and Gallia counties, linked to the Welsh heritage of that area; Ohio's Amish Country Scenic Byways

in Holmes Couty; and the Scenic Olentangy Heritage Corridor along that river in Franklin and Delaware counties. Many of these byways are located in heritage areas and are part of their promotional and development efforts.

Ever since the 1980s Ohio has seen increasing public and private investment in restoration of both individual landmark buildings and of whole historic districts. Much of the private investment has been spurred by widespread public interest in preserving, visiting, and living in traditional and authentic historic communities; by programs such as Main Street, which has made it less risky and more economically rewarding to invest in older communities, large and small; and by the Historic Rehabilitation Tax Credit, which rewards investment in historic income-producing buildings by offering significant savings on federal income taxes. Many hundreds of rehabilitation projects all across the state have created attractive new affordable housing, as well as market-rate apartments, in old commercial buildings, warehouses, factories, and other buildings not usually considered residential in nature. These projects have also produced new commercial and office space to meet increased demand as traditional downtown areas have revived economically. Cumulative investment nationwide has totaled tens of billions of dollars; Ohio's share of that investment has been several hundred million, and interest in such projects continues unabated. Thousands of temporary construction jobs and permanent new jobs have resulted from this widespread investment in Ohio's older communities.

One of the largest private projects was the creation of Tower City Center in Cleveland, which in the 1990s transformed the under-utilized Cleveland Union Terminal beneath the landmark Terminal Tower into a shopping and entertainment complex. Since then, and undoubtedly spurred by Tower City, downtown Cleveland also has seen major investment in the Warehouse District, the former industrial area called The Flats, and in the Gateway Neighborhood, where construction of a new baseball stadium and basketball arena sparked a flurry of residential and commercial projects that remade many run-down but sound older buildings. Euclid Avenue in particular has seen major investment from Public Square through the theater district of Playhouse Square and out to the Cleveland State University complex.

In Columbus and Cincinnati there have been many redevelopments of older office, commercial, and warehouse buildings into new apartments and condominiums. Investment has taken place both in the downtown areas and in the older first-ring suburbs, where sound and spacious housing could be found at reasonable prices. In Columbus, the real estate arm of Nationwide Insurance has created a whole new sports and entertainment district that is anchored by a rehabilitated former farm implement warehouse. The heart of the district is a park crowned by the Union Station Arch, all that remains of the Columbus Union Station that once stood nearby. Preserved by a small group called Citizens for the Union Station Arch, the arch had been in a small city park and was moved to the larger park as the district began to develop.

Smaller cities and villages have received their share of investment, too. Places such as Tipp City, Perrysburg, Lancaster, Delaware, Ashtabula, and Marietta have seen significant levels of historic building rehabilitation. Many of these efforts have been complemented by government-funded streetscape and infrastructure improvements. In addition, organizations such as Heritage Ohio and Preservation Ohio have played important roles in encouraging investment in historic areas. Heritage Ohio promotes downtown development programs and runs the statewide Main Street program. Preservation Ohio provides advice and expertise on building rehabilitation techniques and in securing appropriate developers for unused or threatened properties.

Not all private investment has been for profit-making projects. The Dennison Depot Museum in Tuscarawas County, for example, is housed in a historic railroad depot and celebrates both local railroad history and the depot's service as a World War II canteen for traveling servicemen. Primarily a privately-funded local effort, the museum has been a huge success that has spurred other investment in Dennison.

The Bob Evans Farms museum, housed in Bob's former home in Rio Grande, Gallia County, chronicles the story of the sausage and restaurant company from its founding in the late 1940s. Undertaken entirely by the company, the project preserved an important historic house built in the 1820s and offers changing exhibits on local and Ohio history.

In Zanesville a local group has preserved the Nelson Gant House, which stands along the old National Road. Gant was an African American who had been freed from slavery in Virginia and became a prominent Zanesville businessman. In Canal Winchester near Columbus, the local historical society has preserved a railroad depot, a schoolhouse, and a grain mill to celebrate these buildings' roles in local history.

In Springfield, the Turner Foundation has emerged as a major historic preservation supporter. The foundation has made strategic investments to keep important local historic resources and neighborhoods from being lost. Springfield also is fortunate to have preserved the Westcott House, a Prairie Style home designed by Frank Lloyd Wright, through a concerted public-private effort. In Toledo, construction of a new Minor League baseball stadium has stimulated private investment in the under-utilized older structures around the stadium.

These are only a few examples of the many historic preservation projects undertaken both for profit and simply to preserve important historic resources and keep them open to the public. What is important is that the right mix of economic incentives and public investment can trigger restoration of historic properties that might not have occurred otherwise.

There has also been major investment in historic structures by the state of Ohio, both on specific projects at state-owned buildings and by means of capital appropriations through the Ohio Cultural Facilities Commission. Restorations of state-owned buildings have included the Ohio Statehouse, completed in 1996, which restored both the original 1861 Statehouse and the 1901 Annex, linking them with a compatible new atrium; and the conversion of the former Ohio Departments of State building in Columbus to the Ohio Judicial Center, which houses the Supreme Court of Ohio and associated agencies.

The Ohio Cultural Facilities Commission has administered state appropriations for a wide range of cultural, historical, and sports facilities all over the state. Each project also usually includes other major public and private funding sources. Some projects involve only new construction, but very often they result in the restoration of historic buildings for cultural purposes. These state-supported projects can be found in major cities and in many smaller communities as well. A small sample of the very diverse collection of projects includes the COSI Toledo science museum; the Decorative Arts Center of Ohio in Lancaster's historic Reese-Peters House; the Art Academy of Cincinnati; the Broad Street Historical Renovation in Elyria; the Fort Piqua Hotel in Piqua; the McKinley Museum in Canton; the new Cleveland Browns Stadium; the Canal Park ballpark in Akron; Chester Academy in Meigs County; and the museum ship lake steamer *William G. Mather* in Cleveland. All these projects have created new centers for cultural and recreational activities in their communities and have proven ideal components of public and private efforts to promote cultural heritage tourism in Ohio.

The myriad ways Ohioans have responded to the state's economic challenges have been innovative, thoughtful, and creative. Establishment of new small enterprises; creation and marketing of niche products; and self-employment in fields that did not even exist a few years ago have provided opportunities and helped build new economic foundations to replace the lost jobs and businesses that once supported the state and its citizens. With a population that is increasingly diverse in race and ethnic background, Ohio has been able to provide meaningful work for both new arrivals and long-term residents. Public and private investment in businesses, in downtown areas, in historic landmarks, and in information technology, has helped to stimulate job growth and reverse economic decline.

At the same time, challenges remain. Agriculture still is Ohio's largest industry, but the debate over where and how much farmland should be preserved is ongoing. Parts of some of the state's cities still

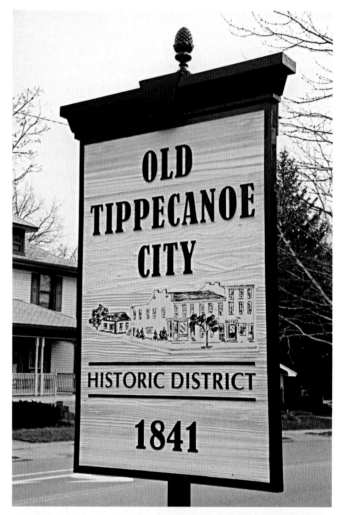

Ohio's cities, small towns and villages are filled with historic properties that are being rediscovered and rehabilitated. They contribute to each community's unique and distinctive character. Photos by Jeffrey Darbee

The National Historic Landmark Ohio Statehouse has been completely restored and is open to the public seven days a week. Photo by Richard Lesch

suffer from disinvestment and lack of economic opportunity. Unemployment remains stubbornly high in some counties, and high school graduation rates are lower than they should be. Poverty is a reality of life for too large a part of Ohio's population. And, in an age of expensive energy, major decisions still have to be made about how people and goods will move about; how we will heat and cool our buildings; and how we will generate the electric power to run it all.

The history of Ohio, however, tells us clearly that Ohioans have risen to past challenges and can be counted on to do it again.

*Wright brothers replica at the National Museum of the
USAF, Wright-Patterson AFB. Courtesy, National Museum
of the USAF, Wright-Patterson AFB*

X

CHRONICLES

OF

LEADERSHIP

Ohio historians would hardly mention Max Morehouse in the same breath as Thomas Alva Edison, Harvey Firestone, or Neil Armstrong. But in his own way Morehouse captured and held aloft for a brief moment the entrepreneurial spirit that has blessed the Buckeye State and its people.

Morehouse was a Columbus dry goods merchant, the proprietor of Morehouse-Martens—The Home Store. His small mark in history was made November 7, 1910, when he sponsored Phillip Parmalee to fly two packages of silk from Dayton to Columbus, the first air cargo flight.

Although Morehouse did not set the world on fire, many others from Ohio did. It is hard to imagine a world today without the pioneering spirit of Ohioans that began with the first settlers in the Northwest Territory. From the beginning they were blessed with natural abundance. The mighty Ohio River, which provided a route for the French explorer Robert La Salle and the pioneers that followed, is still one of the nation's great commercial waterways.

To the north Lake Erie fostered industrial growth unsurpassed by any state in the Union. All manner of industry came to life along its shores, lined with harbors for vessels bearing iron ore, coal, and grain. Later the St. Lawrence Seaway offered the giant ships access to the open sea.

In between the river and the lake was a natural wealth that put food on the nation's table and muscle on emerging industry. Ohio's great seal highlights the state's rich and varied agricultural heritage. Ohio agriculture is still a major and competitive force in the markets of the world.

It is doubtful that the Buckeye State's renowned economic strength would have prospered without the water, coal, iron ore, natural gas, and crude oil found within its borders. These basic resources contributed to the commercial development of so many industries: steel, glass, automotive, rubber, paper, petroleum, chemical, and hundreds of others.

Ohio's partners in its remarkable progress have been adventurers and leaders of vision. Foremost among these, perhaps, have been the eight presidents of the United States from Ohio. Others, such as astronauts John Glenn and Neil Armstrong, have stepped out of this world for their place in history.

But there are many Buckeye entrepreneurs who have made their mark through vision, courage, and leadership: the Wright brothers of Dayton; Edison, the unsurpassed inventor; Charles F. Kettering, the automotive genius who invented the self-starter; John D. Rockefeller, a self-starter himself who began penniless, founded Standard Oil, and became the world's richest man; W.A. Otis of elevator fame; and Dr. B.F. Goodrich and Harvey Firestone, pioneers of the tire industry.

Today's entrepreneurs, whose stories are found on the pages that follow, continue to add to Ohio's rich and diverse history, and they have chosen to support this important literary and civic project. Some have been a part of the Ohio scene for more than 100 years; others are relative newcomers, who have built on the vigor and prosperity of their predecessors. Ohio can be proud of the achievements of these innovators.

A. LoPRESTI & SONS, INC.

A. LoPresti & Sons, Inc., located on East 40th Street in Cleveland, Ohio, specializes in produce and food distribution and has a long standing reputation for quality food, satisfied employees, and exceptional customer care. The owners of the company proudly embrace the culture of a family run business. They, like their fathers before them, successfully maintain lasting relationships not only with customers, but also with employees. Their secret to sustaining both is simple: treat customers and employees as if they were family. This philosophy began four generations ago with the great-grandfather to them all, Augustino LoPresti.

In 1908 Augustino conceived the idea of buying fruits and vegetables from local growers and selling them to Cleveland's townspeople. He began by loading up a small flatbed cart, pushing it through the streets of downtown Cleveland, and selling produce to individuals and small businesses. His customers began to depend on the appearance of LoPresti's red pushcart, pleasant smile, and quality produce. As a result, his company grew. He worked diligently from his home located on East 14th Street and soon transformed his dining room into an office and expanded his garage into a warehouse. His accounting system was straightforward—account receivables were kept in his left pocket, and payables in his right. It was a good day when the left pocket was weightier than the right!

LoPresti's young son, Carl, grew up

The delivery vehicle of choice—from the red pushcart in 1908 to a fleet of twenty-five trucks and trailers.

Open house for the new warehouse on Crayton Avenue in 1961. Mary LoPresti surrounded by her three children, cousins, and employees.

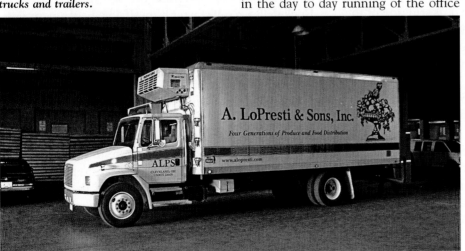

with the company operating out of his own home. It was only natural that he would eventually become part of the family business. Carl continued in school, but each day after classes he joined his father in packing and loading produce from his family's garage.

By the mid-1920s Carl was still young, but represented a strong presence in his father's business. It was at this time that Carl met and fell in love with a woman named Mary Dinor. Not only did Mary become Carl's life partner in marriage, she also helped the business grow considerably and was a substantial support to the company in every way. Carl and Mary wasted no time and quickly had three children, Gus, Joe, and Frances, who all became integral parts of the growing family business. Frances helped in the day to day running of the office

and Gus and Joe made early morning deliveries before they went to school.

At age thirty-five Carl suffered an acute attack of appendicitis. Sensing the seriousness of his illness and the consequences it could have on his family and the business, Carl asked to speak with Lawrence Piazza, a cousin and employee of the company and someone he trusted implicitly. Lawrence met with Carl and agreed to help should anything happen to him. Sadly, Carl passed away that same day.

Although Carl's children were teenagers at the time of his death, they helped Lawrence and Mary run the business. Another cousin, Virginia Morris, joined the team, and the company stayed on track and continued to grow. With the customer base expanding, the need for delivery trucks and more warehouse space became evident. The family decided it was time to move the operation out of their home and into a 10,000-square-foot warehouse on Crayton Avenue.

Gus took over the business realm, Joe the warehouse and drivers, and Lawrence the purchasing and receiving. Frances and Virginia ran the office. Mary could always be found in the kitchen cooking homemade meals for employees, customers, and any hungry soul that stopped by. Her life was A. LoPresti & Sons until she passed away in 1975. Lawrence, Gus, and Joe continued to work together expanding product lines, territories, and customers.

Gus passed away in 1994, Joe in 1995, and Lawrence in 2000. Frances still works part time in accounts payable.

Now, the fourth generation shareholders Daniel LoPresti, Mary Jo LoPresti, Patricia LoPresti, Mary LoPresti Turnes, along with Michael Wiedower, the company's first non-family CEO, oversee the mission and vision of the company. Augustino's pushcart has been replaced by a fleet of thirty refrigerated trucks and trailers. The family garage has expanded into an 180,000-square-foot distribution center, and the hand written accounting has been replaced by a state-of-the-art computer system. The product line has increased to over 7,000 items representing produce, specialty items, groceries, frozen foods, fresh chicken, seafood and meat, dairy products, and fresh processed produce. The product line even includes cleaning supplies and paper products. The territory once covered by a pushcart now includes the expanse of Northeastern Ohio. The company distributes to more than 1,200 customers including caterers, restaurants, schools, healthcare facilities, and hotels.

Patricia LoPresti, daughter of Gus LoPresti, credits her employees with the

Mike Wiedower, president with Daniel LoPresti, Patricia LoPresti and Mary Jo LoPresti.

The current 180,000 square-foot-distribution center on East 40th Street, Cleveland, a stone's throw from the 1908 home origins.

company's continued success. She also considers them family. "We adopt our employees into our family...without their dedication, we are nothing." Even on the company website, the employment page has "adoption" under the heading of employee opportunities. The page reads, "...consider being adopted by our family."

In turn, employees treat customers like family. A salesperson might get a last minute call from a frantic caterer who finds himself in need of food items. That employee may make the delivery himself—even if it's after business hours.

A. LoPresti & Sons' personnel stay current on food trends and keep ingredients for unique dishes and specialty items in stock. They generously offer menu ideas and cost saving suggestions to keep returning customers happy. This

enduring level of commitment not only nurtures the business, it elevates the respect of the culinary community.

Several associations including The American Dietetic Association, The American Culinary Federation, The Cleveland Area Restaurant Association, and The International Food Service Executive Association recently honored the late "Gus" LoPresti by creating a scholarship in his name. Gus, grandson to the patriarch of the company, had to leave school at age fourteen in order to help run the family business. He had a tremendous respect for education, so it is fitting that the August LoPresti Scholarship Fund would honor school and college students with his same commitment to family and community. The scholarship, which has awarded over $30,000, is not given based on financial need or scholastic achievements; it is given based on a student's dedication to the food service industry and a passion for giving back to the community

A. LoPresti & Sons celebrates 100 years of serving the community of Northern Ohio in 2008. From humble beginnings of a dream and a little red pushcart, the company has become one of the largest food distributors based in Ohio. It will continue to serve its greater family community for many generations to come.

ARTHUR G. JAMES CANCER HOSPITAL
AND RICHARD J. SOLOVE RESEARCH INSTITUTE
AT THE OHIO STATE UNIVERSITY

"All cancer will eventually be wiped out; there's no doubt about that. I don't know how long it will take ... but I'm sure the day is coming."—*Dr. Arthur G. James*

When the Arthur G. James Cancer Hospital and Richard J. Solove Research Institute at The Ohio State University ("The James") opened on July 9, 1990, it represented the culmination of decades of hard work by its founder and namesake, Arthur G. James, MD.

Though the path to creating the hospital was a long and winding one, Dr. James was spurred on through the years by a passion to address the individual needs of each patient and to make strides toward eradicating cancer in its many forms. With The James being consistently ranked among the nation's best hospitals for cancer care by *U.S. News & World Report*, Dr. James' efforts demonstrate how the vision of one person can have a profound effect on the fight against cancer.

The hospital opened with little fanfare; in a small ceremony, a single patient was wheeled over from the adjacent Ohio State University Hospital and greeted by Dr. James and others upon

The Statue of Hope located on the front lawn of The James.

Arthur G. James, M.D.

arriving. But the gravity of the event was understood by the seventeen patients who were admitted to The James on that first day: Ohio and the Midwest at last had a stand-alone cancer hospital.

Although Dr. James retired from general practice that same year, he remained at Ohio State in an academic capacity and was active in fundraising for the hospital. Failing health dictated his full retirement in 1996, but he left with the satisfaction of having achieved his ultimate professional goal of bringing a cancer hospital to central Ohio.

This accomplishment was no small feat given the profound need for comprehensive cancer care. Until very recent times, cancer was a great mystery. How it forms and spreads was largely unknown; scientists in the 1700s believed

that cancer was a poison or even contagious. With the dawn of cellular pathology, much more was understood about the nature of the disease and its effects on the body. Modern researchers came to understand that cancer is formed by the unregulated proliferation of mutated cells. Yet even though the disease had been better defined by the 1900s, it still tended to be a dire diagnosis, one with little hope of recovery. Each potential medical solution created a host of other problems resulting from damage done to the body in attempting to remove the cancer. For example, once the medical community began to surgically remove tumors in the early 1800s, the threat of infection left a grim survival rate.

Even in the twenty-first century, cancer has remained an elusive foe. This is in large part due to its many forms, varied causes and hidden nature. More sophisticated treatments such as radiation and chemotherapy have increased a patient's odds of survival dramatically, but these treatments are often harsh on already-weak bodies.

Despite the difficult treatments and emotional battles faced by patients with this disease, the fight against cancer must progress. The James has been one of the leaders in pioneering a new approach to cancer treatment, one that takes into account the needs of each individual patient. Medical treatment is accompanied by support systems to help patients and family members cope with the

Lobby at the James.

The James and The Ohio State University Medical Center from 9th Avenue.

effects of the disease. A top-notch team of doctors, clinicians, oncology-trained nurses, researchers, rehabilitation therapists, pharmacists, dietitians, psychologists and social workers brings highly specialized skills and full-spectrum compassionate care to patients.

Because cancer is the sole focus of The James, its multidisciplinary teams are able to work closely together to provide the best possible approach for their patients' healthcare. Each member of the team works diligently to customize a treatment plan for each patient, specific to his or her needs. Today, The James offers some of the most sophisticated programs for cancer diagnosis, treatment and prevention, all of which are directly correlated with the extensive research that is ongoing at the institution. This personalized approach to medicine is one of the reasons The James is continually listed as one of the Top 50 cancer-care

facilities in America by *U.S. News & World Report.*

The hospital's care extends far beyond its own walls. The James has reached out to the community by creating outpost JamesCare sites for those patients who live farther away. These sites allow patients to receive first-rate care, only closer to their own homes. This is an extremely important and valuable service for patients, in terms of not only geographic convenience but by also limiting travel time and discomfort for sick patients. This is only one of the ways that The James shows that it always has its patients in mind.

The James also creates a wealth of resources for its patients, including its own health and wellness publication, *Frontiers.* The monthly magazine is filled with thoughtful and informative articles that serve to educate people coping with cancer as well as their family members. It also includes tips for overall health and wellness and serves as a support tool as well, connecting patients and readers.

The James also makes significant efforts to educate the community on healthy habits that will help minimize cancer risks. Healthful eating habits and stopping smoking top the list of positive actions a person can take to stay well and avoid cancer risks. To help people accomplish this goal, The James sponsors its own smoking cessation program aptly named Kick It! When cancer is detected early, treatment options and survival rates increase dramatically. The James therefore widely advocates pre-screening, getting the word out to all to take the time to get proper check-ups and screenings such as mammograms, colorectal exams and prostate exams.

Patients and their families are also able to connect through the many support groups coordinated through the JamesCare for Life program, a comprehensive oncology rehabilitation program that seeks to balance treatment by offering ways for people to heal their minds and spirits. This provides a forum for those affected by cancer to share in challenges and celebrate victories with others who are in a similar situation. Some support groups address specific types of cancer, while others focus more generally on coping, adaptation and adjustment, care giving or quality-of-life concerns. Additional services from JamesCare for Life include Look Good, Feel Better, which is a collaboration with the American Cancer Society. This class teaches appearance-enhancing skills for specially designed for women undergoing cancer treatment. MusicCare is also offered. This is a program that employs music's healing potential during treatments and surgeries. When it comes to patient well-being, anything that may be therapeutic on a physical, emotional or spiritual front is explored for patient benefit.

Support groups are available for those who are ill, those who have survived cancer and for family members, including children. Special support groups offer a wide range of services for children and have been created to help children cope with the cancer in their lives, whether it affects them or someone they love. The James extends these free support services to *any* child who has a loved one who

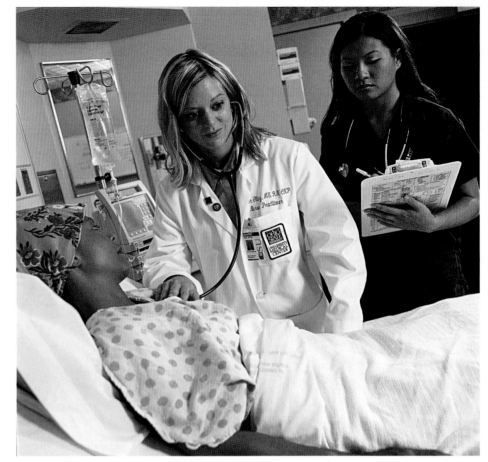

has been diagnosed with a terminal illness, not just cancer. All children from the community are welcome to participate.

The James also has a Children's Healing Garden, a labyrinth located behind the OSU Child Care Center. The garden was made possible through a collaboration between The James, the Child Care Center, the OSU College of Arts and the OSU School of Architecture.

Doctors and Nurses at The James are specially trained to care for oncology patients.

Children can make tiles in honor of lost loved ones, giving them some closure and peace.

The James is the patient-care component of the Ohio State University Comprehensive Cancer Center. Ohio State is one of only thirty-nine institutions in the United States designated by the National Cancer Institute as a "comprehensive" cancer center. The James has a three-pronged approach that elevates it to world-class treatment level. The hospital doesn't merely work to create personalized patient care to achieve and maintain optimal health; it also sees to it that healthcare professionals are trained in the most innovative and cutting-edge techniques. To bolster this aim, the hospital also conducts cancer research involving the most promising treatments for prevention strategies.

More than 265 researchers representing fourteen colleges at Ohio State work within the Comprehensive Cancer Center from a variety of disciplines, each searching for better understanding, treatment and education options to help reduce the effects and incidence of

Radiation oncology—staff looking at x-rays.

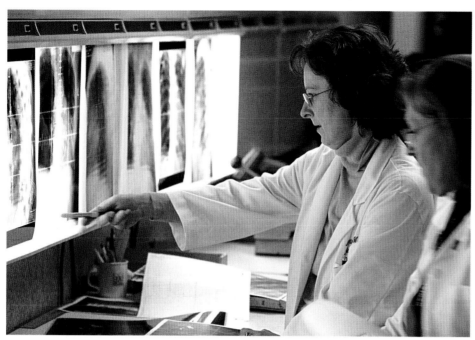

Healthcare professionals at The James believe they can accomplish their goals by focusing on high standards of patient care, sophisticated research efforts and ongoing patient education.

cancer. The James is pioneering some of the most advanced cancer treatments in the world in such promising areas as genetics, genomics and bioinformatics. Research at The James is divided into seven distinct interdisciplinary programs: cancer control; experimental therapeutics; immunology; molecular biology and cancer genetics; molecular carcinogenesis and chemoprevention; pediatric oncology; and viral oncogenesis.

Within these different disciplines, Ohio State has assembled a team of top researchers to aggressively explore the many avenues that may give insight into cancer prevention and treatment. Cancer researchers at Ohio State look at the various forms and causes of cancer from every angle in their efforts to find better methods of preventing, diagnosing and treating the disease. At The James, there is constant research in the areas of development of anti-cancer drugs, improved methods of prevention, advanced diagnostic methods, as well as superior treatment through molecular oncology, surgery, immunotherapy, radiation, chemotherapy, nutrition and many other types of medicine. Thanks to this research, the hospital can offer the most

up-to-date diagnostic tools, treatment options and clinical trials.

This builds on a strong legacy of cancer research at Ohio State. Even before The James opened, the University's cancer program had gained acclaim for some prominent achievements, including early advancements in radiation medicine, the discovery of hairy cell leukemia and an effective cure for it, and the development of a vaccine for feline leukemia.

Since 1990 medical scientists at The James have made even more exciting contributions to the global cause against cancer. These strides have included showing the natural cancer-preventing

qualities of specific fruits and vegetables such as black raspberries, strawberries and blackberries, tomatoes, broccoli, cauliflower, cabbage and kale. Researchers at The James have also been leading the way in uncovering the link between genetics and cancer, discovering alterations in microRNA genes of human cancers and becoming the first to show that expression of these genes can be used in cancer diagnosis and prognosis.

With the ongoing work by dedicated physicians, nursing staff, researchers, administrative staff and a whole host of other important team members, great progress is being made to understand and tackle the obstacles presented by cancer. With their contributions, cancer is no longer the dire and hopeless diagnosis it once was. Now, there are better methods of detection, better ways to fight cancer and better odds of lasting wellness. Now, there is hope.

Dedicated to carrying on Dr. James' legacy, the medical professionals and researchers at The James will continue pursuing excellence in cancer research, education, treatment and prevention. The hospital also plans more community action, branching out by adding beds and developing new outpatient facilities. Through these efforts, The James may help realize its founder's dream of a world without cancer.

The James' annual Cancer Survivors Day.

COOLIDGE WALL CO. L.P.A.

Coolidge Wall is not only one of the oldest law firms in Ohio, but also among the longest continuing business operations in Dayton. The recent celebration of the firm's 150th birthday coincided with the bicentennial of Ohio's admission to statehood in 1803, and with the centennial celebration of Orville and Wilbur Wright's first powered flight in 1903.

Founded in 1853 as Gunckel & Strong, the firm has operated continuously ever since, changing its name from time to time as generations of lawyers have continued the practice. Lewis Gunckel and Hiram Strong were united by a shared commitment to excellence. Gunckel once defined the necessary ingredients for a good lawyer as "character, study, and work." These became the hallmarks of their legal practice.

To maintain the firm's records, Gunckel and Strong purchased a letter copying press that created copies of documents on translucent Japanese rice paper. The press was used for almost 100 years, until the paper became unavailable during World War II. The copies were bound together in serially numbered leather volumes, producing an enduring record of the firm's practice from its inception in 1853.

In 1862, when it became clear that the Civil War would not end quickly, Strong felt compelled to volunteer for military service in the 93rd Ohio Regiment, at the age of thirty-six, leaving his wife, his four children, and his legal practice in Dayton. He rose to the rank of colonel and was named commander of the 93rd Ohio Regiment. During Strong's military service, the two

Letter copying press.

Lewis B. Gunckel, 1826–1903.

partners maintained a steady correspondence. The descriptions of client problems, fee disputes, and strategy for a case going to the Ohio Supreme Court provide a fascinating snapshot of the firm's day-to-day practice in the 1860s.

When Strong was mortally wounded at the Battle of Chickamauga, Gunckel continued the work of the firm with the same dedication to high standards for legal practice and community service. He worked in Ohio and nationally for a facility to house the soldiers returning from the Civil War. Dayton was chosen as the national headquarters for the National Home for Disabled Volunteer Soldiers. That headquarters is now known as the Dayton Medical VA Center. Gunckel's work was recently recognized through his selection for induction into Dayton's Walk of Fame.

In 1896 Gunckel was a founding father of Associated Charities of Dayton, an organization that continues today as Family Services Association. Gunckel and his father-in-law, Valentine Winters, were instrumental in the creation and development of the Winters National Bank in Dayton, which continues as part of JPMorgan Chase Bank. Gunckel and Winters also led the successful community fund drive in Germantown to establish a public library which still serves the Germantown community.

In about 1900 the legal baton passed from the aging Lewis Gunckel to his associate Lee Warren James. Unlike Gunckel, who was an early graduate of the University of Cincinnati Law School, James became a lawyer through the apprentice system, and then proceeded to the highest levels of legal practice. James was part of the inner circle for the first public offering by National Cash Register in 1926; he argued cases in the United States Supreme Court; he had a satellite office on Wall Street in New York; and finally he spent his retirement years at the Metropolitan Club of New York.

James' successor in the firm leadership was Joseph Bradford Coolidge, a scholar and legal perfectionist who graduated from Boston Latin High School, Harvard College, and Harvard Law School. As a former headmaster of the Dayton Latin School, Coolidge brought his schoolmaster and taskmaster talents to the firm, with a rare combination of great intellectual skill and tremendous business acumen. It was during his long tenure that the legal practice became known as the "Coolidge Firm," with a reputation for excellence that has endured to the present.

Since the death of Brad Coolidge in 1965, the Coolidge firm has grown significantly in size and has developed many

Joseph Bradford Coolidge, 1886–1965.

new areas of practice to accommodate changes in the law, legal practice, personal rights, and the structure of the business community. The firm has also adapted to the modern challenges of computer technology and a global economy. The letter copying press had to give way to electric copiers. Telephones and telefax became integral to the practice. The firm originally registered "Coollaw" as its Western Union Cable address. Then, as the world of communications moved from telegraph to Internet, the tagline would become its website address: www.coollaw.com.

The firm's history reflects both cultural and commercial milestones in Dayton community history. During the 1890s the famous African American poet, Paul Laurence Dunbar, operated the elevator in the building in which the firm was located. Firm lawyers would have been among the first to have access to his poetry, as he peddled his earliest books to his elevator passengers. In the 1920s, the firm began to work with inventor Charles Kettering, particularly in the Kettering family's acquisition of Winters National Bank, and subsequently in the family's development of Kettering Medical Center and its generous community philanthropy over successive generations.

In more recent times, the firm's clients have included such diverse personalities as the Ohio Players, a rhythm and blues music group whose 1970s funk sound is enjoying an enormous rebirth, and Pete Rose in his battles

Gunckel & Rowe, Federal Reporter—1st series, volumes 1-3, 1880.

with Major League Baseball and the Internal Revenue Service. Probably not since Colonel Harlan Sanders visited the firm in the 1970s has a client's presence caused the stir that it did when Pete Rose was scheduled for an appointment.

As the firm moves forward, it continues to pursue a broad range of legal practice areas, including corporate-business transactions, real estate, taxation, estate planning, healthcare law, environmental regulation, employee benefits, labor, and public sector representation. The practice continues to reflect and adapt to changes in the nature of the Dayton economy, the legal profession, and the level of governmental regulation.

The lawyers from Coolidge Wall also continue the firm's long-standing commitment to community service and the belief that strengthening the quality of life in the community furthers the business and personal interests of all community members. Lawyers from the firm now actively lead and support an array of civic, charitable, and cultural organizations.

Coolidge Wall is a legal professional association licensed by the State of Ohio. With more than forty lawyers, it presents

Some of the current members of the Coolidge Wall law firm, standing around the Gunckel desk that has been a part of the firm's history since its inception in 1853. Left to right: Glenn Bower, Merle Wilberding, Steve Herbert, Ron Pretekin, and Joe Gruenberg.

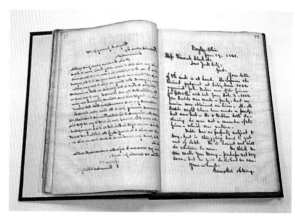

Gunckel & Strong, Attorneys at Law, copy letter book. Letter to Viscount Clark Co., New York City, January 19, 1861.

a unique combination of talent and commitment to the highest principles of legal practice. The lawyers of the firm still meet the needs and expectations of their clientele with the standards set by Hiram Strong and Lewis Gunckel in 1853—character, study, and work.

HEINZERLING FOUNDATION

The Heinzerling Foundation is a private nonprofit organization dedicated to the care, education and treatment of non-ambulatory children and adults with multiple disabilities, including severe or profound mental retardation. Individuals are admitted solely on developmental criteria without regard to the ability to pay. The Foundation, which operates three facilities in Central Ohio that house 213 individuals, works tirelessly to provide compassionate care to its residents.

The Foundation began modestly in 1959 as a labor of love for Otto and Mildred Heinzerling. The couple had raised three children of their own and opened their home to many others through their in-house daycare. The Heinzerlings found a new calling when Otto heard a presentation given at the local Civitan Club. It was there that he became aware of a group of children who were seriously underserved: severely or profoundly mentally retarded babies. These children were nearly forgotten in the system, relegated to very short, very lonely lives.

The Heinzerlings felt compelled to take action. They mortgaged their own home in order to open a residence for retarded children. "Peck O' Wee Ones," a twelve-bed facility, opened on September 15, 1959. The Heinzerlings covered all bases at the first facility, with Otto running the office and raising money for

Staff members help a resident into a specialized van to go on a field trip.

Otto and Mildred Heinzerling.

the home while Mildred lovingly cared for twelve babies all hours of every day.

Within four years, Peck O' Wee Ones was incorporated as an Ohio nonprofit organization, and within another, federal tax-exempt status was granted by the IRS. The Heinzerlings' hard work was also being recognized by others; the civic group Sertoma International awarded Otto Heinzerling its prestigious Service To Mankind Award.

As Peck O' Wee Ones continued to fill this critical need in the community, the organization grew. Otto Heinzerling began to raise funds to build a larger facility that would enable the organization to provide services to more children. However, neither he nor Mildred would live to see the eventual expansion of the Heinzerling Foundation and the extent of the services it would provide for Ohio families.

After both Heinzerlings passed away, their family made the decision to continue their legacy. Their son, Robert A. Heinzerling, D.D.S., stepped in to carry on his parents' work. In 1974 he renamed the original facility

Heinzerling Memorial Foundation in honor of Mildred and Otto and vigorously pursued the expansion his father had begun. In 1979 a brand new 22,400-square-foot facility opened, followed a few years later with the Heinzerling Developmental Center (HDC), which added a continuum of care to the Foundation's operation. The Developmental Center was specifically designed to handle the needs of children from the Memorial Foundation who were growing into older and larger individuals. In addition, HDC offered a first-class residential option for adults with multiple disabilities living in Central Ohio who needed this type of care.

The Heinzerling Foundation has worked to provide these individuals with ongoing care and opportunities for growth and development as they grow into adulthood. The range of services provided by the Foundation follows a developmental model delivered via an interdisciplinary team approach. Professionals from the areas of medicine, education, therapy, nutrition, social services, and personal care work together with parents and guardians to make thoughtful decisions that impact the lives of residents in positive and meaningful ways. One resident, who has lived at the Foundation since infancy and whose doctors predicted would not live very long, is now thirty years old, attends educational programs, helps the receptionist at the front desk, wheels her own wheelchair and often laughs with staff. This is a significant accomplishment that current administrator Christine "Chris" Rafeld attributes to the excellent care and nurturing provided by everyone at the Foundation.

"When you are dealing with people with IQ scores below 40, and many with scores below 25, the general perception may be that they can't do very much—but that's not our focus at all," Chris Rafeld explains. "We believe that every single person who lives here has value simply because he/she is a human being. Every person has potential and it is our job to discover what that is."

The Heinzerling family remains actively involved in the administration of the Heinzerling Foundation (as Peck O' Wee Ones was officially renamed in 1980). When Dr. Robert Heinzerling passed away in 1989, his wife, Kathryn, a registered nurse, took the reins as the Foundation's executive director, where she oversaw the administration and continued expansion of the organization until her retirement in 2001. At that

A staff member sings with a resident at camp.

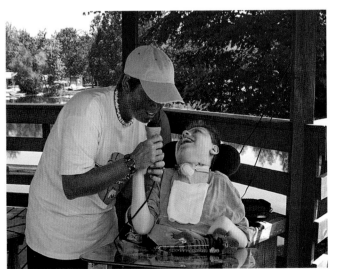

Heinzerling Memorial Foundation, home to the younger residents. Across the street is Heinzerling Developmental Center, home to the adult residents.

point, longtime administrator John A. Taylor was appointed to the executive director post. Robert E. Heinzerling, Otto and Mildred's grandson, and Robert A. and Kathryn's son, became the Foundation's administrator. He now fulfills the executive director role at the Foundation, following in the footsteps of his grandfather, father and mother before him. "I am honored to continue the legacy of my grandparents and parents," states Robert. "I fully understand and support the important role the Foundation plays not only in the lives of the individuals who live here, but also in the community as a whole."

The dedicated staff at the Heinzerling Foundation is instrumental in the organization's continued success. The multi-disciplinary team works around the clock, much as Mildred and Otto Heinzerling did for the first twelve residents, to make sure that they are cared for on every possible level. Given the wide range of disabilities and disorders that are represented at the Foundation's three facilities, such as cerebral palsy, orthopedic abnormalities and severe developmental delays, a great deal of collaborative effort is necessary to provide each resident with a program that best suits him or her.

The staff goes far above and beyond the normal call of duty in their efforts. While 98 percent of the Foundation's funding comes from state and federal sources, these funds only meet the basic needs of the residents. In addition, residents receive a very meager allowance from Social Security in the range of $30 to $40 per month for all clothing, personal items and recreational activities. The Foundation receives support from the community and holds events to raise funds and awareness of its mission. Additionally, Heinzerling staff often does internal fundraisers such as bake sales and raffles in order to augment the resident activity fund and ensure that residents are provided with whatever items they need to enrich their lives.

While working for the Foundation is deeply rewarding and challenging for every staff member, those who choose to work at the Foundation tend to have the deep level of commitment necessary to provide the signature care associated with the Heinzerling name. "Our purpose really hasn't changed much from the beginning," Chris Rafeld notes. "We've certainly expanded and changed location, but our mission remains the same."

HIRAM COLLEGE

In the second half of its second century, Hiram College has changed dramatically and yet—in the most important ways—not at all.

Yes, there are new, state-of-the-art buildings such as Gerstacker Science Hall and the Coleman Sports, Recreation, and Fitness Center, and there are new majors such as a bachelor of science in nursing. There is even a master of arts graduate program focusing on the interdisciplinary studies that are the heart of a Hiram College liberal arts education.

What remains unchanged, however, is the college's devotion to providing innovative, egalitarian higher education of nationally recognized excellence. From its founding by the Disciples of Christ (Christian Church) in 1850 as the Western Reserve Eclectic Institute, the college has stood as a testament to these underlying principles.

Thirty-one Disciples churches from seven counties in the Western Reserve, which settlers from Connecticut carved out of Northeast Ohio, created a non-sectarian institution dedicated to educating men and women from diverse backgrounds. The Ohio legislature, on

This photo of James A. Garfield, twentieth president of the United States, was made at about the time Garfield, a former student, returned to Hiram in 1856, first as a teacher and then as principal of the Western Reserve Eclectic Institute, predecessor to Hiram College.

March 1, 1850, recognized the Eclectic Institute as a preparatory institution. Among the early leaders who guided the institute to college status was James A. Garfield, who would become the twentieth president of the United States.

Garfield isn't just a famous name associated with the college. His legacy lives on in the twenty-first century in one of Hiram's six Centers of Excellence, the Garfield Institute for Public Leadership, which prepares students to assume the responsibilities of public leadership by developing expertise in matters of public policy, both foreign and domestic. The institute is solidly grounded in Hiram's traditional liberal arts education and also serves to educate the public by bringing to the campus people whose own responsible leadership enables them to help clarify issues of public policy.

Students and visiting experts alike find a growing college perched on the hilltop in the picturesque village of Hiram. Garfield came here in 1851 and rose to prominence as a student through his intellectual ability and personal charisma. After two years at Williams College to complete his studies, Garfield returned to Hiram as a classical scholar and taught Greek, Latin, mathematics, and geology before becoming the institute's principal and broadening its curriculum while reinforcing its nonsectarian character.

Though he left Hiram in 1861—twenty years before he became president—

The students and faculty of Hiram College in 1891 were, as they have been since the College's inception, men and women of many races from diverse backgrounds. They are gathered outside Old Main.

Garfield returned often and his influence remained in the form of colleagues and friends such as Almeda Booth, teacher of English, classics, and mathematics from 1851 to 1866, and Burke A. Hinsdale, a student of Garfield's who became president of the college.

The Garfield-Hinsdale relationship established a pattern of close professional and personal association between Hiram professors and their students. "The relationship between professor and student has to do with culture and tradition," says Adam Cathcart, assistant professor of

Hiram College's strong science curriculum has always attracted serious students who have gone on to medical and veterinary medicine schools and other graduate programs.

Legendary Professor John S. Kenyon, the "Dean" of American phoneticians and a writer, was, most of all, teacher to generations of Hiram College English students. The John S. Kenyon Chair in English honors his memory.

history, who quickly adapted to this culture and embraced the tradition. "It goes all the way back to Garfield and Hinsdale. The relationship comes from energy that springs from intellectual dialogue and respect for ideas. At Hiram, this relationship is not just talk. It happens all the time."

Throughout its history, this ability to build a sense of community among both students and faculty members has made Hiram a comfortable place for those who come from abroad as well as those who are the first in their families to attend college. Nearly 40 percent of Hiram students are first-generation collegians who find a warmth that has prompted author Loren Pope to rave about the quality of Hiram's liberal arts education and the way in which it is delivered. "No college anywhere, and certainly no university," Pope writes in *Colleges that Change Lives*, "works more good magic on young minds and souls than beautiful Hiram College in a lovely Ohio village of the same name."

Pope calls Hiram College "a national asset" and has included it in each of the

three editions of his book, which is subtitled: *40 Schools That Will Change the Way You Think About Colleges.* Student, faculty, and alumni have told Pope that Hiram College is "amazing" and "incredible," a place that constantly echoes the Garfield-Hinsdale collaboration, where professors' concern for the students spills out the doors of the classrooms and into the students' lives. "Ten years later," Pope writes of revisiting, "I got the same fervent superlatives from students and alumni about how the Hiram experience had made them better persons and better thinkers, had given them confidence to become winners, and had made them open-minded, caring world citizens."

Among the reasons such a global learning environment exists is Hiram's innovative study abroad program that is facilitated by the one-of-a-kind Hiram Plan. Unlike other colleges and universities, Hiram divides its semester into twelve-week and three-week segments. The twelve-week session is Hiram's long-term learning segment. Students explore a number of academic subjects in a time frame that enables extensive research

Gerstacker Science Hall is among the newer buildings on the Hiram College campus and has become the science beacon of this liberal arts college, a place where new ideas are born of cross-fertilization between previously disconnected fields.

Hiram College students enjoy getting together at the Kennedy Center, one of the campus focal points.

and study. Classes meet two or three times per week for two hours a session. This enables detailed study of several topics and emphasizes long-term comprehension and conceptual development. Courses typically culminate with a detailed research paper or other final project that reflects both the depth and breadth of knowledge cultivated during the session.

During the three-week session, Hiram students are immersed in a highly focused exploration of one topic. In the three-week, students enroll in a single course that meets four days a week for an average of three to four hours per session. During this session, students and faculty explore one topic in-depth and intensively. This single course format removes other academic obligations from the schedule. It also allows faculty to be truly creative in how they teach. That may mean a day-trip to the renowned Cleveland Museum of Art or three weeks studying in Malaysia with a Hiram faculty member. An upper-class student may use the three-week to fulfill an internship requirement at off-campus sites like the Cleveland Clinic or to complete a research project at Hiram's on-campus biological field station.

By combining the long-term learning of the twelve-week session with the intensive research and study of the three-week, the Hiram Plan prepares students for success in graduate school and the professional workforce. The three-week, especially when studying abroad, brings the students into even closer association with their professors, often forging the kind of bonds that can be traced back to Garfield.

The unique Hiram Plan is not the college's first example of originality. The school has a history of curriculum innovation. From 1934 to 1958 Hiram pioneered the Single Course Study Plan, in which students took only one course at a time, in short, intensive terms.

More recently, Hiram College has been in the vanguard of institutions that are addressing the cost of the education they provide. In 2004 Hiram initiated its Tuition Guarantee. This guarantees students that the tuition and fees they pay

The Les and Kathy Coleman Sports, Recreation, and Fitness Center offers Hiram College students, faculty, and staff state-of-the-art facilities, whether for NCAA Division III athletics, intramurals, or simply to work out.

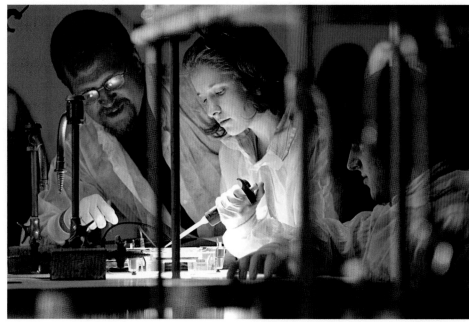

Associate professor of biology Brad Goodner, holder of the Edward J. Smerek Chair in Mathematics, the Sciences, and Technology, involves students in genomics research.

in their first year will remain the same throughout their four years.

"At Hiram," says President Thomas V. Chema, "we're taking a leadership position with our approach to college costs. Nationally, these costs are spiraling out of the reach of many families. Additionally, in Ohio, far too few of our residents pursue a college education because of rising and unpredictable annual increases in costs. We're pleased to be in a position of strength that has allowed us to take steps to make our costs both affordable and predictable."

Hiram tuition is among the lowest of the colleges in the prestigious North Coast Athletic Conference, including Wooster, Allegheny, Earlham, Wittenberg, Ohio Wesleyan, Denison, Wabash, Oberlin, and Kenyon. Likewise, Hiram's Weekend College is comparably priced with other non-traditional, adult-learner programs.

Hiram was the first in Ohio—and the second in the country—to offer Weekend College, and did so without diluting the engaging, demanding, traditional liberal arts program for which it is known and respected. Weekend College, with its every-other-weekend class format, celebrated its thirtieth anniversary during the 2006–2007 academic year and has produced 1,740 graduates.

Whether in the traditional or weekend program, students, as Loren Pope points out, come away from Hiram

College changed. Likewise the college, because of its commitment to innovation, continues to change.

Hiram created a nursing program in 2007, for example, because the college wanted to respond to the shortage of registered nurses, and because it believes, given its history of strong, successful science programs, that it is well positioned to educate a new generation of health professionals who will become the critically thinking, caring leaders of their profession. Neither students nor college has had to forfeit the advantage of a traditional liberal arts education to enable students to obtain the specific skills needed to succeed in an increasingly competitive world.

With a $1-million, five-year grant in 2006 from The Burton D. Morgan Foundation of Hudson, Ohio and the Ewing Marion Kauffman Foundation of Kansas City, Missouri, Hiram College began creating still another innovative program, one that will inspire entrepreneurship across its campus and throughout the liberal arts disciplines. At Hiram, education that works is, and for more than 150 years has been, the college's promise.

REMINGTON PRODUCTS CO.

Every day millions of Americans walk with a little more spring in their step thanks to Remington Products Co. Among other products, the Wadsworth-based company churns out cushioned shoe insoles for the footcare market's best-known brands, including ProFoot, Dr. Scholl's and Foot Petals. Even though the company's cushioned insoles have improved comfort for millions, the footcare business's seventy-three-year history hasn't always been a walk in the park.

Joseph Remington discovered a need for shoe cushioning in the 1930s while selling rubber galoshes for B.F. Goodrich's boot and shoe division. When B.F. Goodrich moved his department to Massachusetts, the Ohio resident resigned and decided to strike out on his own. He devised a way to make heel cushions and arch pads out of sponge rubber and created a machine to manufacture them.

With his new invention and an entrepreneurial spirit that coursed through generations of his extended family (he was related to the famed family that gave America Remington firearms, Remington shavers and hundreds of other products), Joseph launched Remington Products in 1934. He set up

Remington Products employees in 1952.

shop in his basement where his three young sons—twenty-year-old Joe Jr., eighteen-year-old Bill and eleven-year-old Richard— helped out. Annual sales for those first few years hit $12,000. Joe, Jr. soon decided that the shoe business wasn't for him and left. Bill ended up working for the company until he retired. Richard rejoined the company after college and a stint in the Army and stayed until retirement.

Joseph kept the business in the basement for about five years, hiring as many as five or six college boys to work

part-time. The manufacturing process required the workers to pound die-cut rubber blanks with leather mallets, which caused quite a racket. Luckily, none of the neighbors complained. If they had, Remington Products could have been shut down. In those days it wasn't legal to run a business from your basement.

Around 1940 Remington Products moved into a factory in Akron in a space that was no larger than a barbershop. Focusing on selling cushioning components to American shoe manufacturers, the family business ambled along at a leisurely pace for many years. Some years, it made money. Some years, it lost money. One of the firm's bestsellers during the 1940s was an insole called the Weaver Wonder Walker, named after Doc Weaver, an athletic trainer for the St. Louis Cardinals. Thanks to popular products like these, Remington Products grew and moved into a 9,000-square-foot facility in Akron. By the end of the 1950s the manufacturing concern had outgrown that space. That prompted a move in 1960 to an 18,000–square-foot facility about thirty minutes away in Wadsworth.

By that time Joseph had retired and his son Bill had taken over the firm as

Remington Products founder's family.

president. His other son Richard had assumed the role of vice president. Bill always had a great interest in the company's manufacturing processes and operations. He began automating procedures, which streamlined operations, and improved efficiency. His talent for operations was tempered, however, by a lack of interest in being a salesman. That's something that reined the company in and prevented greater growth.

During the 1960s the third generation of Remingtons began working at the manufacturing facility. Bill's son Timothy, who is now president of Remington Products, started doing odd jobs there in the summer of 1966 at the age of thirteen. Children weren't allowed to work in a factory until the age of sixteen so Timothy helped out in the office sweeping floors and such. In 1968 when Timothy was a junior in high school, he worked afternoons and was officially put on the payroll. Upon his high school graduation in 1970 he joined the family business full-time.

The 1970s proved to be a turbulent time in the shoe industry. Manufacturers were exiting the U.S. *en masse* and heading offshore to China and other countries where labor was cheap. Remington Products was losing custom-

Remington products.

Bill and Tim Remington in Hong Kong in 1993.

ers fast. A few times things got so bad the company nearly had to shutter its doors. The Remingtons realized they had no choice but to seek out new markets to pick up the slack. One new customer—the military—basically saved the company by placing huge orders for foam cushioning for missiles.

Remington Products survived that rocky period and by 1980 the manufacturer hit $1 million in annual sales. The 1980s proved to be another tumultuous decade, however, beginning with a few good years and then skidding downward by 1986. The 1980s were also marked by a change in leadership at Remington Products. Timothy took over as president

in 1983 with Bill remaining on board as chairman of the board. Bill also continued working in the factory doing what he loved best—manufacturing—until his death in 1995. Richard continued as vice president until he retired in 1990.

Now that he was in charge, Timothy was determined to turn around the limping business. Beefing up the sales department was the first step. To that end, Timothy hired his brother-in-law Jeff Wert to take over that department in 1988. Wert, who had some experience in shoe repair, quickly made an impact on the bottom line.

Since that time Remington Products has been on the upswing. One of the main reasons for the growth was a change in focus from selling to shoe manufacturers to creating products for the footcare aftermarket—insoles and cushioning products that are sold in retail environments. One such product created in the mid-'90s was the Dr. Scholl's DynaStep. Remington Products produced millions of the popular insole, which helped fuel growth.

With the company expanding more rapidly, Remington Products needed more space. Unfortunately, adding on to the Wadsworth facility wasn't an option. The firm had already expanded the building three times, bringing it to a total of 50,000 square feet. And there simply wasn't any more space available. Instead, in 1996 the operation moved into a nearby 100,000-square-foot facility, also in Wadsworth.

From this modern facility, the manufacturer currently produces about 2,000 different products, including its biggest seller, the Triad for ProFoot. Remington Products manufactures about 10,000 pairs of the Triad insole each day. But not all of the company's products are headed for the footcare industry. Remington Products now creates items for numerous industries, including medical, sporting goods, military, industrial, apparel, packaging, automotive, electronics, and consumer products. Products rolling off the production line include foam cushioning for kayaks, bulletin boards, and furniture for day care facilities.

Remington Products employees in 1985.

at home with their family or friends, so you may as well make the work environment as pleasant as possible. That philosophy trickled down to Timothy, who also encourages a relaxed and happy work force. In fact, there's a bit of a family feeling at Remington Products, where many employees are long-timers with more than 20 years of service at the company.

While employees have become like family, many actual Remington family members have come and gone. There were as many as ten Remingtons on the payroll at one point. Timothy admits that so many family members under one roof caused a bit of friction in the normally relaxed office. But the majority of Remingtons made their exit, leaving only Timothy and his brother-in-law currently on board. With no fourth-generation Remingtons on staff, it appears the business won't remain in the family beyond the third generation. Even so, the family is proud of the major strides Remington Products has made—growing from a basement business into a multi-million dollar manufacturing concern.

Creating so many different products for so many different industries isn't easy. The business spends about $750,000 to $1 million each year in capital expenditures, mainly in operating systems to improve efficiency and quality. Producing so many products is also extremely complicated from a scheduling standpoint. For example, the company might have 200–300 different molds that can be used for a single process. On top of that, a single product may involve five or six separate processes. Keeping production running smoothly is a constant challenge and a main focus for Timothy.

To ensure quality and improve operations, Timothy made a decision about five years ago to become ISO 9001 certified. The ISO standards focus on quality management and aim to improve customer satisfaction. The decision has paid off handsomely for Remington Products, with continuous improvements being made in the quality of both the products and services provided.

A major component of the manufacturer's quality initiative: the approximately 100 employees working at the Wadsworth facility. All of the employees at Remington Products are encouraged to help find new ways to improve the quality of products and services. Keeping employees engaged in their work has never been a problem at Remington.

Since Bill took over back in the 1950s, the company has aimed to create a relaxed and fun atmosphere. Bill always felt that most people spend more time at work with their coworkers than they do

Remington's current 100,000 square-foot facility.

HIRZEL CANNING COMPANY AND FARMS

A good product at a good price: that, according to the Hirzel Canning Company History, was all it took to move merchandise when Carl Hirzel founded the company in 1923. Over their eighty-year history, however, the Hirzels have discovered that their role in the community is much more complex than that. Hirzel Canning Company has played and continues to play a part in Ohio's evolving history because of the family's enduring belief that agriculture is not just about the product, but about the people.

Agriculture has always been a critical industry in Ohio. Native Americans supported their families there by raising corn, beans, squash, and pumpkins; European settlers did the same throughout the 1800s. Ohio was the top corn-producing state in the union by 1849, and corn continued to be the state's primary crop until after the turn of the twentieth century.

It seems natural that when Swiss American brewmaster Carl R. Hirzel found himself out of a job at the beginning of Prohibition, he might have moved to Ohio to grow corn. But he didn't. He bought a sixty-acre farm outside of Toledo and grew cabbage. Cabbage grew well on the land, but the

Carl R. Hirzel, president 1923–1944.

efforts of Carl R. Hirzel's son Karl A. as a door-to-door cabbage salesman proved futile. After one particularly good harvest and a particularly unsuccessful sales year, Carl found himself with a basement full of cabbage and empty pockets. Never one to give up, he bought a kraut cutter and began to make sauerkraut.

Thus Carl founded the Hirzel Canning Company. It may not have occurred to him at the time that the hundreds of pint jars his wife Lena packed by hand would provide not only for his own family, but for his descendants into the fourth generation and beyond. It is certain, however, that he founded the company to help his family get through a difficult time. It wasn't just about the product; it was about the people.

A high quality product certainly helped, though. Within a year of the first production, Hirzel sauerkraut had become so well respected that grocers began to ask Carl for canned tomatoes as well. In 1924 he began to produce canned tomatoes under the label "Star Cross"—a name that derived from the star of the American flag and the cross of the Swiss flag.

The business grew steadily over the next two decadès. Then, with the onset of World War II, it skyrocketed. Demand for canned food products was very

high during the war, and Carl saw an opportunity to expand the company line to include tomato juice, tomato puree, catsup, beets, and carrots. Hirzel's business flourished.

However, the years immediately following the war were difficult for the company in more ways than one. Both Lena and Carl passed away during the war—Lena in 1941 and Carl in 1944—and their children were left in their mourning with the problem of restructuring the company in what was by then a glutted postwar market. Not until Karl A. Hirzel took over as president and incorporated the business in 1947 did things begin to move forward again.

Karl A. realized that in their current market situation, Hirzel would have to innovate to survive. Over the next few decades, he and his family members created a number of cutting-edge canning and storage techniques and machinery. Their tomato bulk-handling system, which debuted in 1969, used water to "float" tomatoes out of a truck without damaging them, was the first successful system in the U.S., still used throughout the world.

Marketing also began to play a bigger role in the business during this period. After World War II, Americans began

Karl A. Hirzel Sr., president 1944–1975.

Karl A. Hirzel Jr., president 1975–2004.

Stephen A. Hirzel Jr., president of Hirzel Canning Company, 2004–present.

to demand more international foods. Hirzel responded by cutting unprofitable items such as beets from their product line and upping the production of Italian tomato sauce. They changed the color of their labels during a lull in the late 1950s and discovered that sales jumped immediately.

In 1975 the third generation of Hirzels—Karl A. Hirzel Jr., president (1975–2004); Joseph, William, John,

Modern method developed by Karl A. Hirzel Sr., of washing tomatoes from the trailer.

Marilyn, and brother-in-law Louis Kozma as comptroller—took over management of the company. By then, Hirzel Canning Company had already expanded to include a second processing plant in Pemberville and the Silver Fleece brand, under which the company sold sauerkraut. Business was good. But the family could see they had to keep innovating to make it even better.

In 1981 the third-generation Hirzel brothers came out with a new product line called Dei Fratelli—Italian for "of the brothers." Proof of the power of branding, sales increased dramatically. In time, the Dei Fratelli line would account for 80 percent of all branded product sales.

Although the Hirzels have used this and a few other marketing strategies over the years, their numerous technological innovations prove that their greatest contribution to the industry has been technology. Joseph Hirzel, now the chairman of the company, explains, "This is not an industry that hasn't advanced. We use very sophisticated machinery." For example, he cites the aseptic tomato storage system Hirzel uses to prevent 100 percent of potential spoilage. They were the first company in the country to succeed with an aseptic bulk storage system, which is used to store tomatoes for off-season production.

It might seem ambitious to expect farm workers to learn how to use "sophisticated machinery," but for the Hirzels, it's standard procedure. They

expect much of their employees because they believe in them as people. "Your company's only as good as your people," Joseph says off-handedly, as if he were stating an obvious fact. And for a family-owned company operated by eleven members of its fourth generation, perhaps it is.

As Hirzel nears its 100th anniversary under the leadership of Karl A. Hirzel Jr.'s son Stephen A. Hirzel, president (2004–present), their major concern is ensuring that people continue to understand the value of agriculture, while agriculture continues to meet the needs of people. Through the Kitchen Incubator Program of The Agriculture Incubator Foundation, they provide licensed-processing assistance to young people interested in the food industry. Hirzel also practices organic farming and works with dairy farmers to create biodigesters and alternative forms of energy.

"Technology is so awesome," Joseph says. "We need to use it for the betterment of humanity." Such a far-reaching perspective on agriculture may be unique to the Hirzel family. It suggests not only that they will enjoy future success, but that Hirzel Canning Company will continue to play a role in the history of Ohio and of the United States for years to come.

Originally, tomatoes were delivered in baskets to be emptied by hand.

KALMBACH FEEDS

Milton Paul Kalmbach, founder of Kalmbach Feeds, had been working as a nutritionist in North Central Ohio for several years when he began to realize that he could offer customers more. For some months, he and his wife Ruth considered opening a feed business in Upper Sandusky. But they had not yet finished preparing themselves when Milton's boss got word of their intentions and fired him, leaving Milton jobless with a family of six to support. Confronted with the possibility of losing everything he had, Milton found the strength to pursue his dream of opening Kalmbach Feeds and fulfill his vision of offering customers a better product for less.

Milton was born the youngest of nine children to a plumber on October 24, 1930. He was raised during the Depression and grew up on the streets of inner-city Philadelphia, where at age seven, accompanied by his father, he would drag his wagon around to collect junk. His father encouraged these excursions because he believed they would teach Milton to be industrious and to earn money. According to Milton's son, Paul Kalmbach, Milton's primary experience with animals might have come from an old harvest facility for cattle and

Milton, Ruth, and Paul Kalmbach inside the Kalmbach Feeds manufacturing plant in 1981.

hogs that operated in his neighborhood while he was growing up.

It may be difficult to imagine that a boy coming from such a background would develop an interest in agriculture. In fact, Paul states that for a person from an urban background to join the industry is exceedingly rare. But Milton not only knew that agriculture was what he wanted to do; he also knew how to go about it. Starting at age ten, he began selling newspapers and soon earned around twenty-five dollars per week. (The average newspaper sold for between

two and three cents, of which his share was a little less than one cent per paper.) Meanwhile, he worked to convince his mother (his father had died on his fourteenth birthday) that he should be allowed to attend an agricultural high school. As with his paper business, he succeeded.

After high school, Milton enrolled in the College of Agriculture at Penn State University. There he met Ruth Elizabeth Rider, with whom he immediately fell in love because, as he states in his memoirs, "she was good-looking and a wonderful person." Ruth was a country girl, the daughter of a dairy farmer, with an excellent mind for business. On March 15, 1952, Milton made what his son Paul calls "the smartest decision of his life"—he married her.

In 1956, only a few months after the birth of their first son, Paul, Milton graduated with a bachelor of science in dairy husbandry. He later continued his education at the University of Connecticut, where he earned a master's degree in poultry nutrition. That degree, no doubt, provided the opportunity for a job with Ohio Farmers Grain and Supply in Fostoria, where he went to work in 1959.

The animal feed industry was undergoing some significant changes during this period, some of which have con-

The Kalmbach Family, Milton, Ruth, Paul, Jeanette, Laura and Rita in 1965.

tinued to this day. Since the end of World War II, smaller sole proprietorships had begun to consolidate at ever-increasing rates. Minor producers who did not consolidate found it increasingly difficult to survive on their own. A job with the Ohio Farmers Cooperative, which later joined with Landmark, Inc. to become the 167-member Countrymark, Inc., might have been an easy path to success for Milton.

But Milton believed he had more to offer customers: better products, greater profits, better reliability, and extraordinary service. In 1962, when he learned that a feed mill in Lovell, five miles north of Upper Sandusky, was for sale, he sat down with Ruth and began to figure how much it would cost them to open their own business and, more importantly, whether it was worth the risk to their growing family. By now, they had four children: Paul (age seven), Jeanette (age six), Laura (age four), and Rita (age two).

They decided that their first step should be to secure the financing: $15,000 for equipment and $15,000 for working capital. First, they approached Ruth's father for a $10,000 loan. Despite some misgivings about the

Kalmbach Feeds Manufacturing plant—1979.

Milton and Ruth Kalmbach, celebrating their 50th anniversary in 2002.

current direction of the agricultural industry, he agreed to help out, so the couple was able to buy the mill on April 2, 1963. To get the business moving, they needed $20,000 more. Milton began to pursue funding from several sources, including the Small Business Administration (SBA). He requested that his applications be kept confidential to avoid jeopardizing his job.

One Sunday morning in late July, however, the SBA announced in the

Columbus Dispatch that they had approved a loan in the amount of $20,000 to Milton Kalmbach. Milton's boss, who had already heard and questioned him about the purchase of the local mill, called him into the office and fired him. It happened so quickly, Milton explains in his memoirs, that without the help of fellow employees, "[I] would not even have gotten the personal items from my desk."

The Kalmbachs had stepped suddenly and unintentionally past the point of no return. They had the money from Ruth's father, but the heralded SBA loan came through with so many restrictions that accepting it would have strangled their newborn business before it started; therefore, they had no choice but to decline it. (Paul would later say that the principle of relying on hard work and the Heavenly Father, rather than on the government, was well taught in the Kalmbach household.) The Kalmbachs' only choice was to move forward as quickly as possible. On August 30, 1963 they received a loan for $20,000 from Crawford County National Bank in Bucyrus, Ohio—and not a moment too soon.

Within six months, the Kalmbachs purchased all the necessary equipment to run the feed mill, bought a truck to haul the feed, and hired their first two employees: Ray Cattran as plant manager and Vernon Grubel as truck driver. In March 1964, Kalmbach Feeds had its first customer: Wayne Duck Farm, a large duck breeder and former customer of Ohio Farmers. They explained to Milton that they had been expecting an order of feed from Ohio Farmers that had not been delivered, and they wondered if Kalmbach could produce it by the next day. After a sleepless and frenzied night of production, Kalmbach delivered it the following morning.

That level of service was extraordinary, but as Milton saw it, he didn't have any other choice. According to Paul, his father often said, "If I hadn't made money in that first year, we wouldn't be here today." Not only did he earn enough money to keep food on the table, but he also earned enough to pay off the $20,000 loan by 1967—and to begin work on a new plant by 1969.

From 1964 to 1969, the business grew at the extraordinary rate of 45 percent per year. The next five years it grew at 15 percent per year. The staff grew also from the initial two employees to around twenty in the early 1970s. By 1971 the new plant—an entirely modernized facility which is still in use at Kalmbach Feeds today—was completed. Kalmbach Feeds had become, to say the least, a success.

Then, in 1975, Milton suffered a debilitating stroke that left him in the intensive care unit for three weeks. When he emerged, the entire left side of his body was paralyzed; he could neither speak nor walk. The family was shaken. Upon coming to terms with their own grief, they realized, too, that it would be necessary for someone else to run the business while Milton recuperated. He passed the baton to his wife.

Ruth had always been intimately involved with the family business—as were most wives in the agricultural industry during that time, Paul explains. "So many wives [in agriculture] were equal partners with their husbands that until I got to college, I didn't even know women's lib existed," he says. In regards to his parents, Paul says, "My dad would

The Kalmbach Feeds Research Farm, just outside of Upper Sandusky, Ohio in 1990.

not have accomplished near what he did without her."

Prior to her husband's stroke, Ruth had run the business office, overseeing such tasks as purchasing, accounts payable, accounts receivable, and shipping. Now she had the responsibility of keeping the business going and taking care of her husband and family. Paul describes his mother as "a 100 percent partner to my dad," but during the time of his recovery, she became a 200 percent partner. Ruth said that this was the most difficult time of her life.

The family's faith was critical in their ability to overcome in that difficult time. "The Lord was very good in those years," Paul says, because He allowed the business to grow very moderately—from 4 to 5 percent a year. Had the business expanded too rapidly, his mother may not have been able to hold it together. Had it declined, it would have added significantly to their troubles. From 1975 to 1979, business at Kalmbach Feeds remained steady, as if waiting for the family to come back together and move forward again.

In late 1979, that is exactly what happened. Paul, who had been away for some time at college and then working, returned to Upper Sandusky and started

working in sales for his father. Through sheer courage and extraordinary faith, Milton had taught himself to speak and to walk again. The business began to grow again, at a rate of approximately 10 percent per year.

Milton P. Kalmbach—new college graduate.

The Milton P. Kalmbach Complex, built in 2007.

There would be many events, both good and bad, that would cause Paul to worry over the next twenty-seven years—particularly after he became president of the company in 1995. He tells one story of a plant fire in which the wiring for the entire plant was melted into large, plastic blobs. By tracing each copper wire from one side of the plant to the other, thirty men working around the clock were able to untangle the mess and rewire the plant within seventy-two hours, with hardly any loss in production. Then, too, faith and trust in the Lord was important. "We were five minutes from being out of business," Paul says. "I saw it as the Lord truly being good to us."

His response demonstrates how many of the business' trials diminish in importance when placed in a larger perspective. "A lot of people reading this are going to say, 'Man, Paul, you've really overstated how easy it's been,'" he laughs. "It's not easy. But there have been a lot of successes. Our team has had the privilege of selling and servicing many of the best families in agriculture."

Ruth, Milton, Paul, and Cheryl Kalmbach at groundbreaking of the new plant.

Pictured above is Kalmbach Feeds as it had grown to be by 2006.

Kalmbach Feeds' basic philosophy, "Treat others as you want to be treated," underscores the importance of those relationships and the faith that helped build them. The motto has always meant more to the family than just words on a page; it has been a plumb line by which they measure their success. Because of that, Milton and Ruth Kalmbach succeeded in a world where small business owners were not even expected to survive.

In 2007 Kalmbach Feeds completed its largest expansion ever with the construction of a new, more efficient, state-of-the-art manufacturing plant. This plant was named in honor of Milton Kalmbach who passed away April 14, 2007. Milt had been involved with the day-to-day activities of the company for forty-four years—right up until his death. The company has also added manufacturing facilities in Indiana, Michigan, and Kentucky and is now in a better position than ever before to continue to deliver the best products at the best value for their customers and future customers.

"We've made a lot of mistakes over the years," Paul admits, "but we have the best team and the best products we have ever had. Our future will be determined by how well we, as a team, execute the golden rule." The company will face many obstacles: an ever-changing industry, a challenging socio-economic climate, and the passing of the baton to the next generation to name a few. But just as in the past, Paul says, great customers, very dedicated team members (who now number over 100), and the blessing of God will be the keys to the team's success in the future.

THE MEYER COMPANY

The Meyer Company, once known for its dairy products and retail convenience stores, is now intrinsically linked to Tomlinson Industries, a division of the company, world renowned for its faucets, dispenser fittings and commercial food service equipment. The Meyer Company acquired Tomlinson Industries in 1974. This transaction was a mutually beneficial one. Tomlinson increased its product line and customer base through the resources of The Meyer Company. The Meyer Company financially benefited from Tomlinson's success. These two once separate companies have origins tracing back to the mid to late 1800s

Gerhard Fred Meyer, the founder of The Meyer Dairy Products Company, was born near Hamburg, Germany in 1859. When young Gerhard was fourteen years of age and the threat of war caused the political and financial world of Europe to be thrown into confusion, he sought to leave Germany to seek a better life in America; a place he was told filled with promise and opportunity.

H. F. Meyer.

When Gerhard, in the middle of winter, decided it was time to seek his future in America, he "ran away from home". Gerhard's parents had suspicions, and because they feared for their son's safety and were dubious of his travel plans, they took and hid his shoes. He left anyway.

Cleveland, Ohio was Gerhard's final destination. He had been told that he had relatives there and there were also a large number of German immigrants in Cleveland. Undoubtedly he encountered many hardships on his journey (his first night in America he spent sleeping under a bridge somewhere in New York), but he finally made it to Cleveland.

Gerhard did not give up. He was an extremely dedicated and hard worker. Eventually he saved enough to purchase some farmland in what is now known as downtown Cleveland. He was in his early twenties when he settled down, married and had a family—three sons and two daughters.

To provide fresh milk and dairy products for his family, Gerhard bought a cow. To his surprise, the cow gave more milk than his family required. He began selling the surplus milk to neighbors and realized there was a profit to be made. He bought a wagon and began making routine rounds dipping out milk to his customers. Eventually, demand outweighed supply and Gerhard began purchasing milk from neighboring farmers to accommodate his customers. Business grew and Gerhard purchased several horse-drawn wagons and horses, then employed his sons to make the rounds. A plant was built to pasteurize the milk and The Meyer Dairy Products Company was officially in business.

Henry Fred Meyer, Gerhard's middle son, was more interested in an education than in the day-to-day running of the family business. Despite his father's

Pictured on the far left is George Meyer—H. F.'s brother—with milk delivery men for other routes.

An early, "over the road vehicle."

disdain for education, "H. F." as he was known, attended Case Western Reserve University in the engineering school. He graduated with a degree in mechanical engineering, but at his mother's request he returned to work for the family dairy. A small fleet of wagons and more horses were added to the assets of the company and its customer base expanded.

In 1916 as World War I was progressing, H. F. enlisted in the Army Air Corp and went to pilot training school in Memphis, Tennessee. Not only did H. F. receive his pilot's license, he met the woman who would become his wife. When the war ended he returned home and concentrated all his efforts on expanding the operations of The Meyer Dairy Products Company. A fleet of milk trucks were added and the customer base continued to grow. By the mid 1940s, the Meyer Dairy Products Company had become one of the largest retail dairies in Ohio.

In the mid 1950s, there was a shift in the retail dairy business as more and more

customers chose to purchase milk at their grocery store. The company began to lose customers. About this time H. F.'s sons became more active in their father's business. The oldest son was William (Bill). H. F., Jr. (Fred) was the middle son and Malcolm (Mac) was the youngest. The three were part of the company's daily operations and soon realized changes would have to be made to ensure the company's survival.

In 1962 the company started a chain of convenience stores called Open Pantry to provide retail outlets for Meyer's dairy products. The stores did produce a good outlet for the dairy's products and were very successful in their own right. Soon it was realized that store expansion could not generate enough volume to make the dairy viable. In the mid 1960s, the dairy was given to a competitor with the understanding that all employees would be retained with all their seniority and benefits.

Although the company parted with the dairy operations, they retained the stores which continued to be successful. Upon the sale of the dairy the oldest son, Bill, retired and the youngest son, Mac, pursued his own business in New York. The middle son, Fred, continued to run

the Open Pantry stores and pursue other business interests to lessen the dependence on the success of the convenience stores.

Over the succeeding years, many opportunities were explored. Some successful, some not, but it was decided that the reliance on the convenience stores needed to be diminished. The company was involved in starting the first medi-vac helicopter operation in Cleveland. There were endeavors in home building, ink production, pet stores, roofing materials and injection molding. The company also had its own small business investment company (an SBIC) which provided financing and other opportunities for its many activities.

One of the businesses acquired was a company in New York started by Mac Meyer. The business was successful, but illness in Mac's family necessitated a sale. Some years after the company, Inland Vacuum was purchased, the stock was taken public and is currently listed.

In the early 1970s, the company name was changed to The Meyer Company to reflect that the dairy no longer existed.

During the '70's, Fred Meyer was interested in growing the company in new directions and was open to sound opportunities. In 1974 the president of Tomlinson Industries, John Chernak, and a longtime personal friend of Fred's, said that Tomlinson Industries was going to be sold due to estate and family decisions. Fred thought the acquisition of the company made sense.

Tomlinson Industries had been a prominent company in the Cleveland area for almost as long as The Meyer Company. The founder of Tomlinson was A. E. Tomlinson, son of an English immigrant. In 1895 Tomlinson had opened a peanut stand next to a dance hall in Old Scenic Park, Rocky River, Cleveland. Tomlinson became fascinated with the inner workings of the compact steam engine and began to consider its value and marketability for

The Dairy in the 1940s on the original farm site.

other businesses, including the food service industry. In 1911 he started the Tomlinson Steam Specialty Company and, as the company grew, he began to see other ways of improving food service products and equipment. For example, faucets for coffee urns and soda fountain dispensers were being produced haphazardly in small shops. None of these faucets were very dependable or uniform in structure. Tomlinson saw an opportunity for further growth and purchased a patent for a ground plug dispensing faucet.

About this time, A. E. Tomlinson's son, R. E. "Tommy" Tomlinson, began to assist his father in the family business. Tommy joined his father in the meticulous work of creating a new and original patent for the faucet. In 1924, after completing his studies at Ohio State University, Tommy Tomlinson was made Vice President and General Manager. The 1920s and '30s were a difficult time for

the company as capital was limited and expansion was slow. Tommy was obligated to be a part of every aspect of the company. He was Receiving Clerk, Assembler, Salesman, Accountant and any other job required to produce and sell faucets for liquid food dispensers.

In 1929 Tomlinson Industries pioneered several advancements in manufacturing various faucets. The concept of a removable faucet head was created by Tomlinson and the company introduced the use of brass forgings as opposed to brass castings. Sales increased a little by the late 1930s. World War II rudely interrupted sales which became almost nonexistent. Wartime restrictions created another time of hardship for the company. By 1946 wartime restrictions were lifted; the void created by them needed to be filled. Tomlinson was ready to produce and did so. Substantial growth for the company ensued. Modernization and new areas of

exploration were occurring in the food service industry. Different types of liquids required specialty faucets for dispensing. Tomlinson created new specialty and custom-made items for a new and growing base of customers.

Tommy Tomlinson's daughter was married to John Chernak. Tommy, using all his powers of persuasion, enticed John to leave his employment as an attorney with a prominent law firm and join Tomlinson Industries. Tommy passed away in 1966 and John, recognizing that the company needed to expand its product and customer base, set about to do both.

By 1974, after both successes and failures in expansion, Tomlinson Industries was stable financially, but had room for growth. The Meyer Company was doing well, but was constantly on the lookout for diversification opportunities. Since the presidents of both The Meyer Company and Tomlinson Industries had been friends for many years, when it became evident that Tomlinson Industries could be acquired; it was clearly an opportunity for both organizations. In 1974 Tomlinson became a division of The Meyer Company.

A decade later the Open Pantry stores were sold and Tomlinson became The Meyer Company's most successful division. Under John Chernak's leadership, a number of products were added to service largely the food equipment industries. Cup dispensers, high chairs, cast iron steak plates, various items for commercial kitchens and a number of other products were successfully

An electric truck—it was only good in warm weather.

Gas powered truck in the early 1930s.

added to the product line. Of course, the main product continued to be faucets for dispensing a wide range of liquids and semi-liquids. In almost every country in the world, you can find Tomlinson products.

The company is now headed by Mike Figas, the son-in-law of Fred Meyer. Mike Meyer, Bill's son, is in charge of engineering, research and product development, so the Meyer family is still represented after well over 100 years. Since there are a number of nieces, nephews, grandchildren and great-grandchildren, there is a good possibility that family members will be involved for another 100 years.

Two separate companies with strong legacies now share a history and a future, one that seems certain to continue for generations.

THE OHIO BRIDGE CORPORATION

Since its debut in 1952 U.S. Bridge—also known as The Ohio Bridge Corporation—has built thousands of bridges that span rivers, roadways and railroads across America. The manufacturer's award-winning, custom-designed truss, beam and pedestrian bridges can be seen in cities and towns from Massachusetts to Florida to California. The firm's colorful history not only spans more than seven decades, it also bridges three generations of the Rogovin family, which founded the bridge manufacturing company.

Brothers Herman and Theodore "Ted" Rogovin didn't set out to launch a bridge company. The Ohio natives originally started a business making steel culverts, the corrugated steel tubes that go under roadways. In 1936, in the midst of the Depression, and unable to find employment, the pair took out a $5,000 loan from the Quaker City National Bank to purchase riveting machines to fabricate the steel culverts. With that loan, the brothers founded American Culvert & Fabricating Co., which still exists today. They set up shop in Cambridge in a 500-square-foot office and a 5,000-square-foot manufacturing

Ted and Herman.

plant. With about five employees, the Rogovin brothers quickly got production underway.

Even though their business was new, Herman and Ted were not newcomers to the notion of entrepreneurship. Their father Sam, who had immigrated from Russia in the 1890s, had instilled it in them at an early age. After Sam arrived in the U.S., he opened a scrapyard in Cambridge, which he ran until he passed away when he was approximately ninety years old. Herman and Ted both helped

out at the scrapyard while growing up, learning what it takes to run a business. As a boy of nine, cutting apart a gasoline tank on a Model T with a torch, Herman's arm was broken when the tank exploded and wasn't properly set because the family was too poor to pay a doctor. It remained crooked through his life. Ted and the family supported Herman during tough economic times in the Depression when he became the first member of the family to ever attend college. Herman graduated in 1936 from Case Institute of Technology to become a registered professional engineer, a license of which he was justifiably proud his entire life.

With their new venture underway, Herman traveled the state handling sales while Ted ran the shop. The business was growing at a steady clip until the U.S. entered World War II at the end of 1941. With no steel available, the brothers reluctantly shuttered the business for the duration of the war. Herman headed off to Cleveland to work for Fisher Body building wing nacelles of B-29 bombers. When the war ended in 1945 Herman moved his family to Zanesville, about twenty-five miles away from Cambridge. He and Ted revived their dormant business and again began supplying steel culverts. The business thrived and within

Somerset County, New Jersey.

a few years, it had grown to about ten employees.

The year 1952 proved to be a pivotal one for the American Culvert & Fabricating Co. That's the year the firm built its first bridge. Commissioned by a local county in Ohio, the bridge marked the debut of a shift in focus for the manufacturing concern. Steel culverts couldn't span rivers and Herman and Ted both saw greater potential in bridge-building. Because of this, they decided to concentrate their efforts in this direction and created a new business entity that same year to reflect the new emphasis. They called the new venture The Ohio Bridge Corporation and began manufacturing the first all-welded steel truss bridges in the country.

The brothers began selling, manufacturing, and erecting bridges throughout the state of Ohio. The firm's target list of customers included local governments, townships, counties, and small towns. The company designed and manufactured the bridges in its own plant, which had moved next door and over the years expanded several times to meet the growing needs of the company. Once they were built, the bridges were loaded onto trucks in sections and hauled to their final destinations. Ohio Bridge also handled the construction efforts, sending three or four multi-talented crew members to erect the bridges on-site.

Ohio Bridge quickly earned a reputation for providing high quality custom bridges. To this day, each bridge is custom built. That's because each bridge project has so many variables, including different lengths, different widths and different highway loadings. Highway loadings are determined by what's traveling on the bridge—pedestrians, cars, gravel trucks, etc.

In 1987 the firm branched out once again. This time, however, the expansion was of a geographic nature. The company sold its first bridge outside of Ohio in upstate New York. Following that sale, Herman and Ted made the decision to target customers outside of Ohio. The pair felt that their company name, Ohio Bridge, might be a hindrance for a national operation so they registered a new trademark: U.S. Bridge.

Under that brand name, the firm began actively selling throughout the nation, now to counties, state governments, private developers and federal agencies.

By that time the second generation of Rogovins had begun contributing to the family firm. Herman's son Arthur "Art" Rogovin started working full-time for the company in 1972. Herman's other son Richard "Dick" Rogovin, a lawyer, returned to Ohio from Pennsylvania and went into private practice, being retained by the company as the firm's attorney. Art and Dick also joined their father and Uncle Ted as the company's

Richland County, Arizona.

Stark County, Ohio.

board of directors and met every Saturday at the family farm near Zanesville to discuss business strategy.

Even though a second generation had become involved with the family firm, the founders Herman and Ted were reluctant to relinquish control. Likewise, they were hesitant to make changes or to modernize. For example, Art and Dick had to work hard to convince them that computers, fax machines and galvanized finishes were essential for future growth; that it was critical to obtain the quality certification of the American Institute of Steel Construction, and that bridges could be sold on the Internet. Sometimes the discussions became heated, but the four of them always operated by discussion and consensus, no matter how long it took.

Art and Dick were patient, recognizing that although their father and uncle were nearing the age of retirement, they would never stop working. The word "retirement" simply doesn't seem to exist in the Rogovin family vocabulary. After all, Sam had labored in his scrapyard until his death at about age 90. Both Herman and Ted inherited that work ethic and continued working in the family business until they passed away in their 90s—Ted in 1998 and Herman in 2004. Richard, now 68, joined a new law firm, Frost Brown Todd, three years ago where he remains a hard-working partner with no plans to ever retire.

Despite their advanced ages, Herman and Ted remained active in the day-to-day operations and in the strategic planning at U.S. Bridge. In fact, Herman remained so intellectually sharp that he was still solving complex engineering problems in his late 80s. For instance, one bridge in West Virginia was posing a particular problem that had stumped the engineering staff: how to remove and reinstall the trusses while maintaining the entire floor system without bracing. To no one's surprise, it was Herman who came up with the solution.

Erie, Pennsylvania.

Cochise County, Arizona.

Prior to his death, Herman shared an office for about five years with Dick's son Dan Rogovin, the third generation to join the family business. Dan came on board in 1999 and gained tremendous insight into running the business while sharing an office with his grandfather. Following the deaths of Herman and Ted, Art assumed the role of president and Dan stepped into the position of vice president. The firm's board of directors now includes Art, Dick, Dan and Ted's daughter, Carole Schwartz.

The new leadership has made significant changes at the family business. For instance, the firm has added new styles of bridges to its portfolio. Today, U.S. Bridge offers a wide variety of bridges, including truss bridges, beam bridges and pedestrian bridges—all manufactured from steel and in several different mod-

els as can be seen on the company's website, www.usbridge.com.

The truss bridges provide an economical design solution that accommodates roadway widths from one to three lanes, local utilities, sidewalks and skewed alignments. Beam bridges are available in short-span models and long-span models. Short-span beam bridges, up to sixty feet in length, allow for easy installation and don't require any specialized equipment. For more complex long-span beam bridges, U.S. Bridge possesses the necessary equipment, materials and expertise to design, manufacture, and even install them.

Each type of bridge at U.S. Bridge is available with a number of treatment options, including galvanized, self-weathering and painted. The galvanizing process ensures an attractive, maintenance-free surface. In fact, U.S. Bridge is so confident in the galvanizing process, it became the first bridge manufacturer to negotiate and offer a thirty-five year rust-free warranty from its exclusive galvanizer, V&S Columbus Galvanizing. U.S. Bridge built the first all-galvanized steel truss bridge in the county of Delaware, Ohio and won an award from the American Galvaniz-

ers Association. Careful measurements of remaining zinc through the years, supports the company's belief that galvanized coatings can survive for more than ninety years in most rural locations.

The self-weathering steel option develops an attractive protective coating that eliminates the need for painting, also making it a maintenance-free option. Examples of self-weathering bridge projects include a 130-foot-long pedestrian bridge in Lorain County, Ohio and a 106-foot-long steel truss bridge in Essex County, New York. The final treatment option, painting, is available in a variety of coatings and a wide range of colors to fit with the surrounding environment. In some cases, customers ask for painting over galvanizing which, while more expensive, ensures the longer life of the painted surface.

In addition to manufacturing new bridges, the family business has also made a name for itself in bridge rehabilitation and historic bridge restoration. For historic restoration projects, all attempts are made to save the original bridge components, but when that isn't possible, U.S. Bridge creates new components that meet current structural codes. Preservation and rehabilitation projects include a Lawrence County riveted truss bridge, the Oxford Road Bowstring Arch Truss in Hamilton County (which received a County Engineers Association of Ohio Historic Preservation Award) and an historic overhead truss in Newark, Ohio which was disassembled, restored, galvanized and re-erected.

Today all of the bridges and bridge components are produced at the firm's expanded office and manufacturing plant. The office currently measures about 10,000 square feet and the plant has grown to approximately 155,000 square feet. The plant houses some sophisticated equipment, but the firm still relies heavily on highly skilled manpower, and its bridges are still considered to be custom "hand-built" products.

Approximately 150 people are currently employed at U.S. Bridge, which still uses the Ohio Bridge name within Ohio. Many of them are longtime workers with more than twenty or twenty-five years with the company. In order to

Burlington-Colchester, Vermont.

better utilize those human assets, the leaders at U.S. Bridge recently hired a consultant to review and revamp their plant and business practices. That resulted in leadership delegating more authority to department heads than ever before while increasing plant capacity by more than 50 percent.

In part, it's thanks to the firm's dedicated workers that it has survived for so many decades in an industry that has been changing dramatically. In the late 1800s there were hundreds of bridge manufacturers. Since that time, many of them have gone out of business or have been snapped up by larger firms. To remain a major player in the bridge-making industry, U.S. Bridge has concentrated on expansion and growth.

One of the key elements that has helped fuel growth at U.S. Bridge is Internet marketing. The firm was the first bridge manufacturer in the country to advertise on the Internet and to create a website for marketing purposes. This move proved to be tremendously successful, increasing sales and inquiries both within Ohio and from around the nation. This forward-thinking advertising and marketing strategy helped cement the company's position as the leading manufacturer of rural steel highway bridges with span lengths from 50 to 200 feet.

With many more inquiries coming in

and bids going out, U.S. Bridge has continued its expansion efforts by strengthening its reach across the country. The firm has begun opening satellite offices to accommodate increasing demand. It currently has offices in several locations—including New Jersey, Pennsylvania and Tennessee—so it can better meet the needs of customers outside Ohio. It is also setting its sights beyond the U.S. The firm has created an international division and new subsidiaries in Europe and South America. This new division is poised to take off and should help keep U.S. Bridge in a growth mode for decades to come.

In the words of Dan Rogovin, "I'm very proud to be part of the company that my grandfather and great-uncle founded, that is still in the family and is rapidly growing across the country and internationally. Our success is due to their dedication and the example they set for the rest of us. They rose from poverty through their own efforts and established our business culture, which is to deal honestly and fairly with our employees and customers, to work hard and to always try to do a better job. We are living proof of the American dream."

OHIO CAT

Ohio CAT, headquartered in Broadview Heights, is Ohio's most prominent Caterpillar construction equipment dealership serving eighty Ohio counties, three counties in northern Kentucky, and six counties in southeastern Indiana. With a product line of over 400 different Caterpillar machines and engines, a ready supply of replacement parts, and on-demand product support, Ohio CAT is the leader in supplying the state's construction equipment and engine needs. The company began in 1945, but the history of the Taylor family's involvement in construction equipment sales and distribution reaches back to the late 1930s and Thomas H. Taylor, Sr. At the time, Taylor was a hard working sales rep. working for a local machinery dealership. He spent his adult life working for others, and then, at age sixty-three, Taylor took a chance, bought a business, and began a family legacy in the machinery distribution business which continues to this day.

Thomas H. Taylor, Sr. was not only in the right place at the right time, he was of the right mindset to venture into unchartered territory, taking a calculated risk which has paid off for three generations. In 1945, the company, then known as Ohio Machinery Co., was first

Ohio CAT's Broadview Heights, Ohio Headquarters.

organized as a partnership with four partners. Tom Taylor was not one of them. He was an integral part of the company; however, he was not one of the principals. His title was simply, sales representative. As the company grew, so did Taylor's rank in the company. He was made sales manager, then vice president, then general sales manager. Eventually, Taylor did acquire some ownership interest in the company. However, it was to be sixteen years, after the company's founding, before Taylor had an opportunity to move into a full ownership position.

In 1961 the two remaining partners of the company elected to retire, creating an opportunity for significant change. Tom Taylor had grown with the company and had established a large percentage of its customer base. At sixty-three, an age when most are considering retirement, Taylor bought out the remaining partners, and controlling interest transferred into the family's hands that year. Ohio Machinery Co. became the Caterpillar distributor for the eastern part of Ohio, covering twenty-five counties. At the same time, two other dealerships were formed to handle Caterpillar distribution in the remaining portions of the state.

Under Taylor's leadership, Ohio Machinery Co. began a grand expansion program. With the 1960s mandate to build interstate highways and the need to construct arterial routes across the states, the demand for machines and equipment to do the job grew expeditiously. The timing could not have been more perfect for expansion of Ohio Machinery Co. It was at about this time that Taylor's son, Thomas H, Taylor, Jr., joined the growing business.

Tom Taylor, Jr. joined Ohio Machinery Co. shortly after graduating from the

Caterpillar 994F Wheel Loader loading a Caterpillar 789C Off Highway Truck in a coal mine.

Wharton School of Business in Philadelphia. Tom, Jr. served as a salesman, as sales manager, as treasurer and finally as president beginning in 1969. Subsequently, Tom, Sr. moved to the position of chairman of the board.

During the early 1960s, Tom, Sr. and Tom, Jr. worked hand-in-hand strengthening and growing the company. In 1962 a branch facility in Zanesville was opened, and in 1966 the branch was relocated to a new 25,000-square-foot facility. In 1971 the company's headquarters and main facility was opened for business in Broadview Heights with 91,000 square feet of offices, warehouse space, and service bays. The construction of a new store in Cadiz followed in 1975, allowing for greatly enhanced sales and service capabilities throughout that region which was heavily involved in coal mining.

Reflecting Caterpillar's increasing involvement in the truck engine business, Ohio Machinery Co. built a second Broadview Heights facility in 1980. This location, which is on Ken Mar Industrial Parkway, is devoted specifically to the on-highway truck engine service business. In response to increased demand

Caterpillar D4G Track Type Tractor on a site development job.

for a more varied line of engines, Ohio Engine Power was created as a separate division in 1988. This divisional structure sharpened the focus on sales and service of commercial engines, including industrial and electric power generation units, as well as the truck engine business. It was around this time that the third generation of the Taylor family joined the business.

Kenneth E. Taylor joined the company in January of 1988. Interested in learning every aspect of the company,

Caterpillar 315C Hydraulic Excavator and a Caterpillar 247B Multi Terrain Loader excavating a new basement as part of a home addition and renovation project.

and getting to know every employee, Ken hired on as a management trainee. He spent close to a year learning the parts and service operations at each branch, working his way through each department. He gained experience on every level while accruing knowledge of supervisory activities. "I learned both what we do and who we are through that experience," states Ken Taylor, now the president of the company.

After spending time in Ohio Machinery Co.'s various branches, Ken spent two years as a financial coordinator working with machine sales and putting together finance packages. This was followed by a three-year period in outside sales covering Lorain and Ashland counties as well as the southern half of Wayne County. He spent the following year as vice president of operations until the untimely death of his father, Tom, Jr. The day his father died, November 2, 1994, Ken became president of the company.

Ken Taylor took the helm of the company, now called Ohio CAT, aware of his grandfather's and his father's significant contributions. About his grandfather, Ken states, "He was one of the early members of that group who supported the initial success of the company. He was the quintessential salesman. My father was probably the quintessential administrator and finance person, with a terrific sense of humor. He took the company through years of incredible growth, during the 1970s and 1980s, within the heavy highway construction and coal mining markets." Ken Taylor learned by example from both his father and grandfather, but he also gained an understanding of what his own contribution needed to be—an enhanced corporate focus on customer service in the interest of totally satisfying both existing and new clients.

According to Ken, there is an element of customer service in every aspect of Ohio CAT's business. Customer service is important in the sales process, in rental, in credit and in sales finance. However, customer service is most important in the company's product support operations. All fifteen Ohio CAT locations offer complete product support, and it is widely believed that product support is what earns a customer's business after the initial sale. Employees provide shop and field service as well as special services such as oil analysis and machine technical support. "Technology is moving along so quickly, with machines now all equipped with advanced hydraulics, electronics and computers, and it is a major job just to keep up with the technology," states Dean Samek, a

Two Caterpillar 789C Off Highway Trucks.

retired Product Support Manager for the company.

One educational program that started and continues under Ken Taylor's tenure is Ohio CAT's Exceptional Customer Service Training Program. All Ohio CAT employees receive this training, and it provides employees the customer service philosophy and tools the company expects employees to utilize in their daily interactions with customers. Also supporting the customer service focus is Ohio CAT's MVP Exceptional Customer Service Award Program (MVP stands for Most Valuable Performer). Taylor believes in individually acknowledging and rewarding the hard work and exceptional customer service provided by his employees, and this is what the MVP

President George W. Bush speaking to members of the International Union of Operating Engineers at the union's training facility in Richfield, Ohio, Memorial Day, 2004.

Program is designed to do. On a quarterly basis, MVP nominees may receive cash awards for going above and beyond their required duties, and the company's MVP of the Year earns a four-day, three-night travel award for having delivered what senior management determines to be the most significant act of customer service during the previous year.

Another educational program which has been created since Ken Taylor became president is the "Think Big" Program. In 1996 Ohio CAT teamed up with three other out-of-state Caterpillar Dealers to develop a college program to train future service technicians. Owens Community College was the school selected due to its proximity to the four dealerships' territories, as well as its excellent diesel and mechanical programs. Students receive state-of-the-art technical education on the latest Caterpillar equipment and engines through a combination of classroom instruction, hands-on laboratory instruction, and supervised occupational work experience at a Cat Dealer service facility. In the twelve years Ohio CAT has been involved with the Think Big Program, more than sixty students have successfully completed the

Caterpillar 267 Multi Terrain Loader in a logging application.

curriculum. After graduating, students are offered full-time positions with Ohio CAT as service technicians.

The service-minded nature of Ohio CAT's employees even extends beyond the requirements of the job, reaching out to the communities in which the company operates. Ohio CAT has a Guiding Philosophy that directs the company and its employees to "be an asset to the communities in which we operate," states Ken Taylor. Making corporate contributions is one important way in which Ohio CAT fulfills that philosophy. In October of 2005, 138 Ohio CAT employees contributed $12,222 to the American Red Cross 2005 Disaster Relief Fund for Hurricane Katrina victims. Through the company's disaster relief matching program, Ohio CAT contributed that same amount in addition to a $20,000 corporate contribution bringing the total contribution to $44,444, which offered support to those who were directly impacted by Hurricane Katrina.

Also, in the aftermath of Hurricane Katrina and Rita, the Ohio CAT Power Systems Division was called into action to respond not only with rental products (rental power and rental temperature control equipment), but with technicians' expertise to restore the main fuel pipeline which feeds the east coast. Having limited items for comfort and living, the technicians worked tirelessly, at times sleeping on the ground and having only limited food supplies. Their efforts resulted in a rapid restoration of the pipeline's capabilities.

In 2003 Ohio Machinery Co. acquired the operating assets of the Cat Dealer in western Ohio, more than doubling the size of the company and expanding its coverage to nearly the entire state. At the time of the acquisition, employment grew from 415 employees to 850, and sales increased from $175 million in annual revenue to $400 million. In addition, the company changed its name to Ohio CAT, signifying the formation of one team of dedicated employees committed to serving Ohio's Caterpillar customers.

The structure of the expanded company today consists of three divisions: Equipment, Power Systems and Growth Opportunities. The Equipment Division specializes in the sales and rentals of new and used Cat machines and replacement parts. The Power Systems Division concentrates on the sales and rentals of engines, with a major focus on serving customers in need of power generation equipment, such as hospitals and data centers. The Growth Opportunities Division handles non-Cat products, many of which are Cat powered, offering machines that are complementary to Caterpillar equipment.

The future is strong for Ohio CAT as the company grows its market share and extends its products and services to the governmental markets, the agricultural markets, and the aggregates markets throughout the state. The mutually beneficial relationship between Caterpillar, as a manufacturer, and Ohio CAT, as a distributor, profits both companies, but also provides solutions and support to their shared customers across the state of Ohio, northern Kentucky and southeastern Indiana.

Caterpillar 994F Wheel Loader.

PRICE BROTHERS COMPANY

Harry Steele Price, Sr. was born in 1876. Sixteen years later, in 1892, when a fire struck Harry's home, his parents and siblings lost everything. Harry and his father got involved in lumbering to earn money for the family. With others, they cut down fifteen trees a day and sawed 300 logs per week. He also worked with his father transporting railroad ties—sometimes 800 per day. Exhausted from this kind of labor, Harry sought other work. He took a job working for a builder. Paid seventy-five cents per day, his first job involved helping build a barn near East Jordan, Michigan.

At age twenty, Harry began his business career by constructing a five-room farmhouse near the rural township of Advance, Michigan, where he grew up. He contracted to build that house for the sum of eighty dollars. Employing one other builder who worked with him from sunrise to sunset and lived in a tent on the site, Harry had the house built in about three weeks. He earned a profit of twenty-one dollars after meeting his payroll of nineteen dollars, a dollar a day for the worker—who happened to be his brother, Ed.

Enjoying this new work, Harry became an independent builder in East Jordan, in February 1899—the date he

Harry Price Sr. stands in a section of 84-inch reinforced concrete pressure pipe produced for Dayton's 5-mile water transmission line connecting wells near Wright Field with the city's water treatment plant.

Harry S. Price

claimed as the establishment of the present Price Brothers Company. He took evening correspondence courses and learned how to read blueprints, a step that put him ahead of his competitors. His slogan was to build well and build for tomorrow. Although generations and technology have come and gone, his motto is still alive and well within the company.

Successful for more than 100 years, the business he started, Price Brothers Company, portrays a rich history and leaves a powerful legacy. The parent corporation began as a general construction company—a builder of hydroelectric dams, bridges and structure—to become a manufacturer of concrete and con-

crete-and-steel products, principally pipes and prefabricated building components. The company's journey is a story that involves hard-working people, progressive engineering solutions, and years of technical innovation. Today the company has plants and subsidiary organizations in many cities in the U.S. and around the world.

In 1899 Harry married Grace Beers, also of Advance, Michigan, and they had three children—a daughter, Margaret, and two sons, Gayle and Harry Jr.—all born in houses that Harry had built. His extensive work and travel schedule kept him from spending much time with his family, which later led to a divorce. One of his earliest contracts was for construction of a dam and power plant on Deer Creek, built for the East Jordan Electric Light and Power Company. It was the first dam his company built, and the first of its kind in the U.S. to be constructed of concrete, a substance Harry strongly believed in. Over time, Price Brothers would build forty-nine hydroelectric dams throughout the U.S.

In 1904 the company took on another major contract, to build a courthouse in Bellaire, Michigan. Sixty years later, Harry would take a trip to see the building and be thrilled to find it in very good shape. The courthouse got Price Brothers a lot more work, including the Bellaire powerhouse and dam in 1910.

In 1911, Harry and his three brothers, Bert, Ed, and Fred, officially went into business together as Price Brothers Company, a Michigan corporation. Initial capital was $1,000 cash plus all the brothers' personal property. Ed and Fred eventually went into contracting on their own, but the name remained. Harry sensed, when his son Gayle was only nine years old and Harry Jr. was only eight months, that his sons might join the company one day.

After the flood of 1913 that devastated Dayton, Ohio, in an act of community generosity the citizens of the area raised $2 million, without help from the U.S. government, to create and finance a system that would protect the valley from future flood disasters. Price Brothers won contracts three years later to supply concrete revetment blocks to

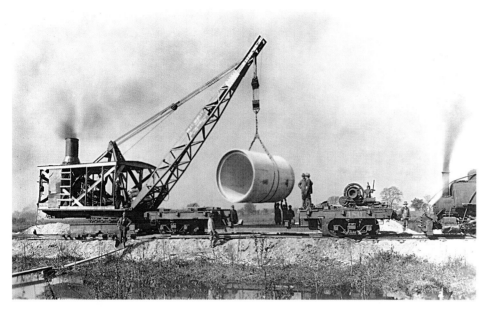

Moving and installing the huge pieces of concrete pipe for the 1926 Dayton water line was accomplished using this rail-mounted steam-powered crane, plus a large work crew was required to excavate the trench and muscle each pipe section into position.

line the levees to prevent future floods. The multi-year contracts led to the permanent relocation of the company operations to Dayton, where its corporate headquarters continue today.

The company began to take on more work for dams, bridges, power plants, ferry docks, warehouses, and other structures in many states during the 1920s. The largest and most significant of these was the Victoria Dam and hydroelectric plant in Michigan's Upper Peninsula. At the time it was built, Victoria was one of the largest multiple-arch dams in the U.S. The work included hauling steam shovels, dragline cranes and thirty-seven-ton generators four to five miles over snow covered primitive roads. Price Brothers kept costs down by quarrying and crushing their own rock, using sand from the riverbed, and setting up portable mills to saw lumber from native timber. The workforce labored seven days a week, ten hours a day, sometimes working at night. When the dam was dedicated on New Year's Day, 1931, Harry realized that this was an historic engineering achievement. But for him, the dam was more a symbol of how hard work and determination can

make a dream real, and bring new prosperity to a depressed area.

Also in the late 1920s, the company produced concrete pipe for a major project in Dayton. This eighty-four-inch diameter pipeline remains in service eight decades later, providing potable water to Dayton and surrounding suburbs.

The recession hit in the 1930s and caused the company to branch out wherever it could find work. The innovative Price Brothers began producing reinforced concrete pipe for gravity sewer applications, and also started a dredging business.

In the 1940s, Gayle and Harry Jr. played an increasing role in the management of the company, just as

Harry Sr. had hoped years earlier. Their presence initiated a shift from construction to manufacturing. The company continued to develop concrete products, including prestressed concrete cylinder pipe (PCCP).

Harry promoted this new pipe to skeptical engineers and water utility owners, believing that it was the most reliable pipe for transporting water. In post-World War II, the new Price Brothers purchased the Lewistown Concrete Pipe Company, located in Hillside, Illinois, ten miles west of the Chicago Loop. Harry Jr., who had to learn the technology of prestressed concrete pipe, was convinced that the company needed to continue the manufacture of concrete pipe and that the installation of pipeline needed to be left to other firms.

Today, PCCP is used by virtually every major municipality in the U.S. to transport large quantities of drinking water and wastewater under pressure. Power plants in the U.S. and around the world use PCCP for its vital water-cooling process. The design of PCCP solved several problems with other pipe materials of the time. It used less hard-to-find steel, was corrosion resistant, cost less than other pipe materials, and featured a steel joint ring design that was reliable and easy to install. Today the company continues its PCCP development to

Victoria Dam.

convey water under pressure. Every day, more than 100 million people rely on Price Brothers Company pipe for water or power.

Also in development was a pre-cast concrete building component system called Flexicore that would later be licensed worldwide. It began with a rubber tube hose that, when inflated, would expand uniformly while shortening in length. Such a tube could be inflated and concrete cast around it. When deflated, the tube would elongate, shrink, and strip itself clean from the concrete core. Price Brothers was now in the business of making holes in concrete. For decades this proved to be a significant manufacturing and marketing device for the company. The sturdy Flexicore floor and roof slab saved many lives in a 1953 tornado that struck New England.

In 1947 Price Brothers was confronted by a new challenge. A principal competitor had found a way to make small diameter concrete pressure pipe by placing the internal concrete lining of the steel cylinder centrifugally instead of casting it with an interior mold. This was a significant development. One could now

Eight years after completing the St. Lucie contract, the Palatka plant was able to produce all sizes of Price Brothers PCCP and covered more than forty acres.

This rail crane lifted and moved each section of seventy-eight-ton, sixteen-foot-diameter Price Brothers pipe to its final position off shore. The St. Lucie outfall extends 3,400 feet out to sea.

make pipe, smaller than forty-eight inches in diameter, stronger and more economically. Price Brothers decided that in order to be a viable competitor, they needed a new plant that used this more efficient method of manufacturing. A survey they conducted revealed that 30 percent of the U.S. population lived within 350 miles of their home base in Dayton, Ohio. So, that's where they built their first permanent pressure pipe plant that allowed them to make both small and large diameter pressure pipe. The Dayton plant was up and running by early 1950. Within another ten years, more plants were built and the company grew.

In 1953 Gayle B. Price, who at age fourteen had worked construction jobs for his father, became president of Price Brothers Company. Gayle had earned a degree in civil engineering from Antioch College, taking over from his successful, self-taught father. He and his brother Harry Jr. were to co-direct the company for more than a quarter of a century. Two years later, Gayle's son, Gayle B. Price, Jr., came to work for the company. Gayle Jr. focused his efforts on improving the company's concrete sewer pipe business and grew it to seven plants in the Midwest.

Harry Sr. died in 1958, at age eighty-two, at the time still fishing, hunting and enjoying an active life. His elder son, Gayle B. Price, had become president of Price Brothers; his second son, Harry Steele Price, Jr., became executive vice-president and secretary.

In the 1960s and 1970s Price Brothers left the dredging business and continued to expand its concrete production businesses, purchasing several pipe operations. Responding to customer needs, the company diversified into large-diameter, filament-wound fiberglass pipe. The company also established the Dyna-Frame structural system, acquiring patents that launched them into the manufacture of columns and beams, double tees, and Corewall® insulated wall panels. Flexicore continued to thrive and set up eleven licensees around the country.

Work began on the company's first major international venture in the 1980s, the Great Man-Made River

Price Brothers engineers designed this special transport vehicle to lift and move each section of Stress-Tite pipe to and from the storage areas.

Project in Libya. Price Brothers purchased two PCCP plants (Kansas City, Kansas; and Perryman, Maryland); built a PCCP plant in Palatka, Florida; expanded the fiberglass pipe business; added and later sold a fiberglass machinery business; and became a supplier of products used in municipal piping projects. The 1990s brought the com-

Many power plant cooling water systems require special concrete pressure pipe fittings such as these large reducers and elbows for an inlet manifold.

Plans for the first phase of the Great Man-Made River Project called for producing and installing more than 250,000 giant sections of PCCP with a diameter of 4 meters

pany ventures in China, also exporting large diameter pipe for power plants, with shipments to Asia, the South Pacific, Europe, and South America.

Gayle B. Price, Jr. became president, CEO, and chairman in 1975 and over the next twenty-three years led many changes, including the addition of non-family members to senior management positions and as outside directors of the company. Gayle Jr. was also instrumental in the company securing work on the Great Man-Made River Project in Libya that has been ongoing since 1983. This $20 billion project is considered to be one of the world's largest civil engineering projects in the last 100 years. It is based almost entirely on Price Brothers technology and designs.

Over the many years since Harry Price had started the company, ownership had become spread over four generations. A decision was made in the early 1990s to liquidate the company. This eventually resulted in an employee-owned and managed company in 1998 when salaried employees purchased the one remaining division, Concrete Pressure Pipe. The company continues to enjoy its position as the leading U.S. and international provider of prestressed concrete cylinder pipe and technology. Since 1943 Price Brothers has supplied pipe to more than 6,500 projects, requiring more than 5,000 miles (26 million feet) of PCCP.

In early 2007 the shares of Price Brothers Company were sold to Hanson PLC of London, UK. Hanson intends to build on the Price Brothers legacy of superior technology, excellent service, and good personnel to create a national pressure pipe business.

Engineering technology and competitive factors have changed fundamentally since Harry S. Price, Sr. built that first house for eighty dollars. His philosophy, however, remains. Employees still work through every problem, choose the best solution and value good relationships with fellow workers, suppliers, and customers. He would be proud of the 107 years of quality construction, and also intrigued by the possibilities of combining with a company the size and capability of Hanson.

RUSCILLI CONSTRUCTION CO., INC.

In 2005 Ruscilli Construction Co., Inc. celebrated its sixtieth anniversary in Columbus, Ohio, honoring four generations of hard work, family values and significant achievement. Since its founding, Ruscilli has built nearly 100 million square feet of space throughout the country while serving as general contractor and construction manager for innumerable local and national projects.

The family's third generation CEO and owner, Louis Jackson Ruscilli, (now known as L. Jack Ruscilli), who joined the firm full-time in 1967, is responsible for introducing design/build and construction management concepts into the company's profile. Once a small trade contractor, Ruscilli Construction is now among the largest full-service construction firms in the midwestern United States.

Growing significantly during the 1980s, Jack invoked "The Ruscilli Way," a set of core company values that regulate the company and influence its associates to be the best they can be at work, at home and in the community. These values are safety, integrity, "can-do" attitude, team cooperation, open communication, quality work, ac-

Louis G. Ruscilli Sr. poses for a portrait with, from left: Louis Jr., Vincent, Phyllis and Albert.

Louis Jr. painted his wife's name right below the gun he manned in a B-24 Liberator during the Second World War.

countability and customer satisfaction.

Although "officially" inaugurated twenty-five years ago, The Ruscilli Way values started at least a century ago, beginning with Jack Ruscilli's grandfather, Louis Ruscilli Sr., born in the southern Italian village of Bovino, a town that dates from 323 B.C., wherein a section of the village, called Madina, is rumored to have been founded in the 1400s by four brothers, then named Ruscillo.

In 1915, at age sixteen, after moving to Elwood City, Pennsylvania to live with family, Louis returned to Italy to serve in World War I. He was captured and held prisoner for three years. Released in 1918, he met and married Anna Venturino, and they returned to the U. S. in 1920.

Louis and Anna eventually settled in the Columbus immigrant neighborhood called Flytown and had four children: Vincent, Louis Jr., Phyllis and Albert. They had moved from Akron, where Louis worked as a tool and die maker for the Goodyear Tire and Rubber Company, then back to Columbus, where Louis found a job with Curtiss-Wright (later, North American Aviation and then Rockwell International).

When Louis Jr. was a teenager he helped his father, holding a light while

Louis Sr. worked with concrete at night. Louis Jr. often asked his father, "Why don't you go into business for yourself? You can make more money." In 1940, even when Columbus had grown into a full-fledged city, there were not many jobs available. But Louis Jr. dreamed of owning his own construction company.

In 1943, at age nineteen, Louis Jr. enlisted in the Army Air Corps and, as a radio operator/gunner aboard a B-24 *Liberator*, served in Spinazolla, Italy, less than thirty miles from Bari, where his parents had met. After more than fifty combat missions over Europe during World War II, he was discharged in 1945 and, with $700 in savings, returned to his wife Mary, whom he had married before enlisting, and to their first child, Louis Jackson. He soon bought a Navy surplus truck and painted the name "Ruscilli Company" on its doors, giving birth to the business of his dreams. When his father refused to join him in the company, he went into business with Thomas Parsons, a carpenter, who was married to Louis' sister, Phyllis.

At the time the company was known as a concrete trade contractor but it was really much more—it was anything anybody needed. If someone sought a roofing and siding job, Louis Jr. and his company took the job and found out how to do it right. During the postwar years, the company grew while focusing on

Mary Ruscilli holds her first-born, Louis Jackson Ruscilli, for this handsome family portrait with Louis Jr., home on leave from the Army Air Corps.

This historical truck is a reminder of Ruscilli Construction's long history, showing the company's original name.

Ruscilli Construction Co., Inc. headquarters, Columbus, Ohio.

concrete and block foundations. By 1947, when work started to pick up, Louis, Jr. managed to lure his father away from Curtiss-Wright with a major job involving the rebuilding of the historic North Market, which had been destroyed by fire. The company also won a contract to build ten steel Quonset huts for storing grain in central Ohio, a job that got them on their feet. At this time, pre-engineered metal buildings, originally developed for the military, came

The first three generations of Ruscillis in the company: Bob, Jack, Louis Sr. and Louis Jr. celebrate the dedication of the company's new home office in August 1977.

into fashion for civilian applications. The firm's expertise soon led to constructing pre-engineered steel buildings with Armco Steel, a business relationship that thrived for almost half a century and earned Ruscilli Construction nationwide recognition. Today, Ruscilli is known as one of the oldest and largest pre-engineered building systems dealers in North America.

In 1955, when Louis Jr.'s son, Jack, turned twelve, he began working summers on his father's construction sites, earning fifty cents an hour. After a few years, several of Louis Jr.'s foremen, who were earning five or six dollars per hour, convinced their boss to give his son a raise. Louis gave Jack one dollar an hour. Tough on all his employees, including his son, when Louis himself showed up at one of his job sites, project work-pace

would increase dramatically. Down in the trenches himself, he inspired workers to move quickly and work hard.

When Jack married Ann Colburn in 1966, he completed his senior year in college studying marketing at Findlay University while Ann taught high school. The family then went through a tough time when Jack's younger brother Jimmy died of leukemia. It was at this time that Louis Jr. invited Jack to work with him full time at Ruscilli Construction Company. Two years later, Jack's brother, Bob, also joined the company where he later followed his father's footsteps by heading up the field operations.

When Jack and Bob joined the Ruscilli workforce full time, their grandfather, Louis Sr., was seventy-four years old and still came to work every day to keep the books and write checks. Ruscilli Construction was gaining a reputation for being a low-cost metal buildings dealer as well as general contractor.

Pre-computer age, all estimates were done with pencil and paper. The company calculated the cost of steel erection by the pound rather than by man-hours. At six cents per pound, a building with steel that weighed 100,000 pounds would cost $6,000 to erect.

Frustrated by the dichotomy of the company's excellent capabilities versus its lack of acclaim, Jack launched an advertising campaign—a radical step for a construction business at the time. Louis Jr. considered advertising a waste of money, but Jack moved ahead with his

"Ruscilli Report" ads that illustrated the company's capabilities and achievements. During the 1970s and 1980s, Jack was utilizing radio, television and direct mail to advertise.

Using strong marketing skills that complemented his father's and brother's construction talents, Jack promoted the company into a top-notch position among central Ohio builders. A diligent and caring worker, Jack would pack his wife and children—Suzanne, Lisa, Gina, and Louis V.—into their car on Sundays to visit construction sites when time didn't allow visits during the week.

In 1968 Ruscilli Construction secured its first $1 million contract for the Purex plant in London, Ohio, which required the purchase of its first large crane. Dissatisfied with what he considered the company's inadequate headquarters, Jack envisioned a 200-acre business park at the intersection of Roberts Road and the I-270 outerbelt and closed a deal that created Ruscilli Investment Co. and started ArlingGate Business Park. Architect Chester "Chet" Croce designed Ruscilli Construction's new headquarters and Coburn Morgan created the interior design, which includes a life-size bronze statue of three construction workers.

Jack continued his marketing strategy by positioning the new office facility so it faced the busy freeway which gave Ruscilli instant recognition as a progressive construction company within the community. While conservative Louis Jr. did not approve of the concept for the new premises, business doubled the next year and he later admitted that it was a good move.

McGraw-Hill distribution facility, Dubuque, Iowa (build/lease project).

In 1978, after moving into the new headquarters, Jack founded Ruscilli Real Estate Services, Inc. to help sell sites in ArlingGate Business Park, as well as locate new building sites for clients who had that need. Today, Ruscilli Real Estate Services, Inc. is one of the leading brokerage firms in Central Ohio specializing in industrial and office sales and leasing, as well as client representation.

A few years later, Jack also founded Ruscilli Development Co., Ltd. to manage other office and industrial land and

Pacer Logistics corporate headquarters, Dublin, Ohio (build/lease project).

to provide leasing opportunities for clients who would rather lease than own their own facilities; such as the 100,000 sq. ft. Pacer Logistics office building in Dublin, Ohio and the 350,000 sq. ft. distribution center for McGraw-Hill in Dubuque, Iowa. Today, both the Real Estate and Development companies are independently operated and are head-

The president of Honda of America Manufacturing admitted that the Ruscilli team accomplished things that even they weren't sure could be accomplished.

quartered at their Perimeter Center Office Park in Dublin, Ohio.

Since the company's first $1 million job, Ruscilli's current annual construction volume has grown to $350 million—approximately $200 million in general construction and $150 million in construction management.

Construction firms from several states wanted the $113 million Franklin County Government Center project in downtown Columbus.

One of the company's largest projects was for Honda of America's $375 million "EX" expansion which required 1 million square feet of new space to be constructed while rehabilitating the existing 1 million square feet of space. During the entire construction schedule, the original manufacturing plant was in full operation and provisions were made to allow the newly assembled automobiles to continually exit through the new

Muirfield Village Golf Club (home of the Jack Nicklaus Memorial Tournament).

addition being constructed. Working with Honda, Jack believes, helped the firm realize that "nothing is impossible if you are focused, plan properly and work as a team." Since then, the company has constructed over thirty plants for Japanese interests. The company was also among the first to initiate a profit-sharing plan and understands that teamwork is what makes a company successful.

During the 1980s, Ruscilli Construction had an office in Phoenix, Arizona and worked on several major projects, including the renovation and restoration of Frank Lloyd Wright's historic Arizona Biltmore Hotel in Phoenix, Rocky Mountain Financial Center in Chandler, and the new underground Hayden Library at Arizona State University.

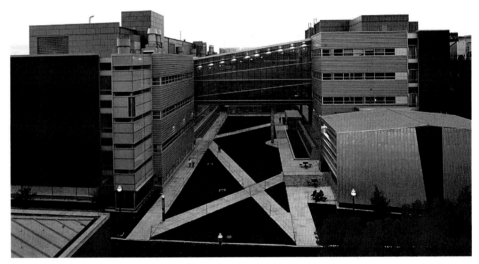

The 1980s also brought tragedy to the Ruscilli family and company as Bob Ruscilli was killed in an automobile accident. As a result, it was the first time in forty years that only one Ruscilli was involved with the company. Fortunately, Bob's son, Robert Anthony Ruscilli, Jr. (Tony), joined the company in 1993 after graduating from Michigan State University with a degree in business administration and; in 2000, Jack's son, Louis V. (Lou), also joined the firm

after graduating from Clemson University with a degree in construction management.

Eventually, Jack became weary of travel and time away from his family and made the decision to sell the Phoenix office and stay in Columbus to focus more on central Ohio. At this time, the company became more involved in construction management providing supervision, scheduling and cost controls on an open-book basis, saving project owners money and time.

The list of Ruscilli's construction projects range from office, retail, assisted living, hospitality, healthcare, religious, educational, recreational and pharmaceutical/laboratory to warehouse, automotive, transportation, manufactur-

The Ohio State University Scott Laboratory Mechanical Engineering Building, Columbus, Ohio.

ing, residential and self perfoming trades. Notable projects, in addition to Honda, include the $113 million twenty-seven-story Frankin County Government Center, Ohio's $65 million Center of Science and Industry showpiece, Ohio State University's $70 million Scott Laboratory, Jack Nicklaus' Muirfield Village Golf Club and Villas (where the Memorial Tournament takes place) and over 500 K-12 schools throughout the state.

Despite mounting competition in central Ohio, the company has entered its second sixty years with an impressive résumé and bright future. A consistent leader in sales volume, Ruscilli has been listed in *Engineering News-Record's* annual list of the nation's top 400 construction firms and is currently listed as central Ohio's largest construction company according to Columbus' *Business First* newspaper.

During 2005–2006 alone, Ruscilli Construction Company was selected to construct the Nazareth Tower senior housing renovation in downtown Columbus; Student Academic Services and Lane Avenue Parking Garage for The Ohio State University; renovation and conversion of the historic Seneca Hotel, also in downtown Columbus; as well as the *Jackson on High* condominiums in the Short North and St. Agatha Church and School Expansion.

Entering its second sixty years is the company's fourth generation—Jack's son, Lou, and Bob's son, Tony. Working with Jack and the company's management team, Lou and Tony have learned the business first-hand, literally, from the ground up. In Jack's words, he feels the company is well-positioned for the future. He boasts that Lou and Tony (the fourth generation) and now co-owners

Carlyles Watch condominiums, Columbus, Ohio.

along with him, are going to be much better than he was at what they do and have already proven to the community and industry that they are a formidable team.

Jack says Lou and Tony have been largely responsible for the dramatic increase in business for their "Ruscilli Residential Division," where they have captivated the Central Ohio market for elderly housing and condominium projects such as the contemporary Carlyles Watch condominiums, 8 on the Square, Dakota I in the Short North, Avenue One condominiums in downtown Columbus, the Metropolitan condominiums in Grandview, Ohio and Prescott Place townhomes in Marblecliff, Ohio. Plus, the new Stratford "age in place" design in Cincinnati, Ohio consisting of 535,000 sq. ft. of cottages, independent and assisted living units, skilled nursing and Alzheimer care, all in one facility.

8 on the Square at Broad and High, Columbus.

Metropolitan condominiums, Grandview, Ohio.

Left to right: Tony Ruscilli, Lou Ruscilli and L. Jack Ruscilli.

Ruscilli Construction projects (top to bottom): Safe Auto corporate headquarters, Columbus, Ohio; Tosoh SMD manufacturing plant, Grove City, Ohio; Lamborghini Ohio showroom, Marysville, Ohio; and, St. Andrew Catholic Church, Upper Arlington, Ohio.

Ironically, Lou and Tony work in tandem in much the same manner as their fathers before them—Lou managing the company's sales, preconstruction and financial services, and Tony managing all operations activities.

It is often said, *the more things change, the more they stay the same*. Sixty-two years following its founding, Ruscilli Construction Company is still managed by the same principles and core values instilled by the Ruscilli family, only the generations have changed.

For more information visit their website, www.ruscilli.com.

Center of Science and Industry, Columbus, Ohio. (COSI)

THE UNIVERSITY OF FINDLAY

Located in one of America's dream towns, The University of Findlay (UF), in Findlay, is northwest Ohio's largest private higher education institution. UF has built an exceptional reputation on a foundation of liberal arts through innovation, tradition, and community. Now celebrating its 125th year, the university encourages students of all backgrounds to fulfill their academic potential and helps them pursue meaningful lives.

The roots of The University of Findlay lie in the Churches of God, General Conference, established in 1830 in Pennsylvania. In 1881 the Churches of God were looking for a location to found an institution of higher education. Eager to add prestige and prosperity to their young town, the citizens of Findlay, who then numbered 4,663, won the bid for the Churches of God College.

Together, the people of Findlay and the Churches of God reached an agreement. Findlay's citizens donated $20,000 and 10 acres of land, valued at $10,000. The Churches of God made up the balance for the construction of the building, which was estimated at $50,000. On February 2, 1882 the Ohio Secretary of State signed the certification of incorporation and the first meeting of the board of trustees was held on February 8.

Findlay Business College students pose in 1921.

Old Main 1889–1890.

Work began in the autumn of 1883. To construct Old Main, limestone, cut stone, brick, and lumber, were brought in by horse and wagon from the local area. In May 1884 builders laid the cornerstone. On September 1, 1886, the institution then known as Findlay College, welcomed its first 70 students. At the time, Old Main was the largest single college building west of the Appalachian Mountains and the only one in the world heated with natural gas.

From the Great Depression to the Second World War, the college over-came many adversities. During the Depression, salaries were cut by 40 percent. The first floor of Old Main burned in 1938. With many men joining the armed forces, the college had only 132 students, most of whom were female, between 1943 and 1944.

The college overcame these difficulties, however, to grow exponentially over the next several decades. In response to an increasing student population, Findlay had two building booms. During the first, between 1955 and 1970, six residences halls, a student union, facilities for fine arts, sciences, physical education, and a library were built. In the 1990s the sciences, visual arts, weight training, athletics, and English riding were provided with modern facilities. Since then, additions have included student living spaces and offices in the UF Village, townhouse apartments, an outdoor sports complex, and the purchase of the former Findlay campus of Owens Community College.

In the 1970s, students in other countries grew increasingly interested in pursuing their education in the United States. Findlay College responded by developing the Intensive English Language Institute—an innovative program through which international students could transition from the educational

system in their home countries to that in the U.S. Findlay also added a number of other unique, market-driven programs at this time, including the renowned Equestrian Studies program and a weekend college tailored to working adults. The success of these programs is exemplified by the fact that the western equestrian team captured its third national title in 2007, with the English team named reserve champion.

In response to these successes and to better serve students, Findlay created a number of specialty majors such as Pre-veterinary Medicine, Hospitality Management, Environmental Safety, and Occupational Health Management. Today, more than 4,500 undergraduate and graduate students matriculate at the university, which offers more than 60 majors leading to baccalaureate degrees, eight master's degrees and a doctor of pharmacy. More than 800 international students from over 30 countries bring multicultural flavor to campus.

In 2007 the university celebrated its 125th anniversary. In 2006 Albert Wilmsmeyer, a local policeman about to

The University of Findlay's English equestrian team was national champion in 2001 and reserve champion in 2007, while the western team earned national championships in 2001, 2005, and 2007. UF is the only institution to have held both titles the same year.

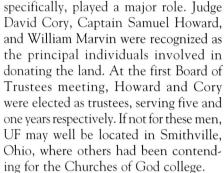

Graduates march through Griffith Memorial Arch in 1968.

retire, came across a packet of deeds in the Findlay Police property and evidence room, of which he was in charge. An anonymous person had handed the deeds over to the police in 1995. The packet recorded land ownership transfers pertaining to the area surrounding Old Main and shed new light on old traditions.

The founding of the College was attributed chiefly to the Churches of God and the citizens of Findlay, but the packet revealed that three individuals,

specifically, played a major role. Judge David Cory, Captain Samuel Howard, and William Marvin were recognized as the principal individuals involved in donating the land. At the first Board of Trustees meeting, Howard and Cory were elected as trustees, serving five and one years respectively. If not for these men, UF may well be located in Smithville, Ohio, where others had been contending for the Churches of God college.

Though their roles in founding the college may have been obscured over the years, the Howards and the Corys are not forgotten in Findlay. A creek called Howard's Run, the Howard United Methodist Church, Howard Street and Cory Street are named for these early, influential Findlay families.

The origin of UF's school colors, orange and black, remains a bit of a mystery. They were adopted in March 1892, when a joint publication of the Ossolian (women's) and Aristotelian (men's) literary societies called *The Ossarist* announced, "The colors black and orange have been adopted by the College." They asserted that all students "will wear them on every suitable occasion." Why black and orange remains a mystery. Since this announcement, nevertheless, these colors have become an integral part of UF's tradition. The athletic teams went by the name "the Orange" until 1937, when the name "Oilers" was coined for the Findlay oil boom during the 19th century.

Another of the longest held traditions relates to the Griffith Arch, the gateway into and out of UF. Every year before classes begin, first-year students march through the arch to signify their beginning at UF. Students do not walk back through the arch until their graduation, paying homage to the light-hearted superstition that those who walk through sooner will not make it to graduation.

The arch honors Miss Caddie A. Griffith, class of 1909. Griffith was known for her "wit, intelligence, and good looks" and her starring role on the girl's basketball team. From 1914–1917 and then 1917–1918, she headed the department of English before going on to serve as dean of women at Franklin College, Indiana, and Ohio Wesleyan

University, Delaware, Ohio. After her untimely death in 1923, her parents erected the entrance to the college in her honor.

After each commencement, faculty line up at both sides of the arch to applaud the graduates as they march back out the Griffith Arch, marking the completion of their degrees. In 1990 the arch was rebuilt 30 feet back from Main Street to allow more room for students to march through as part of a renovation and relandscaping of the front lawn. The newly renovated arch was engraved with the institution's new name, The University of Findlay, which it officially acquired on July 1, 1989.

Today, campus life is vibrant. Residence Life and the Student Government Association host an event-filled brothers and sisters weekend and international and multicultural organizations have their week of social events and activities. The Theta Chi fraternity hosts the annual "Wing Off" every fall, in which students create their own barbecue sauce and compete for the honor of having the tastiest Buffalo wings.

Another strong tradition at UF is excellence in athletics. Twenty-one intercollegiate teams in the NCAA Division II competition and two equestrian teams in English and western riding in the Intercollegiate Horse Show Association (IHSA) are fielded at the university. The equestrian program has risen to the top of the IHSA, with the western teams winning national championships in 2001, 2005, and 2007 and the English team taking the top spot in 2001.

Led by Dick Strahm for 24 years, the Oilers football team won four National Intercollegiate Athletic Association (NAIA) championships. Strahm was inducted into the National Football Foundation College Hall of Fame in 2004, in recognition of his career with a school record 183 wins and the 1979, 1992, 1995, and 1997 national championships. The 2006–2007 season marked the 100th year of men's basketball, the Oilers having one of the premier programs in America. They are consistently ranked among the top 25 of all NCAA Division II schools.

This campus aerial view was taken in 2006.

Since the 1970s women's sports have evolved dramatically. Women's sports did not receive much attention in the early years—competition was limited due to lack of women's athletic programs in many area colleges—though teams included basketball and tennis in the 1930s. Coached primarily by Sharon

Dr. DeBow Freed, University president, appears in academic regalia.

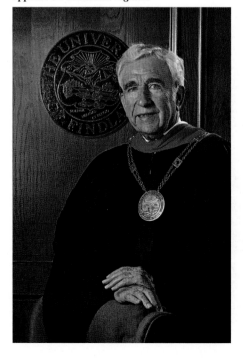

Milligan throughout the 1970s, the Oilers competed in volleyball, basketball, track and field, softball, and tennis.

Perhaps even greater than its athletic and academic traditions, however, is UF's tradition of fostering kind, morally upstanding students. According to university president Dr. DeBow Freed, "The church relationship supports the university's goal of having an atmosphere of Judeo-Christian concern and kindness as a part of everyday life on campus." UF, he states, is home to many good people—caring students, faculty who look on their positions "as a calling, not a job"—and these people form the foundation for the university's success.

Whether athletic or academic, faculty or student, the traditions formed at UF throughout its 125-year history have brought the university through changing times into the 21st century. Dr. Daniel May, vice president for Academic Affairs, explains, "Once you build a tradition of excellence, there's always that expectation." Students and faculty continue to work together to fulfill that expectation. Together, they will continue to innovate and succeed in both academic and other affairs long into the future.

*Lawnfield, James A. Garfield National
Historic Site, is the former residence of
James A. Garfield, 20th president of the
United States. Photo by Hedrich Blessing
Photography. Courtesy, preservation
architects Westlake Reed Leskosky*

UNIVERSITY OF DAYTON

From a boarding school for boys carved out of fertile farmland more than 150 years ago, the University of Dayton (UD) has evolved into a top-tier national private university and one of the ten best Catholic universities in the country.

Indeed, UD is a premiere research institution that ranks top in the nation among Catholic universities for the quantity of non-medical engineering and science research it performs annually. And UD's exchange program with China offers students a global perspective on business, as does the RISE Forum, which invites chieftains from Wall Street to lecture at the school. The university stays on the cutting-edge of education, with an accelerated law school curriculum and offers new degrees, such as Human Rights, that underscore the concept of Catholic education and social justice.

UD is a university on the move with a deep commitment to academic excellence. It offers a one-of-a-kind, challenging education shaped by the Catholic, Marianist tradition. It embraces diversity and provides a friendly, welcoming environment for its 6,600 undergraduates and 3,500 graduate and law students. It's a place where faculty challenge students to forever link their learning to lives of leadership and service. In all, UD offers more than seventy academic majors, which span the humanities, visual and performing arts, social sciences and sciences as well as the professional disciplines of business

Painting of St. Mary's Institute campus in 1911.

Group photo in front of Mary Immaculate Conception statue in 1904.

administration, education and allied professions, engineering and law. UD provides the Dayton region's premiere graduate programs, including doctoral degrees in Catholic theology, educational leadership, engineering, electro-optics and biology.

"Anyone who's ever set foot on campus knows we're all about community—from the front-porch friendliness of the neighborhoods to our outreach efforts in the Dayton community and around the globe," says UD president Daniel J. Curran, Ph.D. "Our research stands among the best in the nation. Our programs are transformative and entrepreneurial. The University of Dayton is gaining national recognition for what we do best."

UD traces its roots to 1850, when it was called

St. Mary's School for Boys. The staff was four Marianist missionaries who came to Dayton from France and learned English from the school's fourteen students. Marianists view Mary, the mother of Jesus, as the model of discipleship. Marianists believe that living, praying and supporting one another in community enriches their faith and strengthens their ability to meet world challenges—especially problems associated with poverty and ignorance. In 1878 St. Mary's Institute was incorporated as a college by the State of Ohio, and the authority to grant degrees came in 1882. The school survived the Great Flood of 1913 that forever changed Dayton. The administration extended the boarding students' Easter holiday so that St. Mary's could offer its facilities to house as many as 600 people who were left homeless.

In 1920 St. Mary's Institute changed its name to the University of Dayton to become the city's adopted university. The most significant development at UD during the years that followed was the enrollment of women in night and weekend courses in 1922. By 1937 women were admitted to all classes and UD became the first Catholic coeducational college in the United States. The University faced tough times during the Great Depression, but the spirit of the Marianists who had survived cholera, smallpox, influenza, wars, fire and flood urged the school onward. The World War II years were lean, but by the mid-1950s enrollment started to increase at a double-digit rate and UD was the fastest growing university in Ohio with the largest private undergraduate enrollment in the state.

UD's Research Institute, or UDRI, was founded in 1956. The University has since achieved a remarkable research record. UDRI, which performs more than $70 million of sponsored research annu-

Immaculate Conception Chapel.

demands of society on higher education. The names of the new majors accurately reflect the shifts in the national and global economies. The University of Dayton is the first American university to sign an agreement to offer graduate education to employees of fifty Fortune 500 companies in the China-Singapore Suzhou Industrial Park. The University is exploring collaborations with Nanjing University, one of the top research universities in China. Engineering technology students from Shanghai Normal University transfer to UD for their senior year.

UD has enjoyed record applications for admission, record sponsored research dollars and tremendous momentum during Curran's presidency. UD has introduced new exchange programs in China, established centers of excellence in nanotechnology and fuels and combustion, renovated facilities, built a sports complex, launched the nation's first

accelerated law curriculum, and started a doctor of physical therapy program. In addition, UD opened the Dayton Early College Academy in 2003. This public high school on campus prepares Dayton area first-generation college students to earn a high school diploma and college credits at the same time. To enhance its residential environment, UD constructed two facilities that combine living and learning—Marianist Hall, a residence hall with learning spaces, and ArtStreet, an imaginative housing and arts education complex in the student residential neighborhood. RecPlex, an ultramodern fitness and recreation complex, opened in 2006.

What makes the University of Dayton distinctive is its unwavering commitment to integrated learning and living rooted in its Catholic, Marianist tradition. The University of Dayton's 95,000 living alumni, including 22,000 in the Dayton region, are leading lives of leadership and service—and transforming their communities. Professors routinely build service-learning opportunities into their courses. This deep sense of mission and vision of educational excellence can be traced back to the Marianists. A UD education doesn't just shape minds. It shapes lives.

St. Mary's Hall.

ally, ranks first in Ohio and second in the nation in materials research funded by the federal government.

Researchers, who have earned a national reputation for their work in aircraft safety, are focusing on making breakthroughs in nanomaterials (the science of constructing new materials with dimensions about the size of five to 10 atoms). The technology could lead to the strongest, lightest materials ever made.

Women, international, and minority students became a larger portion of the student body during the enrollment shifts of the 1960s. Total enrollment in 1961 included sixty-nine international students, representing twenty-nine different countries. New majors introduced in the 1980s and 1990s reflected the changing

THE VERDIN COMPANY

Francois and Michael Verdin were among many Western Europeans who emigrated to the United States in the mid-nineteenth century. They came from Alsace, France as skilled metal forgers, and began a business to repair and manufacture tower clocks. They located their new company in Cincinnati, a city that was alive with economic opportunity.

Since the first Verdins started their business more than 165 years ago, some 30,000 installations of clocks and bells have graced thousands of communities and public places all over the world. Still based in Cincinnati, The Verdin Company is the oldest American maker of large bronze bells, and has worked hard to continue traditional principles, provide excellent customer service, and stay in tune with pioneering technology that augments its products. The company is proud of its longevity and innovation, the hallmark of Verdin business.

Today the Verdin business includes more than clocks and bells. It also creates Verdin-designed, free-standing towers, allowing the time and its accompanying music to become part of any setting. Electronic bells have become an important product for churches preferring the sound of real bells. Tower clocks, once installed only as part of a

Xavier University tower clock, Cincinnati, Ohio.

city hall, church or county courthouse, now lend an identification to shopping malls, residential developments, business parks and banks. Street clocks were used in the 1880s as advertising features for stores. Now they identify towns, neighborhoods, parks and schools, and continue to leave a memorable mark on Ohio history.

Verdin is the oldest family-run manufacturer in Ohio, and the fifty-second oldest family company in the United

States. Verdin's remarkable story begins in 1842, when the company moved the business to the Over-the-Rhine area of Cincinnati, and installed a tower clock at Old St. Mary's Church. When Francois Verdin turned the business over to his son, Alois Nicholas, he started the more than 165-year tradition of passing the family business from one generation to the next. During the second generation, the company invented the continuous winder for clocks and, while working in towers, they also repaired and maintained bells.

In 1927, I. T. Verdin, the company's third generation owner, invented the first electric ringing device for bells ever used in the United States. Until that time, all bells were rung by hand. Selling electric ringers to churches throughout Ohio, Kentucky and Indiana, The Verdin Company business changed forever.

In 1934 Robert Verdin, Sr., Ralph Verdin and Forrest Verdin rang in the fourth generation. Still focusing on high quality customer service, they followed in their predecessor's footsteps by providing bell restoration while modernizing company products via the use of new technology. In the 1950s the Verdins introduced recorded bells, known today as digital carillons.

When many other bell foundries went out of business due to bronze shortages during World War II, Verdin installed and maintained the cast bronze bells that these companies had started. After the war, the brothers expanded their business, thanks to an agreement with the family-owned Royal Dutch Bell Foundry, Petit and Fritsen, becoming a major builder and renovator of bells, chimes, and carillons in the United States.

Since inventing the first electric bell ringer, Verdin has been advancing bell-ringing technology. Each bell striker is custom made using the most updated materials as well as digital programming. As part of the company's latest technological innovation, digital carillons, commonly called digital bells, have changed dramatically with the advent of modern technology.

Verdin ancestors prior to 1927.

Verdin street clock, Madison, New Jersey.

Today, these bells, digitally sampled from cast bronze bells, can play songs, ring a peal, or toll in memoriam. The invention of digital bells has given the sound of bells to all churches, regardless of size, and has made the ringing of bells part of a community, college or downtown event, no matter the size or need.

Verdin tower clocks enhance city squares, courthouses and universities as well as airports, amusement parks, churches, hotels, restaurants, and shopping centers. The tower clock at Xavier University in Cincinnati, Ohio is an example of Verdin designers' inspiration.

Street clocks, first introduced around 1880, are image builders that reflect a community's tradition. Among a variety of communities, the Verdin street clock in Madison, New Jersey is a longtime favorite. Verdin custom-designs these masterpieces with a master clock controller and automatic daylight savings adjustment.

Verdin also constructs bell towers that preserve aesthetic and acoustic qualities of their cast bronze bells. A local favorite is Pulley Tower, at Miami University in Oxford, Ohio. Verdin's clock towers appear in many business parks, shopping areas and on college campuses. They can be built with clocks and bells that ring the hour and play bell music for any occasion.

Today, the fifth generation includes Robert J. Verdin, Jr., James R. Verdin, and David E. Verdin. Still working to

Pulley Tower at Miami University, Oxford, Ohio.

maintain 19th century craftsmanship, the Verdin cousins continue to explore the best ways to maintain industry standards while inventing new products.

In 1981 the Verdins purchased and renovated downtown Cincinnati's Old St. Paul's Church, originally built in 1848, at the time, on the verge of demolition. Restored to its original beauty and charm, the church now houses Verdin's bell and clock museum. Today, still rooted in Cincinnati, The Verdin Company enjoys a glowing reputation all over the world. Its collection of historic items sits in the museum they created on the premises. Groups tour the building or rent it for private functions. The stained-glass windows, arched ceilings, hand-painted murals, and marble and terrazzo floors are a perfect backdrop for the family's collection of antique clocks, bells and bell-ringing equipment.

An heirloom itself, the Verdin Company prides itself in a relatively new section of its business—creating legacy projects that provide a bell or clock as a monument in a distinct setting. Such legacies celebrate a notable event or a community's goal. One legacy is the

Verdin Cincinnati headquaters during flood of 1937.

World Peace Bell in Newport, Kentucky. The 66,000-pound masterpiece was created in honor of the millennium and installed in Newport, Kentucky, to promote world peace. Other legacies include the Lawrenceburg, Indiana Gateway, the Vacc Memorial Tower at UNC-Greensboro, the Alumni Bell Tower at East Tennessee State, Johnson City, Tennessee along with the 88 Ohio Bicentennial Bells.

The art and craft of bell- and clock-making continues at the company's manufacturing facility in Cincinnati. With 130,000 square feet of space, Verdin handles all production operations with a machine shop and plenty of room for full assembly. Verdin craftsmen have constructed towers as tall as 110 feet, built in sections and then assembled on-site.

In a separate nearby facility, the company casts bells up to 1,000 pounds. The process for casting bells has not changed for centuries. Today there are electronic

Verdin Clock Tower at night.

World Peace Bell at night.

A carillon of bells.

tuning devices and mechanical lathes used in the foundry, but the human skills and techniques required for forefront bell casting have remained the same. The secret lies in mixing the copper and tin, casting the bronze, and never using re-smelted metal in the casting process.

Still, Verdin continues to explore and utilize new technology to create clocks of exceptional quality. Tower and street clocks, for example, feature reliable electric works, a control compartment in the base for easy setting and service, and an unbreakable face cover, plus photocell automatic illumination. The technological aspects may be hidden but they enhance each clock's design.

Another example of continuing innovation is the way the company celebrated Ohio's Bicentennial. Verdin designed and built the world's only mobile bell foundry that traveled to each of Ohio's eighty-eight counties to cast a bronze bell in each locale while Ohioans watched.

The equipment for the mobile foundry was housed in two large trailers, so that each of the 250-pound bells could be cast in the county in which it was to reside. On day one in each locale, 500 pounds of bronze ingots were put in the furnace, then heated to 2,200 degrees Fahrenheit. The molten bronze was then poured into a custom-made bell mold, where it cooled and hardened overnight. On day two, the mold was broken with a large sledgehammer, exposing the bell. The bell was then sandblasted to clean and smooth the surface. After another four hours of polishing, the bell was ready to be dedicated. In eighty-eight counties, the bell became a legacy, a gift, a lasting treasure of the Bicentennial. Since then, the Verdin Bell Foundry on Wheels® has traveled to many locations to honor or commemorate a special event or anniversary by casting a custom bell. The Verdin Bell Foundry on Wheels® is a rare innovation that serves to demonstrate Verdin's ability to combine traditional craftsmanship and modern technology.

Among its more recent offerings, Verdin cast a church bell for television's *Extreme Makeover:* "Home Edition: After the Storm." First Emmanuel Baptist Church in New Orleans, Louisiana was a Hurricane Katrina victim. With 1,200 parishioners and a church school, the *Extreme Makeover* team chose the church as one of their recipients in the Gulf Coast to benefit from a community makeover. The Verdin Company cast a 250-pound cast bronze bell with a custom inscription as a gift to the church.

Verdin repairs, refinishes and reconditions damaged bells and bell equipment to recapture their original beauty. More than seventy-five employees work in the Cincinnati facility, and more than thirty service and installation technicians and twenty-five sales representatives work across the country. The company offers a complete maintenance program for all products, and many customers participate in the Preventive Maintenance program to ensure worry-free operation of all products. Verdin is proud that several original electric bell-ringing pieces of equipment, built in 1927, are still fully functional.

Today, family members of the sixth generation are serving apprenticeships, learning all aspects of the business, from customer service to creation, installation and sales—all before taking on greater responsibilities within the company. The Verdin Company continues its research and development, striving to maintain the old-world craftsmanship of its ancestors while creating heirlooms for the future.

Fifth generation Dave, Bob, and Jim Verdin.

Pouring a bell.

WITTENBERG UNIVERSITY

As Wittenberg students embark on the collective quest for what poet William Blake describes as a firm persuasion, "the knowledge that what we are doing is right for ourselves and good for the world at exactly the same time—one of the great triumphs of human existence," they succeed in igniting flames of creativity, compassion, integrity and international awareness in ways that extend far beyond the realms of traditional academics. Founded on the belief that "by having light, we pass it on to others," Wittenberg's altruistic approach to higher learning inspires results particularly rare in our culture, in our times.

Established in 1845 as a Lutheran college and seminary, Wittenberg University has emerged as one of the finest liberal arts colleges in the country and its long-standing commitment to service fuels its luminous flame. Wittenberg contributes a significant number of participants working for organizations such as the Japan Exchange and Teaching Program, Habitat for Humanity and Teach for America. The experiences gleaned have a profound impact on student's lives, propelling thousands of alumni to become actively engaged within their respective communities. "It really changes their trajectory," says

Hollenbeck Hall Atrium.

President Mark H. Erickson, who stresses the importance of cultivating personal and professional integrity. "Although Wittenberg students go on to work in a vast array of professions," Erickson says, "they do it with an eye toward making a difference in the world."

Inaugurated in 2005 as Wittenberg's thirteenth president, Erickson encourages faculty and students alike to strive magnanimously toward developing a global sensibility. Among the many

Wittenberg alumni who have harnessed achievements of extraordinary merit are the founder of the Hong Kong Stock Exchange, the head of the Nissan Foundation, the former president of the United States Olympic Committee and Mr. Ho Pak Kong, director of the largest travel agency in the Far East, who reciprocates his success by funding the education of 100 children from his hometown village in the People's Republic of China. University communications director Karen Gerboth champions the notion that, "we're trying to shape people who will go on to contribute to the greater society and humanity."

Erickson lauds the achievements of one Wittenberg alumna who provided what he describes as "the most phenomenal experience" in his first year as president. Miss Emily Guhde is teaching second grade as part of the Teach for America program at a charter school located in one of the most impoverished districts of Phoenix. While traveling to Arizona for a recent convention, Erickson paid a visit to Emily's class and proudly found her students to be full of possibility, intellectual curiosity and excitement. "You could see it in their eyes,"

Myers Hall.

Erickson recalls after one student's inquiry as to what he needed to do to become the president of Wittenberg. "It was one of those moments that gave me the chills," Erickson recalls. "This child may hold the presidency one day, but only because of the impact Emily Guhde has had on his life, lifting his sights not only to *go* to college but to *become the president!*"

Nationally ranked in the NCAA Division III, Wittenberg supports the pursuit of excellence in both academics and athletics offering more than forty majors, minors and special programs from which students may choose to direct their studies, as well as twenty-three different men's and women's athletics programs, three of which won championships in 2006. Wittenberg boasts a rare marine biology program and outstanding interdisciplinary studies in Russia and East Asia, the latter having secured a $1.9 million grant from the Freeman Foundation—the largest single-foundation grant ever to be received by a Wittenberg program. The grant is being used to ensure all students have an encounter with Asia as part of their undergraduate experience whether through fellowships, lectures, performances or exchanges abroad.

"The world is getting smaller every day," says President Erickson "the more our students truly understand that world, the better prepared they will be to lead it." One program takes students to the Kingdom of Lesotho—a small, independent country within South Africa where students volunteer for various community projects. Kat Hittle, future participant in the Teach for America Program with plans on the horizon for law school, recently traveled to Lesotho and credits the experience with shaping her career path. "The children I worked with at the AIDS orphanage touched my heart, and I touched theirs. And while no one can save the world by themselves," says Ms. Hittle, "one-on-one, humans can make a difference."

Wittenberg's flame was first ignited in 1845 by founder Ezra Keller, a strong-spirited preacher from Hagerstown, Maryland who identified with the American pioneer spirit and recognized

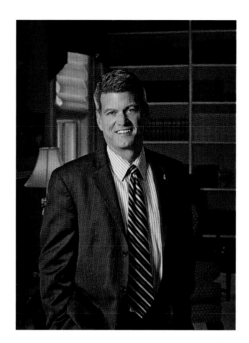

Wittenberg President Mark Erickson.

the auspicious role the church could play in higher education. With a vigorous persuasion for Wittenberg's future, Keller spent months traveling thousands of miles on horseback across what was then still considered a great expanse of untamed wilderness, garnering the necessary funding and support that allowed Wittenberg to establish its home in Springfield, Ohio, and commence its first winter session in the fall of that same year with nine students who paid a mere fifty dollars in tuition. Prior to Wittenberg's conception, only nine colleges existed in Ohio, and only a few thousand students were enrolled among them. Today, the ensemble of Wittenberg programs draws

Hollenbeck Hall.

more than 2,000 students from thirty-eight states and twenty-three countries, and 62 percent of its freshmen come from the twenty-fifth percentile of high school classes. The persistence for continual growth can be felt throughout the campus; the brick and mortar of its first historic buildings were set in place by the hands of the university's very own.

President Erickson upholds the importance of providing appropriate mentorship opportunities as students shape their intellectual capabilities, spiritual identity and future career paths. With a faculty to student ratio of twelve to one, Wittenberg narrows the distance between promise and performance, placing among the top 10 percent of four-year colleges in the number of students who earn their PhDs. Wittenberg's dedicated faculty of 220 instructors is comprised of thirteen Fulbright Scholars, ranking the university first among four-year colleges in Ohio since 2002. Three others received the prestigious honor of Ohio Professor of the Year, placing the institution eighth nationally among more than 500 institutions. Faculty members can often be found leading discussions on campus staged around world news pulled from *The New York Times*, which is delivered daily to residence halls.

The name Wittenberg, borrowed from the university in Germany where Martin Luther taught in the sixteenth century, remains a proud one in Lutheran history. Today's Wittenberg represents the quintessential example of the potential for liberal arts colleges to cultivate and promote the next generation of scholars and global citizens. Bob Rafferty, director of new media and webmaster, supports the university's revered mission of helping students find their firm persuasion by eloquently stating, "Our alumni not only leave with an education that will help them make a living, but they leave with a way of thinking that will help them make a life."

A TIMELINE OF OHIO HISTORY

1669 The French explorer La Salle explores the region between Lake Erie and the Ohio River.

1745 The British build Fort Sandoski on Sandusky Bay, the first British fort in what would become Ohio.

1749 The French explorer Celeron de Bienville travels down the Ohio River, burying lead plates that claim the Ohio Country for France's monarch Louis XV.

1761 Christian Post builds a log house near Bolivar in today's Tuscarawas County, the first permanent house in Ohio.

1764 Colonel Henry Bouquet secures the release of more than 200 white settlers, near Coshocton, held by native tribes during the French and Indian War.

1773 David Zeisberger and Moravian missionaries open first school west of Allegheny Mountains, at Schoenbrunn, to educate Native American children. The mission was abandoned in 1777 as conflicts with native tribes grew.

1780 George Rogers Clark destroys Piqua, a Shawnee village on the Mad River in western Ohio.

1782 Ninety-six converted Christian Native Americans are massacred by

National Road mile markers can still be found along the road in Ohio. Photo by Nancy Recchie

Chillicothe was one of several communities that served as the state capital before Columbus was selected as the permanent seat of government in 1812. Courtesy, Ross County Historical Society

Pennsylvania militiamen at Gnadenhutten in Tuscarawas County. Near Upper Sandusky, Col. William Crawford is burned at the stake, having been captured by native warriors during an expedition against them.

1785 Fort Harmar is established on the west bank of the Muskingum River where it joins the Ohio River.

1787 The Ordinance of 1787 is passed, becoming the basic framework for government in the Northwest Territory. It

provides for public education; freedom of speech, the press, and assembly; and prohibits slavery.

1788 Forty-eight pioneer settlers led by Rufus Putnam, arriving from Massachusetts, establish Marietta, the first permanent white settlement in Ohio.

Campus Martius is built as protection against native attacks.

Cincinnati is founded the same year and is at first named Losantiville, a name made up primarily from Latin words meaning "City Opposite the Mouth of the Licking River." It was later named for the military officers' organization known as the Society of the Cincinnati.

1790 Gallipolis ("City of the Gauls") is founded on the Ohio River by 500 French settlers.

1793 *The Centinel of the North-Western Territory*, the first newspaper north and west of the Ohio River, is published in Cincinnati.

1794 Twenty years of battles with Native American tribes end with the defeat of British and native confederated forces at the Battle of Fallen Timbers near present-day Maumee.

1795 The Treaty of Greenville formally ends hostilities with native tribes and cedes large amounts of native lands, triggering increased white settlement in Ohio.

1796 General Moses Cleaveland establishes a town site on the east bank of the Cuyahoga River. The town would be named for its founder, but with a change in spelling.

The same year, Ebenezer Zane is authorized by Congress to survey Zane's Trace, a pioneer road from Wheeling, Virginia, to Maysville, Kentucky, by way of Zanesville and Lancaster, Ohio.

1799 Ohio's territorial government is established at Cincinnati. The territory's population is just over 40,000.

1800 Chillicothe becomes the territorial capital.

1802 A constitutional convention at Chillicothe drafts a constitution and petitions Congress for admittance to the Union.

1803 Ohio becomes a state, the "Seventeenth Star" on the flag of the United States.

1804 Ohio University, the first institu-

Ohio produced a number of important Civil War generals, including U.S. Grant, who later became president of the United States. On the left is a portrait of Grant by Matthew Brady. On the right Lieutenant General U. S. Grant in Cold Harbor, Virginia, June, 1864. Courtesy, National Archives

tion of higher learning north and west of the Ohio River, is founded at Athens.

1810 Zanesville succeeds Chillicothe as Ohio's capital, but only for two years. The state now has nearly 231,000 citizens.

1811 The steamboat *Orleans* is the first steam-powered craft on the "western waters," traveling down the entire length of the Ohio River.

1812 Ohio's capital returns to Chillicothe for four years. Also this same year, the new town of Columbus is made the permanent seat of the state's government.

1813 The Battle of Lake Erie, in which Oliver Hazard Perry's small navy defeats a much larger British force at Put-In-Bay, securing the Great Lakes for the United States in the War of 1812.

1815 The first meeting of the Union Humane Society, an anti-slavery organization, is held in St. Clairsville in eastern Ohio.

1816 The Ohio General Assembly

meets in Columbus, the new permanent capital, for the first time.

1817 The first issue of *The Philanthropist*, the first abolitionist newspaper in the nation, is published at Mount Pleasant in eastern Ohio.

1818 The first steamboat on Lake Erie, the *Walk-in-the-Water*, visits Cleveland and Sandusky.

1820 Ohio's population has grown to a little more than 581,000.

1824 The first trip by a steamboat on the Muskingum River is made by the *Rufus Putnam*.

1825 Work begins on the two state-constructed cross-Ohio canals, the Ohio and

Erie in the east and the Miami and Erie in the west.

1829 Boat service begins on the Miami and Erie Canal between Dayton and Cincinnati.

1830 Ohio's population is nearly 938,000.

1832 The Mad River and Lake Erie Railroad, the first all-Ohio line, is chartered by the state legislature to run from Sandusky to Dayton.

1833 Oberlin College is founded, the first college in the United States to admit blacks and whites on an equal basis.

The National Road is opened between Cumberland, Maryland and Columbus, Ohio.

1836 Nearly 2,000 lake vessels load and unload cargo at the port of Cleveland.

1837 Vesuvius Furnace, the first hot-blast iron furnace in the United States, is started up in southern Ohio.

1838 The National Road is completed for its entire length from Cumberland, Maryland to Vandalia, Illinois.

1839 The Ohio Statehouse's cornerstone is set in place; completion will not be until 1861.

1840 Ohio's population is more than 1.5 million.

1841 Navigation improvements are completed on the Muskingum River between Dresden and Marietta.

The Hocking Valley Railway made it possible to transport southeastern Ohio coal to Lake Erie and Ohio's industrial cities. Courtesy, The Mueller Collection, Columbus Metropolitan Library

1847 Thomas A. Edison is born in Milan near Lake Erie.
1850 Ohio canal traffic hits its peak, soon to be eclipsed by the growing railroad network.

Ohio's population reaches more than 1,980,000.
1851 Cincinnati and Cleveland are connected by rail via Columbus.

Ohio's last county, Noble, is established.
1853 Antioch College is founded at Yellow Springs in southwestern Ohio.
1857 A national financial panic results in bank failures and high unemployment.
1860 Sharpshooter Annie Oakley is born near North Star in Darke County.

Ohio's population is nearly 2,340,000.
1861 State canal system is leased to private operators for ten years.

30,000 Ohioans answer Lincoln's call for 75,000 Union volunteers.
1863 Morgan's Raiders, a band of Confederate soldiers, terrorize parts of

Cincinnati, known as the "Queen City," had become a major industrial and port city by the middle of the nineteenth century. Courtesy, Public Library of Cincinnati and Hamilton County.

THE LEVEE AT CINCINNATI, OHIO.

southern Ohio.
1865 Ohioan General Ulysses Grant accepts General Robert E. Lee's surrender at Appomatox Court House, Virginia, to end the Civil War. More than half of Ohio's able-bodied men had fought on the Union side.
1868 U.S. Grant is elected president of the United States.
1870 The Hocking Valley Railway is

After numerous architects and considerable controversy and construction delays, the Ohio Statehouse became the dominant feature of Capitol Square in Columbus. Construction extended from 1839 to the first year of the Civil War. Courtesy, Columbus Metropolitan Library, Columbus Circulating Visuals Collection

completed, opening southeast Ohio coalfields to development.
1870 John D. Rockefeller forms the Standard Oil Company in Cleveland. Benjamin Goodrich begins making rubber articles in Akron.

The Ohio State University is founded on the north side of Columbus as the Ohio Agricultural and Mechanical College.

Ohio's population is just over 2,665,000.
1871 The Toledo University of Arts and Trades, later to become the University of Toledo, is opened.
1876 Ohioan Rutherford B. Hayes is elected president of the United States.
1877 The national railroad strike hits rail facilities at Newark, where martial law is declared.
1878 The start of the Scripps-Howard newspaper chain begins with purchase by Edward W. Scripps of the *Penny Press* in Cleveland.
1880 Case School of Applied Science, later part of Case Western Reserve University, opens in Cleveland.

Ohioan James A. Garfield is elected president of the United States.

Ohio was a leader in the development of institutions for the care and education of the handicapped. The Ohio School for the Deaf was established in 1829 and had expanded to the point that this building was completed in Columbus in 1866. Courtesy, Columbus Metropolitan Library, Columbus Circulating Visuals Collection

Ohio's population reaches nearly 3,200,000.

1884 The first electric street railway in the U.S. begins operation in Cleveland.

Striking coal miners set fires, which still burn today, in mines near New Straitsville.

1886 Oil is discovered near Bowling Green in northwestern Ohio.

1888 Ohioan Benjamin Harrison is elected president of the United States.

1890 Ohio's commercial fisheries hit their peak year, with 22,500 tons caught in Lake Erie.

Ohio's population is nearly 3,700,000.

1893 The Ohio Anti-Saloon League is founded at Oberlin.

1894 Jacob Coxey of Massillon leads "Coxey's Army" to Washington, D.C. to demand relief for people unemployed as a result of the Panic of 1893.

1896 William McKinley of Canton is elected president of the United States.

1898 The separatist communal society at Zoar in Tuscarawas County, which had held together for much of the nineteenth century, is disbanded and community property is divided among members.

1899 The first Packard automobile, built by J. Ward Packard, is produced in Warren.

1900 Ohio has 11,000 one-room schoolhouses.

Ohio's population reaches just over 4,150,000.

William McKinley is reelected as president.

1901 Political reformer Tom Johnson, a street railway entrepreneur, is elected mayor of Cleveland.

President William McKinley is assassinated in Buffalo, New York.

1903 Ohioans Wilbur and Orville Wright achieve the first manned and powered flight in a heavier-than-air craft on the North Carolina coast.

Ohio celebrates the centennial of its statehood.

1904 Mark Hanna, power broker in Ohio Republican politics, dies after a short illness.

1906 The cooperative system of education is begun at the University of Cincinnati.

1908 Ohioan William Howard Taft is elected president of the United States.

1909 Leopold Stokowski becomes leader of the Cincinnati Symphony Orchestra.

The Anti-Saloon League opens a permanent headquarters in Westerville.

1910 The peak period of travel by electric interurban railroads begins, just before the start of widespread automobile ownership.

Ohio's population is just over 4,767,000.

1911 The self-starter for automobiles is invented by Charles Kettering of Loudonville.

1913 Massive spring flooding across Ohio costs over 400 lives and does huge damage, triggering final closure of the state's canal system.

1914 The Ohio Conservancy Act permits formation of watershed districts to facilitate flood control.

1917 The United States enters World War I. About 6,800 Ohioans die in the war.

1918 Columbus native Eddie Rickenbacker is celebrated as America's Flying Ace for his success against German opponents during World War I.

1919 Author Sherwood Anderson publishes *Winesburg, Ohio,* a novel about life in a small town and based on Clyde in Sandusky County.

1920 Ohioan Warren G. Harding is elected president of the United States.

The Standard Oil Company was founded in Cleveland in 1870 by John D. Rockefeller. Courtesy, Cleveland State University

A vast system of interurban transit lines connected cities and villages throughout Ohio between the 1890s and World War I and then disappeared almost entirely by World War II. Courtesy, Medina County Historical Society

Ohio's population is nearly 5,760,000.
1921 Wages of Ohio's workers drop 44% during the economic depression of the early 1920s.
1922 Ohio Stadium is completed on the Ohio State University campus in Columbus.
1923 President Harding dies in office.

The site of the Moravian mission at Schoenbrunn is discovered and reconstruction begins.

Garrett Morgan of Cleveland invents the first traffic light.
1924 A tornado devastates downtown Lorain, killing seventy-five people and doing $25 million in damage.
1925 The dirigible *Shenandoah* crashes during a storm in Noble County in southeastern Ohio.
1927 *The American Insurance Union Citadel*, the first skyscraper in Columbus and today known as the *Leveque Tower*, is completed. For many years airplane pilots used the building as a beacon for navigation.
1929 Port Columbus airport, "America's Greatest Air Harbor," opens, offering coordinated air-rail transcontinental service.

Steel becomes the most important industry in Ohio.

The stock market crash ushers in the Great Depression.
1930 Ohio's population is nearly 6,647,000.

The Millfield Mine Disaster in Athens County kills eighty-two miners, the worst mining accident in state history.

Severance Hall in Cleveland, home of the Cleveland Symphony Orchestra, is dedicated.

Cleveland's Terminal Tower office building is completed.
1931 Cincinnati's Carew Tower, part of the complex that contains the Netherland Plaza Hotel, is opened.
1932 A gas explosion in the nearly finished Ohio Departments of State office building in Columbus kills eleven

workers and injures fifty. Completion of the building is delayed over a year.
1933 The stunning Art Deco Cincinnati Union Terminal opens for service with a capacity of 216 daily passenger trains.

Effects of the national depression result in Ohio wage-earners dropping from 740,000 to 472,000 in number, and in industrial production dropping from $5 billion to $3.3 billion.
1934 Ohio imposes its first sales tax, 3 percent.

Work begins on 14 flood-control dams in the Muskingum Watershed Conservancy District.

Troops are sent to Toledo to keep order during labor strife.
1935 The Toledo Industrial Peace Plan is implemented in an effort to arbitrate disputes between employers and employees.
1936 Sit-down strikes occur at Akron rubber plants.

Cleveland hosts the Great Lakes Exposition on its downtown lakefront.
1937 Massive Ohio Valley flooding makes 750,000 people homeless and does hundreds of millions of dollars in property damage.

The CIO goes on strike against "Little Steel" in three northeastern Ohio cities.

The 1913 flood caused destruction in many areas of Ohio. The west side of Columbus was particularly hard hit. Courtesy, Columbus Metropolitan Library, Columbus Circulating Visuals Collection

1938 Teflon is invented by Roy Plunkett of New Carlisle, Ohio.

Only 1,674 one-room schools remain in Ohio, their number reduced by emergence of the township and district school system.

1939 The country continues to emerge from the Great Depression, with industrial states like Ohio benefiting from demand for industrial goods spurred by gathering pressures for war in Europe.

World War II begins with Germany's invasion of Poland.

1940 Ohio's population has risen to just under 6,908,000.

Port Columbus was on the first transcontinental airline route, operated by Transcontinental Air Transport (TAT), the precursor of Trans World Airlines (TWA). Courtesy, Earnest Stork Scrapbook, 1915–1961, Port Columbus Construction, in the Collection of the Biography History & Travel Division of the Columbus Metropolitan Library.

1941 The United States enters World War II after Japan's attack on Pearl Harbor. Some 839,000 Ohioans would serve in the war, with more than 20,000 killed.

1943 Wages for industrial workers have risen by 65 percent from their level in 1940, spurred by the war's demand for goods.

1945 The end of World War II and return of servicemen from overseas spurs the postwar baby and suburban housing booms.

1946 The U.S. Air Force selects a pilot instructor at Wright Field in Dayton, Chuck Yeager, to pilot the first rocket-powered aircraft. He would break the sound barrier in 1947.

The Tuskegee Airmen, successful African American fighter pilots during World War II, are assigned to Lockbourne Air Force Base south of Columbus.

The Lustron Corporation begins manufacturing enameled metal pre-fabricated homes in its plant in Columbus.

Eddie Rickenbacker, a Columbus native, was a well-known race car driver before he became one of America's World War I flying aces. He was also an automobile and aviation entrepreneur. Courtesy, U.S. Air Force

1948 Orville Wright dies.

1949 The General Assembly creates the Ohio Department of Natural Resources.

The Tuskegee Airmen are assigned to integrated Air Force bases across the country and their base at Lockbourne is deactivated.

1950 President Truman seizes control of U.S. railroads to prevent a nationwide strike.

Ohio's population is nearly 7,947,000.

1952 Governor Frank J. Lausche, a Democrat, is elected overwhelmingly to a fourth term in an election otherwise dominated by winning Republican candidates.

Toledo Central Terminal is opened, the last major railroad station built in the United States.

1953 The U.S. Congress learns that it had failed to make formal recognition of Ohio's achievement of statehood; it passes a resolution declaring Ohio's entry into the Union on March 1, 1803.

1955 The Ohio Turnpike is completed across the northern part of the state.

1956 Dr. Albert Sabin of Cincinnati Children's Hospital develops oral polio vaccine, considered more successful and effective than the Salk vaccine developed the year before.

1957 *Collier's Weekly* magazine ceases publication, devastating Springfield, in Clark County, with a loss of several thousand jobs.

1959 The St. Lawrence Seaway connects the Great Lakes with the St. Lawrence River and the Atlantic Ocean.

The Ohio Civil Rights Commission is established.

1960 Goods exported from Ohio total nearly 8.5 percent of all U.S. exports.

Ohio's population is just over 9,700,000.

1962 Ohioan John Glenn becomes the first American to orbit the earth in a space capsule.

Republican James A. Rhodes is elected as Ohio's governor.

1963 The Professional Football Hall of Fame opens in Canton.

The Limited clothing chain begins with a single store at the Kingsdale shopping center in the Columbus suburb of Upper Arlington.

1964 The Ohio General Assembly votes to approve $500 million for highway construction.

1965 Interstate Highway 71 between Cleveland and Cincinnati is in operation, with completion in an area northeast of Medina to follow somewhat later.

Cash receipts in Ohio's farm economy total more than $1.1 billion.

1966 Springfield becomes the first of the nation's larger cities to elect a black mayor.

1967 Ashtabula native Charles Burchfield, a widely-known watercolorist and landscape painter, dies.

OCLC, the Ohio College Library Center, is founded at Ohio State University. It will later be renamed the Online Computer Library Center and is an early computer database.

1969 Ohioan Neil Armstrong is the first human to step onto the surface of the moon.

The Cuyahoga River catches fire in Cleveland, focusing unwanted attention on the city and highlighting river and lake pollution.

Hamburger chain Wendy's International is founded in Columbus by Dave Thomas.

1970 Four students are killed by the Ohio National Guard during Vietnam War protests at Kent State University.

Ohio's population is just over 10,652,000.

1971 Ohio adopts a state income tax.

1973 Ohio voters approve a state-run lottery.

1974 A massive tornado kills thirty-four

Cleveland and other Ohio cities are rediscovering their center cities and are undergoing revitalization. Courtesy, Photohome

Immediately following World War II, the Tuskegee Airmen were stationed at Lockbourne Air Force Base in Columbus. Following President Truman's order to integrate the military in 1947, the Tuskegee Airmen were sent to bases all over the world. Courtesy, National Archives and Records Administration Still Picture Branch

and devastates downtown Xenia.

1975 James A. Rhodes begins his second two-term stint as governor of Ohio.

Former astronaut John Glenn begins serving as one of Ohio's U.S. senators.

1976 The last commuter train in Ohio, between Cleveland and Youngstown, ceases operation.

Dave Longaberger of Dresden opens his first basket store. Two years later he would move on to the idea of selling through consultants at home shows.

A 141-day strike by rubber workers is the beginning of the end for automobile tire-making in Akron.

1977 A serious natural gas shortage occurs during unusually severe winter weather in Ohio.

1980 The Staggers Act, passed by Congress to deregulate the nation's railroads, spurs formation of short lines and regional railroads in Ohio and elsewhere.

Automobile tire production is moved entirely out of Akron to other facilities.

Ohio's population is nearly 10,798,000.

1981 Justice Potter Stewart, once a Cincinnati resident, leaves the U.S. Supreme Court, having served since 1958.

1983 The Honda automobile plant near Marysville is dedicated.

1985 Ohio is ranked fifth nationally as a headquarters location for service corporations, hosting a total of twenty-five such firms.

Cincinnati's Procter & Gamble is the largest manufacturer of over-the-counter drugs in the United States.

1986 Destruction of the space shuttle *Challenger* kills Ohioans Christa McAuliffe and Judith Resnick, as well as five other astronauts.

1988 The Limited clothing chain is listed as forty-eighth in stock value of all the nation's businesses by *Business Week* magazine.

1990 Just over 10,847,000 people now live in Ohio. The increase since 1980 is only about 0.5 percent, reflecting difficult economic times in the 1980s.

1991 The World Wide Web became available for public use and would grow in the number of users by a factor of 3,500 each year.

1992 Bill Clinton wins in Ohio on his way to the presidency, despite general Republican dominance of state politics.

1993 A bloody takeover by inmates at the Southern Ohio Correctional Facility at Lucasville ends after a siege by law enforcement personnel and National Guard troops.

1995 The Rock and Roll Hall of Fame opens in Cleveland, where the term "Rock and Roll" was created by radio disk jockey Alan Freed in the 1950s.

The Bosnian peace agreement is signed at Wright-Patterson Air Force Base near Dayton.

1996 Restoration of the Ohio Statehouse in Columbus is completed.

1997 The Longaberger Company builds a new headquarters building in the form of a huge basket east of Newark, 160 times the size of one of its baskets.

1998 At the age of seventy-seven, John Glenn becomes the oldest American to travel into space.

2000 Nothing significant happens when the calendar changes from 1999 to the "Y2K" year, 2000, despite worries about major disruption in computer systems.

295 million people are using the World Wide Web.

The federal census places Ohio's population at just over 11,353,000.

2001 Ohio ranks among the top ten states in the country for growing or raising corn, oats, wheat, soybeans, sweet corn, tomatoes, chicken, and hogs; and for producing maple syrup and dairy products.

2003 Ohio celebrates the bicentennial of its admission to the Union.

The state of Ohio launches its Third Frontier initiative to build and enhance research capacity, sources of financing,

Native Ohioan John Glenn became the first American to orbit the earth. Courtesy, NASA photograph courtesy of the John Glenn Archives at The Ohio State University.

advanced technologies, and productivity improvements for Ohio businesses.

2005 Conversion of the Ohio Departments of State building in Columbus to the Ohio Judicial Center is completed. The building is the new home of the Supreme Court of Ohio.

2006 The first legal drink is served in formerly "dry" Westerville, near Columbus, once the home of the Anti-Saloon League.

Ohio's population is estimated to be 11,478,000.

BIBLIOGRAPHY

American Greetings Corporation. "The First 75 Years." "American Greetings News."

Andreano, Ralph, ed. *The Economic Impact of the Civil War*. Cambridge, Massachusetts: Schenkman, 1962.

"Autobiography of Thomas Ewing, The." Clement L. Martzloff, ed. *Ohio Archaeological and Historical Society Publications*, 22 (1913): 126-204.

Baughman, James L. "Classes and Company Towns: Legends of the 1937 Little Steel Strike." *Ohio History*, 87 (1978): 175-192.

Beachley, Charles E. *History of the Consolidation Coal Company, 1864-1934*. New York: Consolidation Coal Company, 1934.

Beaver, R. Pierce. "Joseph Hough; An Early Miami Merchant." *Ohio Archaeological and Historical Society Quarterly*, 45 (1936): 3745.

Becker, Carl M. "A Most Complete Factory: The Barney Car Works 1850-1926." *Cincinnati Historical Society Bulletin*, 31 (1973): 48-69.

———, "Entrepreneurial Invention and Innovation in the Miami Valley During the Civil War." *Cincinnati Historical Society Bulletin*, 22 (1964): 5-28.

———, "James Leffel: Double Turbine Water Wheel Inventor." *Ohio History*, 75 (1966): 200-211, 269-270.

Benedict, C. Harry. *Red Metal; The Calumet and Hecla Story*. Ann Arbor: University of Michigan Press, 1952.

Bilstein, Roger E. "Putting Aircraft to Work: The First Air Freight." *Ohio History*, 76 (1967): 247-258.

Blackford, Mansel G. "Scientific Management and Welfare Work in Early Twentieth Century American Business: The Buckeye Steel Castings Company." *Ohio History*, 90 (1981): 238-258.

Blocker, Jack S. "Market Integration, Urban Growth and Economic Change in an Ohio County, 1850-1880." *Ohio History*, 90 (1981): 298-316.

Bob Evans Farms. "The Bob Evans Story."

Bond, Beverley W., Jr. *The Foundations of Ohio*. Columbus: Ohio State Archaeological and Historical Society, 1941.

———, *The Civilization of the Old Northwest*. New York: Macmillan, 1934.

Boryczka, Raymond, and Lorin Lee Cary. *No Strength Without Union; An Illustrated History of Ohio Workers, 1803-1980*. Columbus: Ohio Historical Society, 1982.

Buley, R. Carlyle. *The Old Northwest*. 2 vls. Bloomington: Indiana University Press, 1951.

Butler, Joseph G. *Fifty Years of Iron and Steel*. Cleveland: Penton, 1920.

Canton Hardware Company, The. Canton: Canton Hardware Company, 1934.

Carnegie, Andrew. *Autobiography*. Boston: Houghton Mifflin, 1924.

Carruth, Eleanore. "Federated Department Stores: Growing Pains at Forty." *Fortune* (June 1969): 142-147, 200-202.

Chamberlain, John. *The Enterprising Americans*. New York: Harper and Row, 1963.

Chase, Stuart. *Prosperity; Fact or Myth?* New York: Charles Boni, 1929.

Christiansen, Harry. *Northern Ohio's Interurbans and Rapid Transit Railways*. Cleveland: Transit Data, 1965.

Cincinnati Milacron. "Cincinnati Milacron, 1884-1984: Finding Better Ways."

Clark, Victor S. *History of Manufacturers in the United States*. 3 vls. New York: McGraw-Hill, 1929.

Cleveland *Plain Dealer*, October 10, 1986.

Cotkin, George B. "Strikebreakers, Evictions and Violence: Industrial Conflict in the flocking Valley, 1884-1885." *Ohio History*, 87 (1978): 138-150.

Crout, George C. and Wilfred D. Vorhis. "John Butler Tytus: Inventor of the Continuous Rolling Mill." *Ohio History*, 76 (1967): 132-145, 176-177.

Dana Corporation. "Toward the Year 2000." "Product and Service Guide."

Davis, Harold E. "Economic Basis of Ohio Politics, 1820-1840." *Ohio State Archaeological and Historical Quarterly*, 47 (1938): 288-318.

DeWitt, Catherine C. "Bog Iron in Lake County." *Lake County Historical Society Quarterly*, 13 (August 1971).

Diebold Incorporated. "Diebold Incorporated, Established in Canton 100 Years Ago." Supplement to *Wooster Record*, August 21, 1972.

Downard, William L. *The Cincinnati Brewing Industry: A Social and Economic History*. Athens: Ohio University Press, 1973.

Drismer, Karl H. *Akron and Summit County*. Akron: Summit County Historical Society, n.d.

Duggan, Edward P. "Machines, Markets, and Labor: The Carriage and Wagon Industry in Late-Nineteenth-Century Cincinnati." *Business History Review*, 51 (1977): 308-325.

Farrell, Richard T. "Cincinnati, 1800-1830: Economic Development Through Trade and Industry." *Ohio History*, 77 (1968): 111-129, 171.

50 Years in Steel: The Youngstown Sheet and Tube Company: 1900-1949. Youngstown: Youngstown Sheet and Tube Company, 1950.

Federal Writers Project. *The Ohio Guide*. 1940.

Fine, Sidney. "The Toledo Chevrolet Strike of 1935." *Ohio Historical Quarterly*, 67 (1958): 326-356.

"Five Hundred, The." *Fortune* (April 29, 1985): 266-285.

Fisher, Douglas A. *Steel Serves the Nation: The Fifty Year Story of United States Steel, 1901-1951*. New York: United States Steel Corporation, 1951.

"Four Hundred Richest People in America, The." *Forbes* (October 27, 1986): 106-312.

Garber, D.W. *Waterwheels and Millstones: A History of Ohio's Gristmills and Milling*. Columbus: Ohio Historical Society, 1970.

Gates, William C., Jr. and Dana E. Omerod. *The East Liverpool, Ohio, Pottery District*. California, Pennsylvania: The Society for Historical Archaeology, 1982.

Greater Cleveland Growth Association. "Headquarters Cleveland."

Greif, Martin. *The New Industrial Landscape: The Story of the Austin Company*. Clinton, New Jersey: Main Street Press, 1978.

Gutman, Herbert G. "An Iron Workers' Strike in the Ohio Valley, 1873-1874." *Ohio Historical Quarterly*, 68 (1959): 353-370.

Hampton, Taylor. "Cleveland's Fabulous Vans." *Cleveland News*, August 1955.

Hartwell, Dickson. "The Mighty Jeep." *American Heritage*, 12(1) (1960): 38–41.

Hatcher, Harlan. *The Buckeye Country: A Pageant of Ohio*. New York: H.C. Kinsey, 1940.

———, "Commerce and Culture, The Pattern in Ohio: An Address." *Ohio Historical Quarterly*, 66 (1957): 270–277.

———, *The Western Reserve: The Story of New Connecticut in Ohio*. Indianapolis: Bobbs-Merrill, 1949.

Havighurst, Walter. *Ohio: A Bicentennial History*. New York: Norton, 1976.

———, *Vein of Iron: The Pickands Mather Story*. Cleveland: World, 1958.

Herryman, Maurice. *In Quiet Ways: George H. Mead, the Man and the Company*. Dayton: The Mead Corporation, 1970.

History of Geauga and Lake Counties, Ohio. Philadelphia: Williams Brothers, 1878.

Holmes, Robert E. "Ohio's Industrial Growth, 1900–1957, and Some Possibilities for Study." *Ohio Historical Quarterly*, 66 (1957): 290–299.

Hook, Charles R. *Romance of Iron and Steel: Contribution to the Central Ohio Valley*. New York: Newcomen Society, 1950.

Hoover Company. "How the Vacuum Cleaner Began." "Hoover Historical Center." "Celebrating Seventy-Five Years." "Our Proud Past ... And Exciting Future."

Hulbert, Archer B. *The Cumberland Road*. Cleveland: Arthur Clark, 1904.

Hunter, W.H. "The Pathfinders of Jefferson County." *Ohio Archaeological and Historical Society Publications*, 6 (1898): 95–406.

Hurt, R. Douglas. "Dairying in Nineteenth Century Ohio." *The Old Northwest*, 5 (Winter 1979–1980): 387–399. "Pork and Porkopolis." *Cincinnati Historical Society Bulletin*, 40 (1982).

Hutslar, Donald A. "Ohio Waterpowered Sawmills." *Ohio History*, 84 (1975): 5–56.

Jefferson Furnace. "Celebration of the Ninety-second Anniversary of the Founding of Jefferson Furnace."

Jones, Robert L. "Ohio Agriculture in History." *Ohio Historical Quarterly*, 65 (1956): 229–258.

Jordan, Philip D. *Ohio Comes of Age, 1873–1900*. Columbus: Ohio Archaeological and Historical Society, 1943.

Keir, Malcolm. *The Epic of Industry*. New Haven: Yale University Press, 1926.

Knepper, George. "A Survey of Ohio's Economy." *The Akron Beacon Journal*, December 1985.

Lindley, Harlow, compiler. *Ohio in the Twentieth Century, 1900–1938*. Columbus: Ohio State Archaeological and Historical Society, 1942.

Lippincott, Isaac. *A History of Manufactures in the Ohio Valley to the Year 1860*. New York: Arno, 1973.

Lundberg, Ferdinand. *The Rockefeller Syndrome*. New York: Kensington, 1976.

I.upold, Harry F. *The Latch String is Out*. Mentor: Lakeland Community College, 1974.

Mabry, William A. "Industrial Beginnings in Ohio." *Ohio State Archaeological and Historical Quarterly*. 55 (1946): 242–253.

M.A. Hanna Company. "M.A. Hanna Company, A Corporate History: The First Hundred Years."

Mak, James. "Interregional Trade in the Antebellum West: Ohio, A Case Study." *Agricultural History*, 46 (1972): 489–497.

Marathon Oil Company. "Five Eventful Decades: A History of the Ohio Oil Company, 1887-1937." "The Ohio Oil Company, 60th Anniversary: 1887–1947."

Marion Power Shovel. "A History of Marion Power Shovel's First 100 Years."

Martin, Linda Grant. "What Happened at NCR After the Boss Declared Martial Law." *Fortune* (September 1975): 100–105, 178–182.

Martzloff, Clement L. "Zane's Trace." *Ohio Archaeological and Historical Society Publications*, 13 (1908): 297–331.

Maurer, Maurer. "McCook Field, 1917–1929." *Ohio Historical Quarterly*, 67 (1958): 21-34.

McGannon, Harold E., ed. *The Making, Shaping, and Treating of Steel*. 8th edition. Pittsburgh: United States Steel Corporation, 1964.

McGrath, Edward J. "Reuben Springer, Cincinnatian: Business Man, Philanthropist." *Bulletin, Historical and Philosophical Society of Ohio*, 13 (1955): 271–285

Mead Corporation. "Mead Corporation History."

Millis, John S. "The Impact of Science Upon the History of Ohio." *Ohio Archaeological and Historical Quarterly*, 61 (1952): 227–234.

Mills, William C. "Archaeological Remains of Jackson County." *Ohio Archaeological and Historical Society Publications*, 21 (1912): 175–214.

Moley, Raymond. *The American Century of John C Lincoln*. New York: Duell, Sloan and Pearce, 1962.

Moore, Opha. *History of Franklin County, Ohio*. 3 vls. Indianapolis: Historical Publishing Company, 1930.

Moaner, Aimee L. "For Sohio, It Was Alaskan Oil—Or Bust." *Fortune* (August 1977): 172–184.

Murdock, Eugene E. *Life of Tom L. Johnson*. Ph.D. Dissertation, Columbia University, 1951.

"National Road in Song and Story, The." Columbus: Ohio Archaeological and Historical Society, 1940.

NCR. "Celebrating the Future."

Nevins, Allan. *The Emergence of Modern America, 1865–1878*. New York: Macmillan, 1927.

———, *Study in Power: John D. Rockefeller, Industrialist and Philanthropist*. 2 vls. New York: Scribners, 1953.

Ohio: An Empire Within an Empire. 2nd edition. Columbus: Beer, 1950.

Ohio Cultivator, June 15, July 15, 1848; June 1, 1849.

Ohio Cultural Facilities Commission. *Annual Report FY2006*.

Ohio Guide, The. Harlan Hatcher, director. New York: Oxford University Press, 1940.

Ohio Roster, The 86. Cleveland: Edward Howard, 1986.

Ohio Timeline of State History. www.shgresources.com/oh/timeline/

O'Reilly, Maurice. *The Goodyear Story*.

Elmsford, New York: Benjamin, 1983.

Overman, William D. "The Rubber Industry in Ohio." *Ohio Historical Quarterly*, 66 (1957): 278–289.

Parker Hannifin Corporation. "Parker Corporation."

Pearson, Ralph L., ed. *Ohio in Century Three: Quality of Life*. Columbus: Ohio Historical Society, 1977.

Reichert, William O., and Steven O. Ludd, eds. *Outlook on Ohio: Prospects and Priorities in Public Policy*. Palisades, New Jersey: Commonwealth Books, 1983.

Roadway Services, Incorporated. "A Look at Roadway."

Robertson, Ross M. *History of the American Economy*. 3rd edition. New York: Harcourt Brace Jovanovich, 1973.

Rose, William G. *Cleveland: The Making of a City*. Cleveland: World, 1950.

Roseboom, Eugene H. *The Civil War Era, 1850–1873*. Columbus: The Ohio Archaeological and Historical Society, 1944.

———, and Francis P. Weisenburger. *A History of Ohio*. Columbus: The Ohio Historical Society, 1969.

Rosenberg, Norman L., and Emily S. Rosenberg. *In Our Times*. 2nd edition. Englewood Cliffs, New Jersey: Prentice-Hall, 1982.

Rubbermaid Incorporated. "1985 Annual Report." "Housewares Catalog."

Sass, Jon A. *The Versatile Millstone, Workhorse of Many Industries*. Knoxville, Tennessee: The Society for the Preservation of Old Mills, 1984.

Scheiber, Harry N. *Ohio Canal Era: A Case Study of Government and the Economy, 1820–1861*. Athens: Ohio University Press, 1969.

Schneider, Norris F. *Blennerhasset Island and the Burr Conspiracy*. Columbus: Ohio Archaeological and Historical Society, 1950.

"The National Road: Main Street of America." *Ohio History*, 83 (1974): 114–146.

"Service 500, The." *Fortune* (June 9, 1986): 113–152.

Sherwin-Williams. "Company History." "Sherwin-Williams History."

Smith, Thomas H., *An Ohio Reader*. 2 vls. Grand Rapids, Michigan: Eerdmans, 1975.

Speer, Michael. "The Little Steel Strike: Conflict for Control." *Ohio History*, 78 (1969): 273–287.

Spence, Hartzell. *Portrait in Oil*. New York: McGraw-Hill, 1962.

Stephenson, Bert S. "Iron and Steel Making in Ohio." *Ohio Magazine*, 2 (January 1907): 64–72.

Stevens, Harry R. "Samuel Watt Davies and the Industrial Revolution in Cincinnati." *Ohio Historical Quarterly*, 70 (1961): 95–127.

Stout, Wilber. "Charcoal Iron Industry of the Hanging Rock District." *Ohio State Archaeological and Historical Quarterly*, 42 (1933): 72–104.

———, "Early Forges in Ohio." *Ohio State Archaeological and Historical Quarterly*, 46 (1937): 25–41.

———, *History of Clay Industry in Ohio*. Columbus: Ohio Geological Survey, 4th Series, Number 26, 1923.

Take a Look at Ohio. Columbus: Office of the Governor, n.d.

TIME, September 8, 1986.

Timken Company. "A Brief History."

Travel Industry Association. *Historic/Cultural Traveler Report*. 2003

TRW. "The Little Brown Hut That Could. . . ." "A Company Called TRW: Putting High Technology to Work."

Tucker, Leonard L. "Cincinnati, Athens of the West." *Ohio History*, 75 (1966): 11–25, 67–68.

U.S. Department of Commerce and the President's Committee on the Arts and Humanities. A *Position Paper on Cultural and Heritage Tourism*. Cultural & Heritage Tourism Summit, 2005.

United States Shoe Corporation. "History of U.S. Shoe Corporation From Board Minutes, 1931–1981."

Utter, William T. *The Frontier State, 1803–1825*. Columbus: The Ohio Archaeological and Historical Society, 1942.

Van Tassel, Charles S. *Story of the Maumee Valley, Toledo and the Sandusky Region*. 3 vls. Chicago: S.J. Clarke, 1929.

Weisenburger, Francis P. *The Passing of the Frontier, 1825–1850*. Columbus: The Ohio State Archaeological and Historical Society, 1941.

Wendy's International, inc. "Historical Highlights of Wendy's International,

Inc." "R. David Thomas." "History of Wendy's Advertising, 1973–1984."

Wheeler, Robert. "Water to Steam." *Western Reserve Magazine*, September-October 1978.

Wiley, Richard T. "Ship and Brig Building on the Ohio and its Tributaries." *Ohio Archaeological and Historical Publications*, 23 (1913): 54–64.

Wish, Harvey. *Society and Thought in Modern America*. 2 vls. New York: Longmans, Green, 1950, 1952.

Wood, Marie. *None Called Him Neighbor*. Parkersburg, West Virginia: Marie Wood, 1951.

Wunder, John, ed. *Toward an Urban Ohio*. Columbus: Ohio Historical Society, 1977.

www.ohiobyways.com

www.ohioheritage.com/omsp.htm

www.thirdfrontier.com

Zeisberger, David. *History of the Northern American Indians*. Archer B. Hulbert and William N. Schwarze, eds. In *Ohio Archaeological and Historical Society Publications*. 19 (1910): 1–173.

INDEX